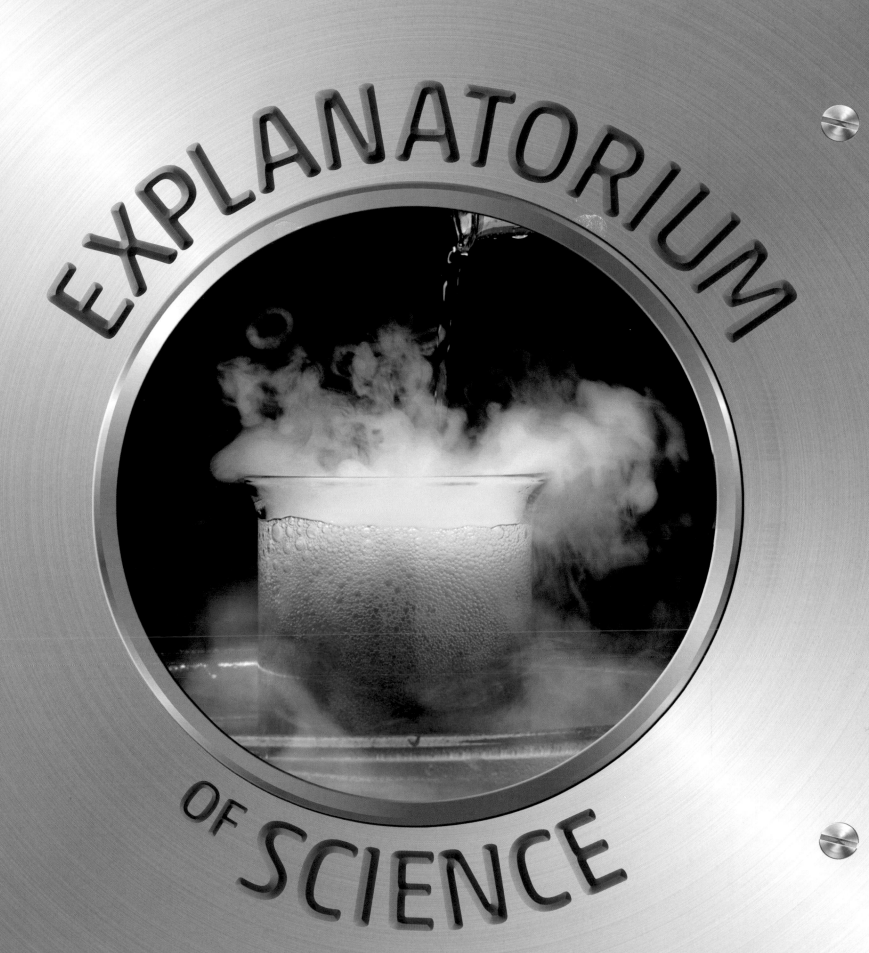

EXPLANATORIUM

OF SCIENCE

EXPLANATORIUM
OF SCIENCE

Senior Editor Jenny Sich
Senior Art Editor Stefan Podhorodecki
Editors Anna Streiffert Limerick,
Georgina Palffy, Vicky Richards, Annie Moss,
Sarah MacLeod, Sam Kennedy
Designers David Ball, Chrissy Barnard,
Sheila Collins, Mik Gates, Kit Lane,
Gregory McCarthy
Illustrators Simon Tegg, Jack Williams
Picture Researchers Nic Dean, Rituraj Singh
Photography David King,
Gary Ombler, Stefan Podhorodecki
Creative Retouching Steve Crozier
Managing Editor Francesca Baines
Managing Art Editor Philip Letsu
Producer, Pre-Production Jacqueline Street
Senior Producer Jude Crozier
Jacket Designers Priyanka Bansal,
Suhita Dharamjit, Akiko Kato
Jacket Editor Emma Dawson
Jackets Design Development Manager
Sophia MTT
Senior DTP Designer Harish Aggarwal
Jackets Editorial Coordinator
Priyanka Sharma
Managing Jackets Editor Saloni Singh
Publisher Andrew Macintyre
Art Director Karen Self
Associate Publishing Director Liz Wheeler
Publishing Director Jonathan Metcalf

Contributors Derek Harvey,
Bea Perks, Dr Kat Day, Hilary Lamb
Consultants Dr Kat Day,
Penny Johnson, Professor Mark Viney

DK would like to thank the Wohl Reach
Out Lab at Imperial College London
for use of the laboratory.

First published in Great Britain in 2019 by
Dorling Kindersley Limited
80 Strand, London, WC2R 0RL

A CIP catalogue record for this book
is available from the British Library.

ISBN: 978-0-2413-5948-8

Printed and bound in China

A WORLD OF IDEAS:
SEE ALL THERE IS TO KNOW

www.dk.com

CONTENTS

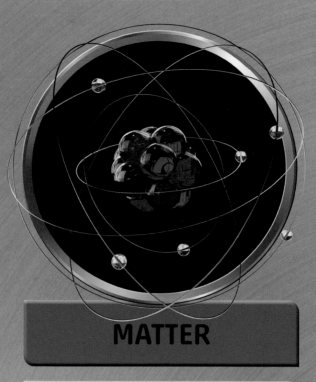

MATTER

REACTIONS

MATERIALS

IMPORTANT

The experiments shown in this book are for demonstration purposes and to illustrate scientific principles. The experiments should not be attempted at home. The author and publishers disclaim as far as the law allows any liability arising directly or indirectly from the use, or misuse of the information contained in this book.

ENERGY

FORCES

LIFE

EARTH

REFERENCE

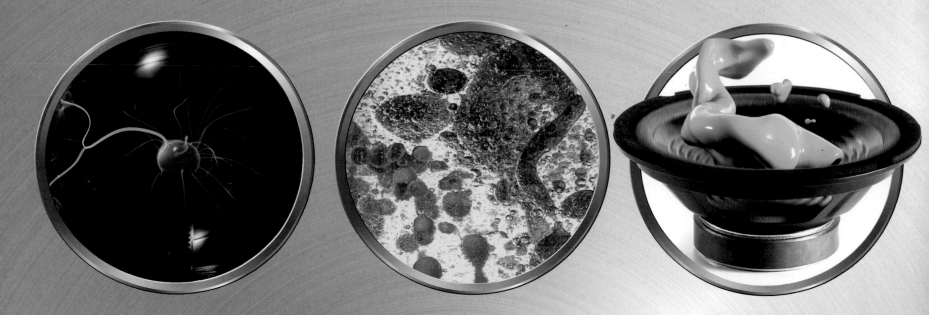

FOREWORD

The first science demonstration I saw was at school. An elderly teacher was sending my class to sleep on a hot afternoon with an endless lecture on the importance of science. He droned on, with his hands behind his back and his head down. We students had heard that this new master was strict and had a fierce reputation, and so we were too terrified to whisper or fidget. After what seemed like an hour, but was probably just 15 minutes, there was a sudden, monstrous explosion behind him. Scared stiff, we watched the classroom fill with dense white smoke. Only later did we realize this terrifying event had been engineered by that teacher. He wanted us to see science in action. From that moment, I regret to say, all of us wanted to make explosions. But that ageing teacher helped us understand that seeing science actually working was a cause of great wonder.

Nowadays, teachers are mostly not allowed to make explosions. But my teacher understood that looking at science is so important. The first scientists, going right back to the ancient Egyptians, used observation and then tried to work out what was happening. This is still true of science today. When I look down a microscope at a few coloured cells, it helps me to work out what is happening inside

somebody's body or in a plant. And very often I have that sense of wonder when I see how beautiful nature is. But it's more than that. I sometimes realize that what I am seeing down my microscope has never quite appeared the same way to anybody else. You too can have that magic chance when you see the world close up and enlarged. And you too, if you decide to study science, may see things that nobody else has ever seen before.

This *Explanatorium of Science* helps us all to see science in action. Most of these remarkable photographs required very skilled camera work to capture events that happen in a tiny fraction of a second. Here you can see the precise moment of an explosion, astonishing chemical reactions, what goes on inside an intense fire, or what happened in the Universe billions of miles away. You can see science actually working. And you, like me, may wonder at the way our world and the Universe exists. And perhaps you too will go on to become a scientist.

Robert Winston.

HOW SCIENCE WORKS

Science is the study of the natural world, from the structure of a tiny atom to the workings of the entire Universe and everything in between. Scientists use observations and experiments to generate evidence and seek answers that will help them to better understand the world around us.

▶ **SCIENTIFIC METHOD**

Much of the work that scientists do happens in laboratories. However, science goes far beyond bubbling mixtures and Bunsen burners – it involves looking carefully at the world and asking questions about what we see. This helps scientists to come up with an idea, called a hypothesis, that might explain what is happening. They then perform experiments to test this hypothesis and determine if it is correct.

WARNING

This book describes experiments and demonstrations that have been done under the careful guidance of an expert. Many of these procedures can be harmful or dangerous if carried out without supervision and should not be attempted at home.

3 HYPOTHESIS
Scientists make a prediction, called a hypothesis, using the knowledge they have, such as "particles move faster at higher temperatures, so the dye will dissolve faster in hot water."

2 RESEARCH
Next, scientists turn their observations into questions, such as "how does temperature affect the way green food dye mixes and dissolves in water?"

1 OBSERVATION
Scientists look around them to make and record interesting observations. They do this in the laboratory or "in the field", which means in the wider world outside.

A factor that is kept the same, such as the amount of green dye added to the water, is called a controlled variable.

4 **EXPERIMENT**
To test the hypothesis, an experiment is carried out. In this example, green dye is added to water of different temperatures and the time it takes to dissolve is measured. Experiments must be repeated to make sure results are reliable.

5 **ANALYZE FINDINGS**
The results of the experiment are carefully analyzed to spot patterns and to see if the results are reliable. Scientists sometimes draw graphs to help them analyze their findings.

6 **ASSESS HYPOTHESIS**
If the results of the experiment support the hypothesis made at the start, the hypothesis is accepted. If the results do not support the hypothesis, it is rejected and a new one is devised.

7 **AN ONGOING PROCESS**
Over time, many experiments are carried out. Lots of accepted hypotheses together can be used to devise a scientific theory to explain observations.

The factor being measured to get results, such as the time taken for the green dye to dissolve, is called the dependent variable.

The factor that is deliberately changed in an experiment (here, the temperature) is known as the independent variable.

Everything around us is made of matter –
the **air** we breathe, the **rocks and minerals**
of the Earth, **our bodies**, and even the **stars** far
out in deep space. Matter can exist in **different
states** – solid, liquid, gas, or plasma – depending
on the conditions. All matter is made up of tiny
particles called **atoms**. These are the **building
blocks** of everything in the Universe.

WHAT IS MATTER?

Matter is anything that takes up space and has mass, from plants and animals to rocks and minerals, and even the gases in Earth's atmosphere. All matter is made up of particles called atoms, which are too tiny to see even with most microscopes.

THE MAKE-UP OF MATTER
Each element has a unique type of atom (see pages 46–47). Some substances, such as the oxygen in the air we breathe, are made of just one type of atom. Others, like the cells in our bodies, are made of many incredibly complex combinations of these different kinds of matter.

Carbon atom

ATOMS
Atoms are the smallest basic building blocks of all matter, and each element's atoms are different. Living matter contains large amounts of the element carbon.

Keratin molecule

MOLECULES
Atoms can join together to form units called molecules. Keratin, the substance in fur and claws, contains carbon, hydrogen, oxygen, nitrogen, and sulfur atoms.

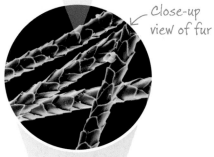

Close-up view of fur

HAIR
Molecules are very tiny, but together they make a structure visible to the naked eye – a single strand of cat hair.

CAT
Each part of this complex organism, is made up of many substances, each containing many thousands of molecules.

This microscope contains naturally occurring metals, as well as glass and plastics.

▶ A WORLD OF MATTER
Everything around you, including your own body, is made of matter. All matter is made from the same set of basic substances, called elements (see pages 48–49). Combined in different ways, these same substances form everything you can see, smell, and touch – and many things you can't.

Hard, spiralled shells such as these are often home to sea creatures.

MICROSCOPIC MATTER
Matter does not only describe the things that we can see. Even tiny things, such as this bacteria, are made of matter. Bacteria are single-celled organisms, ten times smaller than a typical plant or animal cell.

Matter can exist in different states – solid, liquid, or gas. Water is found in all three states but is a liquid at room temperature.

All living things, from butterflies to plants, are made of tiny living units called cells, which constantly renew themselves.

JAPANESE HOLLY FERN

These calcite crystals have a highly ordered structure, resulting in a unique shape.

Even colourless air is made up of matter. The only place with no matter at all is a vacuum – a space where there are no particles, not even air.

HESSONITE

Hessonite mineral forms a type of gemstone known as garnet.

A butterfly is an animal – a complex living organism.

This mineral is made up of the elements calcium, aluminium, silicon, and oxygen.

MONARCH BUTTERFLY

GOLD NUGGET

This fossil is the preserved remains of an animal that lived millions of years ago.

AMMONITE FOSSIL

ANORTHITE

WHAT ARE THE STATES OF MATTER?

Gaseous water is invisible. The white mist we see when water boils consists of tiny water droplets; they form in the air when the hot vapour cools down and condenses.

Substances around us exist in one of three states – solid, liquid, or gas. The state of a substance depends on how much its particles (atoms or molecules) are moving. Changes in temperature affect their movement, and may cause a change of state. Particles move constantly, even those in a solid, as long as the temperature is above absolute zero (-273.15°C or -459.67°F), when all movement stops.

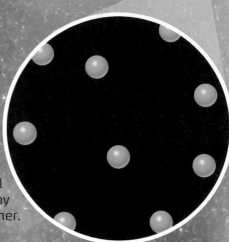

GAS
In a gas, particles move very fast in all directions, and there are big gaps between them. They fill any space, and will escape out of any open container.

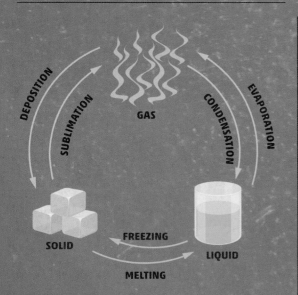

DEPOSITION
SUBLIMATION
GAS
CONDENSATION
EVAPORATION
SOLID
FREEZING
LIQUID
MELTING

LIQUID
In a liquid, all the particles are touching, but they are able to move over and around each other. That is why liquids flow, and take the shape of their container.

CHANGING STATES
Substances change their state depending on temperature. With enough energy, solids melt to become liquids, which can vaporize into gases. If the temperature falls, a gas can condense into a liquid, which can freeze to become a solid. Under certain conditions, some substances jump from solid to gas. This is known as sublimation (see pages 18-19).

▶ THREE STATES OF WATER
Water readily exists in solid, liquid, and gaseous states – seen here as ice is melted over a flame. As the temperature rises, water particles gain energy. They break free from the forces holding them in a fixed position to form liquid water. When the water boils, the particles have enough energy to break away completely and form gaseous water, or steam.

Water boils at 100°C (212°F).

SOLID
The particles in a solid such as ice are tightly packed together. They vibrate, but do not have enough energy to move around, so solids keep their shape – until they melt.

The freezing point of water is 0°C (32°F). As the temperature rises, the ice melts.

HOW A SOLID CHANGES TO A GAS

The state of a substance depends on the strength of the forces between its particles. These forces are affected by temperature and pressure – a change in either can mean a change of state. When heated, most solid substances will melt to a liquid then evaporate into a gas. But some elements may turn straight from a solid into a gas. Here, iodine goes through this change, known as sublimation.

SOLID IODINE
Iodine is a non-metallic element, belonging to the halogen group. Seaweed contains iodine, and it is used in medicine. At room temperature, pure iodine is a dark silvery-grey solid.

❶ THE SET-UP
Pellets of solid iodine are placed at the bottom of a beaker. A flask full of ice is placed on top. Underneath is a Bunsen burner, used to heat up the solid iodine. Soon, the first signs of gaseous iodine can be seen.

A flask full of ice provides a cold surface at the top of the beaker.

The iodine pellets heat up and start to turn into a violet gas.

A Bunsen burner heats up the iodine in the beaker.

► CHANGING STATES OF IODINE
This experiment shows a grey solid turning into a violet gas. It is not a chemical reaction, but a physical one, in which a substance changes state twice. Small pellets of solid iodine are placed in a beaker. When heated, the iodine quickly becomes gas, or vapour. When it cools down again, it changes back from vapour to solid.

BACK TO SOLID
When the hot iodine vapour hits the ice-filled flask, it cools down rapidly, changing into solid iodine crystals. This change of state, from gas to solid, is called deposition.

2 FROM SOLID TO GAS
When the iodine is heated, the forces holding its particles together are broken apart. The particles are released, changing from being tightly packed to moving freely and randomly. The whole beaker fills with violet iodine vapour, which rises upwards as the air in the beaker heats up.

Free particles (gas)

Fixed particles (solid)

Particles BREAKING FREE

In its gaseous state, iodine is bright violet.

HOW SOLIDS WORK

In a solid, particles are packed together tightly and bound by strong forces. However, some types of solid are stronger than others. A metal hammer has particles arranged in a different way to the particles in a boiled sweet, so when a hammer hits a boiled sweet, it is the sweet that shatters rather than the hammer.

▶ PROPERTIES OF SOLIDS
Solids may be stiff or flexible, hard or soft. Some let light through, while others do not. These diverse properties of solids are determined by how their particles are arranged and by the strength of the forces that hold their particles together.

Chocolate is a solid with weaker forces between its particles, so it melts at a lower temperature than some other solids – low enough to melt in your mouth!

Jelly sweets contain particles arranged in long chains. Water becomes trapped between these chains, giving the jellies their springy property.

DEFINITE SHAPE
The forces that hold particles in a solid together are strong, so solids will not change shape without an external force. Unlike a liquid and a gas, a solid can be held in your hand. Its size also cannot be changed. While a sponge may appear smaller when it is squeezed, this is only because water or air has been removed – the sponge itself remains unchanged.

Individual GRAINS OF SAND

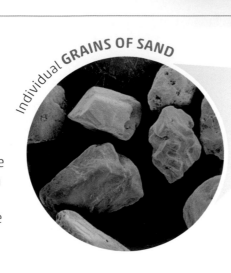

SAND
Although sand can be poured, it is not a liquid. In an egg timer like this one, many sand grains are flowing but the individual grains do not change shape. Each grain of sand is one very small crystalline solid.

Sand piles up, rather than spreading out to fill the container as a liquid would.

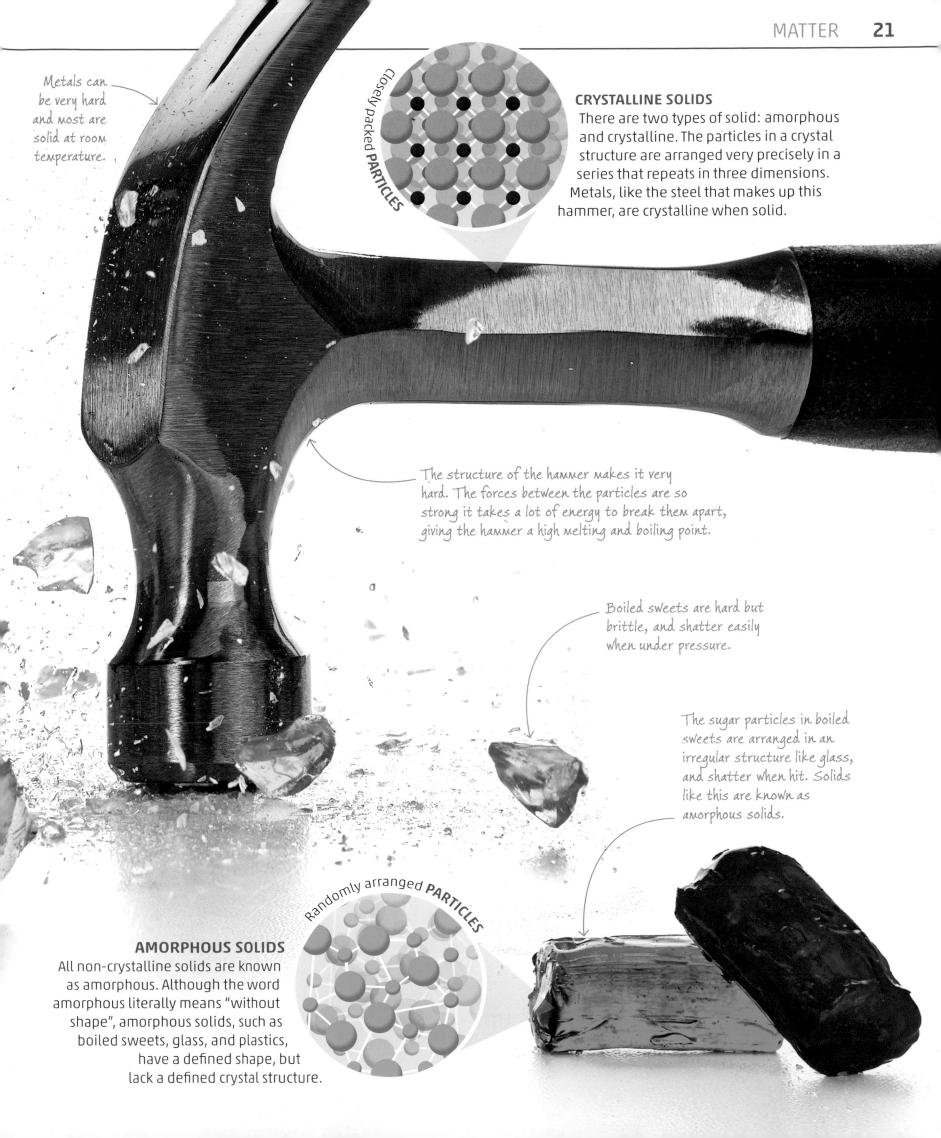

Metals can be very hard and most are solid at room temperature.

Closely packed **PARTICLES**

CRYSTALLINE SOLIDS
There are two types of solid: amorphous and crystalline. The particles in a crystal structure are arranged very precisely in a series that repeats in three dimensions. Metals, like the steel that makes up this hammer, are crystalline when solid.

The structure of the hammer makes it very hard. The forces between the particles are so strong it takes a lot of energy to break them apart, giving the hammer a high melting and boiling point.

Boiled sweets are hard but brittle, and shatter easily when under pressure.

The sugar particles in boiled sweets are arranged in an irregular structure like glass, and shatter when hit. Solids like this are known as amorphous solids.

Randomly arranged **PARTICLES**

AMORPHOUS SOLIDS
All non-crystalline solids are known as amorphous. Although the word amorphous literally means "without shape", amorphous solids, such as boiled sweets, glass, and plastics, have a defined shape, but lack a defined crystal structure.

MANY DIFFERENT CRYSTALS
Minerals, the compounds of different elements that make up Earth's crust, form crystals. Some metals, and a few organic gems, such as shells, do too. Crystals can be large or small – the tiniest cannot be seen without a microscope.

QUARTZ
Crystals of the mineral quartz come in many different varieties, from the grey quartz found in granite rock to violet amethysts (above).

NATIVE COPPER
Nearly all metals have their atoms arranged in a crystalline structure. Copper is unusual in that it can grow delicate, tree-shaped crystals.

Layers of thin, hexagonal **ARAGONITE CRYSTALS**

Mother-of-pearl inside an oyster shell

MOTHER-OF-PEARL
The shiny lining of an oyster shell is made of layers of aragonite crystals, a form of the mineral calcium carbonate.

HOW CRYSTALS GROW

A crystal is a solid in which the atoms are arranged in a highly ordered, repeating 3D pattern. Salt, ice, sugar, and shiny mineral gemstones form crystals. Rock minerals and metals have a crystal structure, too. Some crystals take years to grow inside Earth's crust, while others form by freezing or evaporation. Mineral salt crystals can be grown in a beaker.

① GROWING KIT
Large crystals can be made by dissolving a salt in water and providing a surface, or "seed", for the crystals to grow on. Delicate spikes of salt crystals start growing on the string after a few hours. The solution must be regularly topped up with salt or the crystals will dissolve again.

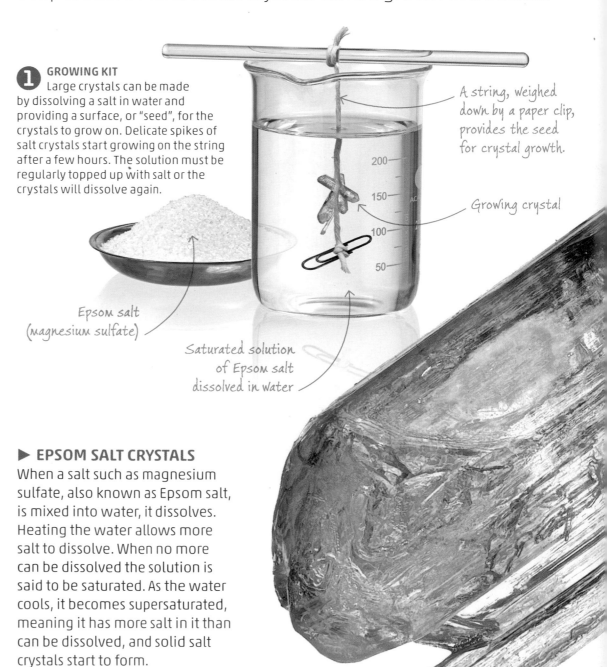

A string, weighed down by a paper clip, provides the seed for crystal growth.

Growing crystal

Epsom salt (magnesium sulfate)

Saturated solution of Epsom salt dissolved in water

▶ EPSOM SALT CRYSTALS
When a salt such as magnesium sulfate, also known as Epsom salt, is mixed into water, it dissolves. Heating the water allows more salt to dissolve. When no more can be dissolved the solution is said to be saturated. As the water cools, it becomes supersaturated, meaning it has more salt in it than can be dissolved, and solid salt crystals start to form.

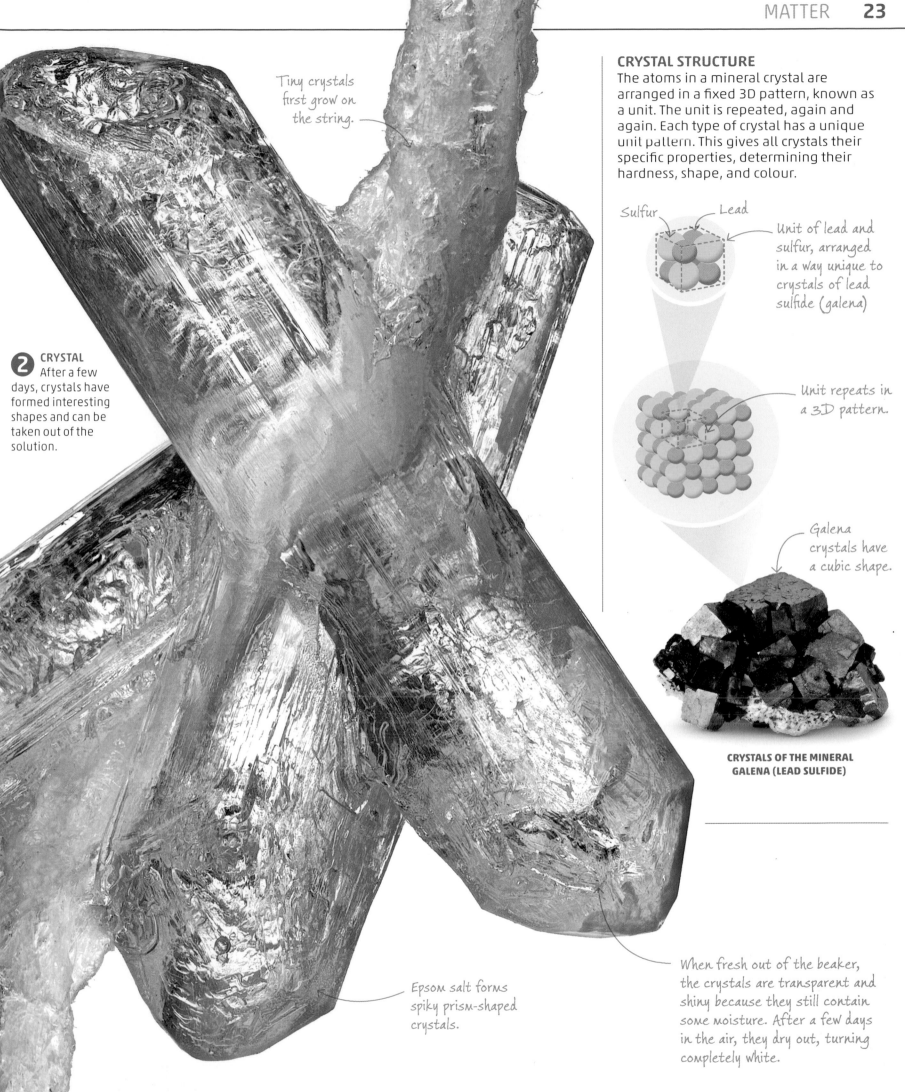

Tiny crystals first grow on the string.

② CRYSTAL
After a few days, crystals have formed interesting shapes and can be taken out of the solution.

CRYSTAL STRUCTURE
The atoms in a mineral crystal are arranged in a fixed 3D pattern, known as a unit. The unit is repeated, again and again. Each type of crystal has a unique unit pattern. This gives all crystals their specific properties, determining their hardness, shape, and colour.

Sulfur   Lead

Unit of lead and sulfur, arranged in a way unique to crystals of lead sulfide (galena)

Unit repeats in a 3D pattern.

Galena crystals have a cubic shape.

CRYSTALS OF THE MINERAL GALENA (LEAD SULFIDE)

Epsom salt forms spiky prism-shaped crystals.

When fresh out of the beaker, the crystals are transparent and shiny because they still contain some moisture. After a few days in the air, they dry out, turning completely white.

WATER
Water flows and splashes easily – it doesn't need to be heated to flow fast. It has the lowest viscosity of the liquids shown here, so it is the runniest one.

OLIVE OIL
Olive oil contains large molecules that tend to stick together. As a result, olive oil is more viscous (thick) than water, and pours more slowly.

LOW VISCOSITY
Water molecules are relatively small. At room temperature, they have enough energy to overcome some of the forces between them, so they move freely around each other.

Forces between WATER MOLECULES

WATER MOLECULE

Forces between molecules are called inter-molecular forces.

HOW LIQUIDS FLOW

All liquids flow, but some flow more easily than others. How fast or slow depends on their viscosity. Liquids with high viscosity flow less easily, while those with low viscosity are runny. Viscosity depends on the shape and size of molecules in a liquid, and how easily they can move around each other.

▲ VISCOSITY RACE
This demonstration tests the viscosity of different liquids. Four liquids are poured from the same height at the same time. Water hits the ground first – it has the lowest viscosity. Olive oil pours more slowly. Honey is even slower and treacle, which has the highest viscosity, takes much longer to hit the ground.

AT BOILING POINT

A liquid boils when there is enough energy for its molecules to break free from the forces keeping them close together. Different liquids boil at different temperatures. Liquids with high viscosity have higher boiling points because more energy, or heat, is needed to break the forces between their molecules.

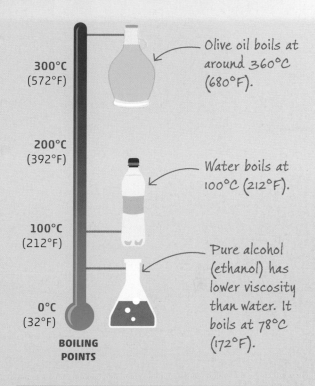

300°C (572°F)

200°C (392°F)

100°C (212°F)

0°C (32°F)

BOILING POINTS

Olive oil boils at around 360°C (680°F).

Water boils at 100°C (212°F).

Pure alcohol (ethanol) has lower viscosity than water. It boils at 78°C (172°F).

HONEY

Slow-flowing and gooey, honey consists of sugars dissolved in water. It contains more sugar than would normally dissolve in water – it is what's known as a supersaturated solution.

More energy is needed to overcome the forces between molecules in a liquid with high viscosity.

BLACK TREACLE

Like honey, treacle is supersaturated, but it is far more viscous. If it is heated, it flows more easily as its molecules have more energy.

The different molecules in HONEY vary in shape and size.

WATER MOLECULE

FRUCTOSE MOLECULE

GLUCOSE MOLECULE

Sticky honey drips slowly.

HIGH VISCOSITY

The molecules in a viscous (slow-flowing) liquid are strongly held together because of the different types of atom they contain, as well as their overall shape and size. This means viscous liquids are less able to flow freely. Sugar molecules such as glucose and fructose are bigger than water molecules, so there are more forces between them.

TAKING SHAPE

Liquids have a definite volume (the amount of space they take up) but no fixed shape. If a certain volume of liquid is poured into a container, it will remain that volume, but take the shape of the container. The volume stays the same because molecules in a liquid sit close together; they can't be compressed. But they are free to move around each other, so liquids can change shape.

HOW SURFACE TENSION WORKS

The surface of a water droplet, or of a lake or pond, is like a thin, transparent skin stretched over the liquid inside. This is because water molecules are strongly attracted to each other. This attraction is especially powerful on the surface of a liquid, where it produces an effect known as surface tension.

As surface molecules have fewer nearby water molecules to attract, they exert a stronger force on their neighbours.

WATER DROPLET MOLECULES
The attraction between the water molecules on the surface of a droplet is especially strong. This is because instead of spreading out in all directions, the cohesive force they exert is concentrated on the molecules below and to either side of them. This creates a "skin" on the surface of the liquid.

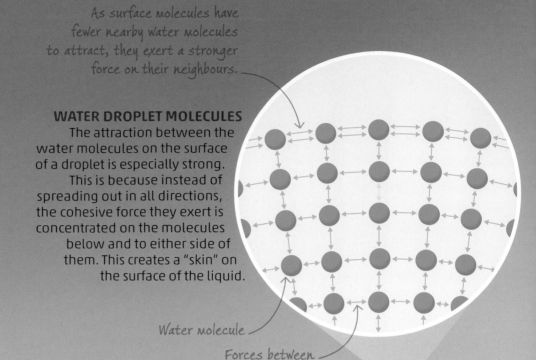

Water molecule

Forces between molecules

▶ **TRAPPED BY TENSION**
The attraction between the water molecules on the surface of this droplet is strong enough to prevent the insect from pushing out of it. Water molecules are attracted to each other by a force called cohesion. Cohesive forces pull the molecules on the water's surface tightly together, creating tension on the outside of the drop.

This insect is a flat bug, less than 1 cm (0.3 in) in length.

WALKING ON WATER
Surface tension makes it possible for small insects to walk on water. This spider's weight is evenly distributed in its legs so it does not break through the strongly linked molecules on the surface.

CAPILLARY ACTION
Water rises up into a narrow space because of surface tension. This is capillary action and it is how plants draw water up through their roots. Capillary action happens due to a force called adhesion that attracts water molecules to their surroundings, causing them to spread out. Adhesion attracts water up the walls of a narrow space. At the same time, surface tension pulls the water molecules into the shape with the smallest surface area, so the whole water column rises.

The narrower the tube, the higher the water can climb.

A narrow tube stands upright in a tray of water.

As the water level in the tube rises, capillary action draws more water up from below.

The insect's antenna was left outside the droplet when it landed.

Surface tension pulls the water into the shape with the smallest possible surface area: a sphere.

Gravity pulls the liquid into a flatter droplet shape.

The nitrogen has been cooled to -196°C (-320°F). It is so cold that it makes moisture in the air condense into visible vapour.

1 **INFLATED BALLOONS**
Two balloons are filled with air at room temperature and sealed with an airtight knot. Gas particles move around inside the balloons, creating a pressure that keeps them inflated. A bowl is filled with liquid nitrogen.

A protective glove is needed as the liquid nitrogen is so cold it can damage skin.

▼ **DEFLATING AND EXPANDING BALLOONS**
When a balloon is inflated, its inside is filled with air particles. These particles bounce against the sides of the balloon, producing a pressure that expands the balloon as far as its stretchy walls will allow. In this demonstration, balloons are placed into a very cold substance. As the temperature in the balloon drops, the particles move less, decreasing the pressure against the balloon's walls and causing it to deflate.

The balloons crumple as the volume of the air inside shrinks.

At -196°C (-320°F) the pressure inside the balloon is much lower than atmospheric pressure.

Frost crystals form on the outside of the cold metal bowl, as moisture from the air freezes.

2 **DEFLATED BALLOONS**
When the balloons are placed in the liquid nitrogen the volume of the gas decreases, until the balloons begin to look flat and empty. The air is still inside them, but the drop in temperature has reduced the energy of the gas particles. They collide with each other less often and come much closer together. They now exert less pressure against the walls of the balloon.

HOW GASES BEHAVE

The particles in a gas move around freely, filling any space available. They constantly bounce into and off each other, and against the walls of any container that holds them. The more energy particles have, the more they move and the more space they create between them. When gas particles cool, they lose energy, move less, and take up less space.

Gas inside is back to room temperature.

The balloon expands as the air inside it warms up.

Any water vapour inside the balloon (from the breath of the person who blew it up) condenses and freezes.

The balloon begins to inflate as soon as it is removed from the bowl.

A white mist forms as water vapour in the air condenses.

③ INCREASING VOLUME
When a balloon is removed from the liquid nitrogen, its temperature rises. The gas particles resume bouncing against the balloon's walls, increasing the pressure inside it. The balloon expands again and its inflated shape is restored.

GAS PARTICLES
As a gas is heated, its particles gain energy, meaning they move faster and hit the walls of their container more often. If these walls are movable, the impact of the gases against them pushes them outward. As a gas cools, its particles lose energy, move more slowly, and hit the walls of their container less. The gas particles now occupy a smaller volume, and the balloon's walls collapse inwards.

GAS AT ROOM TEMPERATURE
At room temperature, gas particles have plenty of energy to move freely. The balloon expands as the particles bump against its stretchy walls.

COLD GAS
If gas particles cool they bump against the balloon's walls less and the volume of the gas is lowered, causing the balloon to shrink.

HOT-AIR BALLOON

Air particles spread out as they get hotter, taking up more space, making the air less dense – this is why hot air rises. Air inside the large fabric "envelope" of a hot-air balloon is heated by a propane burner until it is lighter than the surrounding air, and the balloon rises. Once airborne, the pilot can lower the balloon by opening a vent at the top, which allows hot air to escape. Cool air from below rushes in to take its place, lowering the density so the balloon sinks.

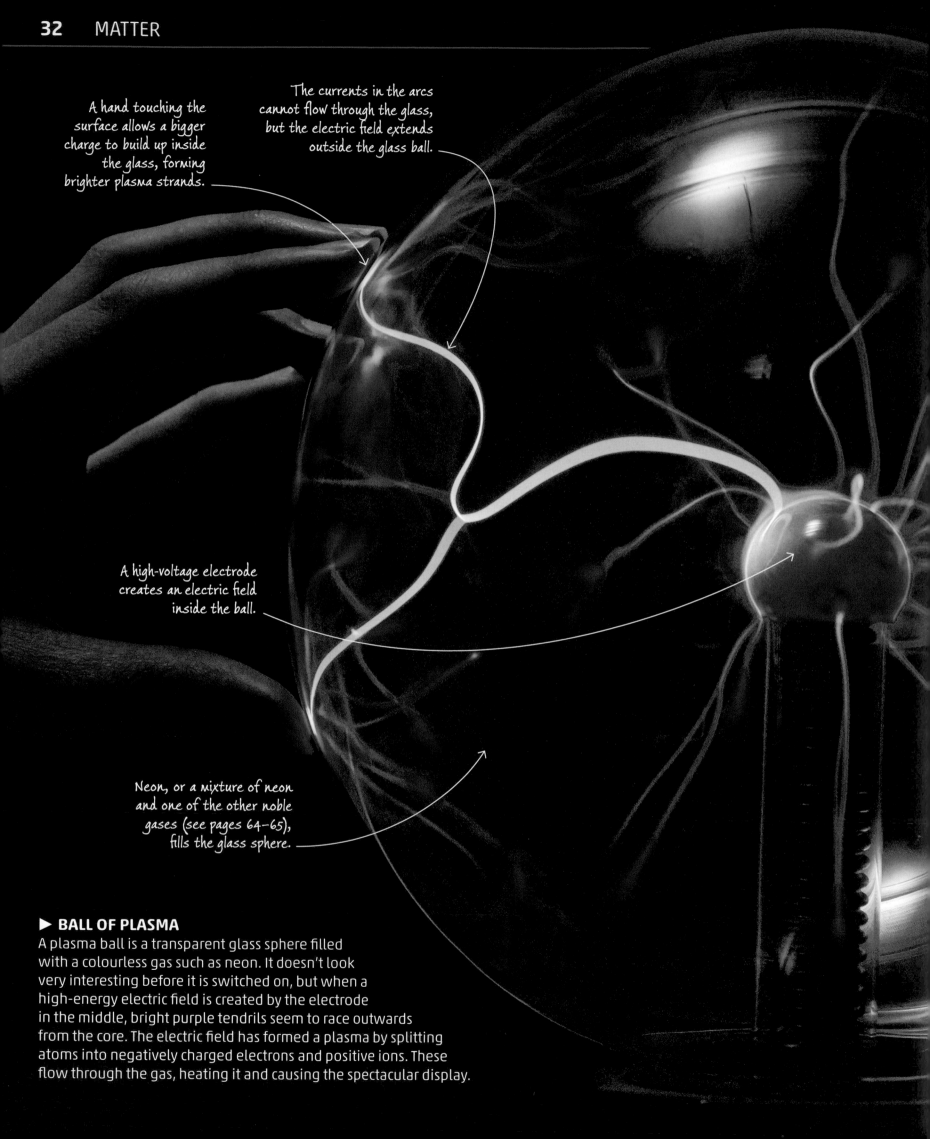

A hand touching the surface allows a bigger charge to build up inside the glass, forming brighter plasma strands.

The currents in the arcs cannot flow through the glass, but the electric field extends outside the glass ball.

A high-voltage electrode creates an electric field inside the ball.

Neon, or a mixture of neon and one of the other noble gases (see pages 64–65), fills the glass sphere.

▶ BALL OF PLASMA

A plasma ball is a transparent glass sphere filled with a colourless gas such as neon. It doesn't look very interesting before it is switched on, but when a high-energy electric field is created by the electrode in the middle, bright purple tendrils seem to race outwards from the core. The electric field has formed a plasma by splitting atoms into negatively charged electrons and positive ions. These flow through the gas, heating it and causing the spectacular display.

WHAT IS PLASMA?

Solid, liquid, and gas are the most common states of matter on Earth, but in the Universe as a whole a fourth state is most common – plasma. A plasma is a gas that conducts electricity because it is made of electrically charged particles. We can create plasma by running electricity through a gas such as neon. This is what happens in a plasma ball.

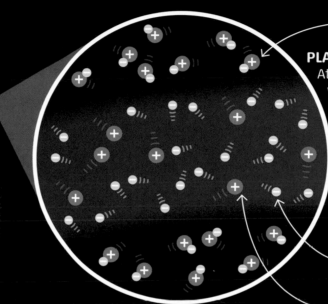

Neutral gas atom

PLASMA PARTICLES
At very high temperatures, or when subjected to a strong electric field, neutral gas atoms split into positively charged particles called ions, and electrons, which have a negative charge. They whizz about freely at very high speeds and emit light when they recombine.

Negatively charged electron

Positively charged ion

PLASMA IN THE SKY
The Universe is full of plasma. Stars, such as our Sun, are made of incredibly hot plasma, and the solar wind and solar flares that extend from the Sun are made of it. Closer to Earth, lightning and auroras are made of plasma.

Thin plasma arcs move around as charges build up on the inside of the glass.

LIGHTNING
Lightning bolts are sparks flowing through streams of plasma created by the electric field around a thundercloud. The hot spark emits white light, and electrons recombining with ions create a blue glow.

POLAR AURORAS
The Northern Lights (aurora borealis), and their southern counterpart (aurora australis), occur when plasma from the Sun interacts with Earth's magnetic field. Charged particles enter the atmosphere and cause the glow.

HOW MIXTURES WORK

When two or more substances are combined but do not react chemically, they form a mixture. Substances in a mixture can be separated by physical means, such as filtration or evaporation. There are different kinds of mixtures, sorted into three main groups – solutions, suspensions, and colloids – depending on whether they contain undissolved particles or not, and particle size.

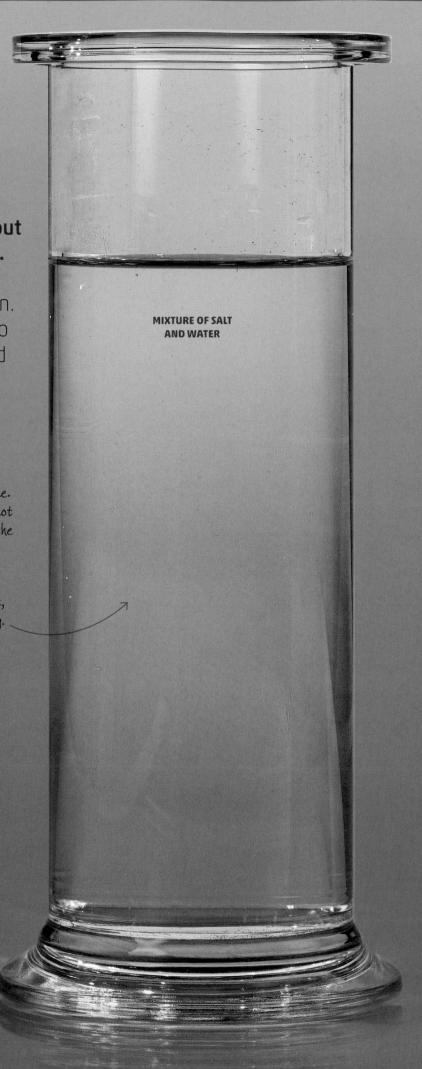

MIXTURE OF SALT AND WATER

The laser emits a powerful beam of light in a straight line. The light from this laser is not usually visible in air, unless the air is full of other particles such as dust or steam.

A solution contains no solid particles, so light passes through without scattering.

▶ LIGHT THROUGH LIQUID MIXTURES

Two jars are filled with colourless liquids. Both are mixtures, but contain different substances. Shining a beam of light through the liquids shows they are different types of mixture. One is a solution and one is a liquid colloid, which contains particles large enough to scatter the light.

1 SOLUTION
The first jar contains a clear liquid consisting of salt dissolved in water. This is a solution: a mixture in which a solid, liquid, or gas (the solute) is dissolved completely in a larger volume of a different solid, liquid, or gas (the solvent). Because the salt has completely dissolved, there are no particles that can scatter light, so the beam of light passing through the jar is not visible.

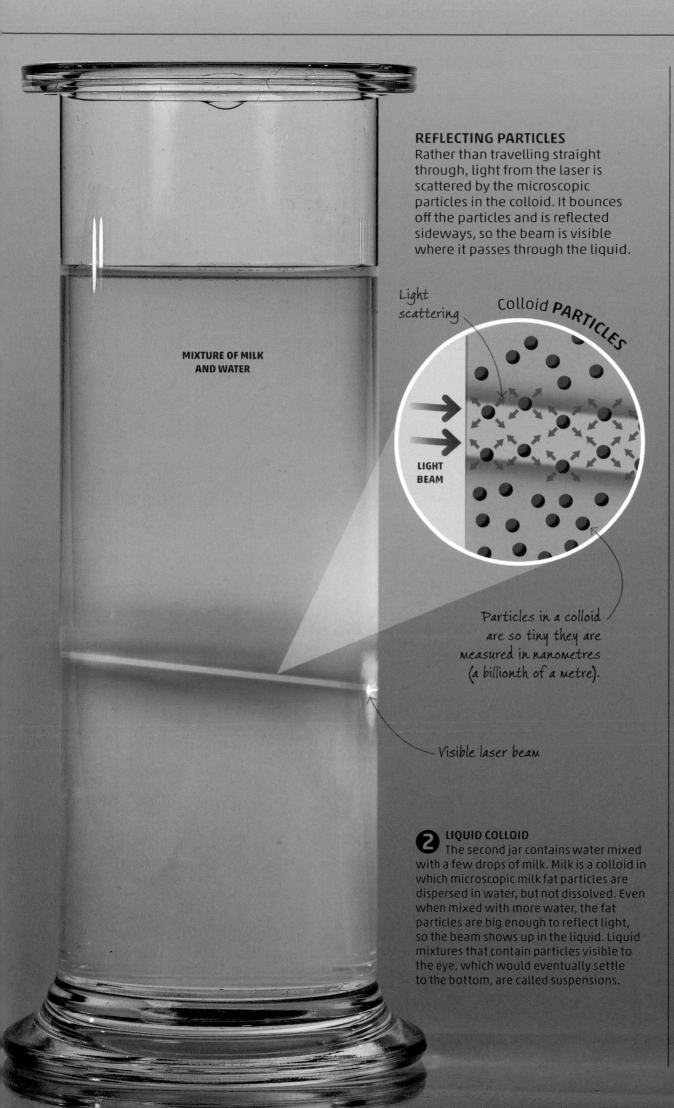

MIXTURE OF MILK AND WATER

REFLECTING PARTICLES

Rather than travelling straight through, light from the laser is scattered by the microscopic particles in the colloid. It bounces off the particles and is reflected sideways, so the beam is visible where it passes through the liquid.

Light scattering

Colloid PARTICLES

LIGHT BEAM

Particles in a colloid are so tiny they are measured in nanometres (a billionth of a metre).

Visible laser beam

❷ LIQUID COLLOID

The second jar contains water mixed with a few drops of milk. Milk is a colloid in which microscopic milk fat particles are dispersed in water, but not dissolved. Even when mixed with more water, the fat particles are big enough to reflect light, so the beam shows up in the liquid. Liquid mixtures that contain particles visible to the eye, which would eventually settle to the bottom, are called suspensions.

WORLD OF MIXTURES

Mixtures can be solids, liquids, gases, or a mix of all these. Synthetic or natural, they can be evenly or unevenly mixed. They consist of at least two different substances but can contain hundreds.

ROCKS
Rocks, such as granite, are uneven mixtures of different minerals, often visible as different colours. Granite mixes as liquid magma before it cools and crystallizes underground.

CLOUDS
When microscopic droplets of liquid water are dispersed in air they form clouds, a type of colloid. When drops grow, they become too heavy and fall as rain, separating from the mixture.

ICE CREAM
Ice cream, like milk, is a colloid of fat particles dispersed in water. It contains other ingredients, too, including emulsifiers that keep it evenly mixed (see page 39), and air.

GAS DIFFUSION

Gas particles move around fast and randomly, bumping into each other and any surrounding particles. As they do, they move away from crowded, concentrated areas, into areas of low concentration. This is called gas diffusion.

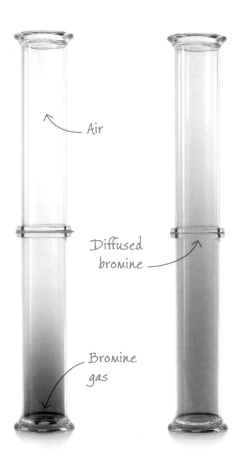

Air

Diffused bromine

Bromine gas

DIFFUSION OF BROMINE

Bromine forms a brown-coloured gas, so it is easy to see how it diffuses in air. The fast-moving bromine gas particles are slowed down by bumping into air particles but eventually the bromine will be evenly distributed in the air.

SMELLY TRAINERS

The smell from a pair of well-used trainers is caused by bacteria and decaying cells rubbed off a sweaty foot. The smell spreads through the air, diffusing to fill all available space. There are more particles, and a stronger smell, near the shoes. Perfume and other scents spread in the same way.

1 ADDING INK
A few drops of blue ink are added to a flask filled with water. As soon as the ink hits the water, it starts to spread out.

Concentrated **INK PARTICLES**

▶ **INK IN WATER**
The particles in liquids move around randomly. When drops of ink are added to water, this random movement means that the two liquids will eventually become evenly mixed, even without being shaken or stirred.

HOW DIFFUSION WORKS

The particles that make up liquids and gases move around randomly, and spread to take up any available space. Diffusion happens when particles of one substance disperse in another substance – moving from an area where they are in high concentration into areas of low concentration.

2 **THE LIQUIDS MIX**
Ink and water particles bump into each other, bounce off, and spread until they're evenly mixed. Stirring or heating would speed up the process, but it is not necessary – the liquids will mix by themselves.

Ink particles **BEGIN TO SPREAD** among water particles.

The ink and water mixture now has an even light-blue colour.

Diffused **INK AND WATER** particles

Ink particle

Water particle

3 **FULLY DIFFUSED**
After a while, the ink particles and water particles are evenly mixed. As in all liquids, the particles continue their movement, even when the diffusion is complete.

WHY OIL AND WATER DON'T MIX

Some liquids just don't mix, no matter how much they are stirred, shaken, or heated. They are called immiscible liquids. The molecules in a liquid are responsible for this behaviour. If two liquids have molecules with similar properties, they will mix. But if their molecules have very different properties (such as oil and water), they will not.

NON-MIX MOLECULES

Oil and water don't mix because of the way their molecules are structured. Water molecules have areas of slight electrical charge. They are described as polar (see page 292). Olive oil contains more symmetrically arranged, non-polar molecules, in which charges cancel out each other. Polar and non-polar substances do not normally mix.

Oil molecules

Water molecules

▶ OIL AND WATER

Oil and water are immiscible – they don't mix with each other even when agitated. This demonstration uses gas bubbles from a fizzy indigestion tablet to disturb oil and water layers in a tall container. As long as the tablet is releasing gas, the liquids mingle in a colourful show. But once all the gas has escaped, the two liquids will separate back into layers.

A fizzy tablet is dropped in.

Oil is less dense than water, so it floats on top.

Water, dyed blue, forms the bottom layer.

1 OIL AND WATER LAYERS
When poured into a container, oil and water form two distinct layers. A fizzy tablet is added and sinks to the bottom of the container.

2 **STIRRED UP, NOT MIXED**
As the tablet dissolves in the water, it releases bubbles of carbon dioxide gas. The bubbles rise up through the oil layer, carrying blobs of water with them. At the top, the gas escapes, and the water falls back to the bottom. As long as there's gas left, the rise and fall will continue.

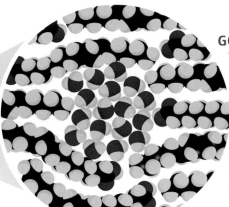

GOING DOWN
Without gas, the water falls back down. Because of the forces holding the water molecules together, they stay in a blob shape until they join the water layer at the bottom again.

Combined, water and gas are less dense than the oil, so they rise together up the column.

EMULSIONS AND EMULSIFIERS

An emulsion is a mixture in which minute drops of one liquid are dispersed in another liquid. Immiscible liquids, such as oil and water, can be held together in an emulsion if an emulsifier is added to stop them from separating. Foods such as salad dressing and mayonnaise are emulsions.

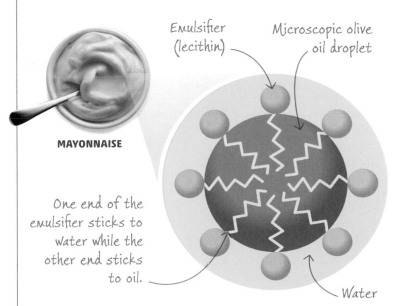

Emulsifier (lecithin)

Microscopic olive oil droplet

MAYONNAISE

One end of the emulsifier sticks to water while the other end sticks to oil.

Water

MAYONNAISE

Mayonnaise is made of olive oil and egg yolk, which contains water and a substance called lecithin. The lecithin works as an emulsifier, stopping the olive oil from separating from the rest of the mixture. The tiny oil droplets stay evenly dispersed in the emulsion.

IS IT LIQUID OR SOLID?

Some fluids flow like a liquid but behave more like a solid if put under pressure. Unlike water and other liquids, they vary in viscosity (how easily they flow), depending on the forces applied to them. They are known as non-Newtonian fluids.

A ripple spreads through the mix as the first vibrations set in.

1 CORNFLOUR MIX
One part coloured water is added to two parts cornflour in a beaker. The mixture is gently stirred until it is a gooey, slimy fluid.

2 FEELING THE VIBRATIONS
The liquid mix is poured into the speaker cone. When the music is turned on the speaker membrane starts to vibrate.

The speaker cone membrane is vibrating at a frequency of 30 Hz – that is 30 times a second.

▶ DANCING CORNFLOUR MIX
This demonstration shows how a non-Newtonian fluid reacts to changes in pressure. Cornflour mixed with water is placed on an upturned speaker cone. When the speaker is turned on, the vibrations it produces make the consistency of the mixture change. The liquid clumps together and appears to dance on the speaker.

3 MOVING TO THE MUSIC
As the volume is turned up, the mix starts leaping into the air. The large cornflour particles get locked into fixed positions, and the mix behaves briefly like a firm solid, before falling back down like a liquid.

CHANGING CONSISTENCY

The mixture is a suspension of cornflour particles in water. If you slide your hand slowly into it, the cornflour particles have time to move out of the way. But the sudden force of a punch doesn't give them enough time to part. The large, uneven particles become entangled and temporarily form a solid barrier that stops the fist.

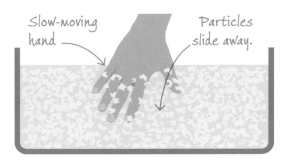

Slow-moving hand

Particles slide away.

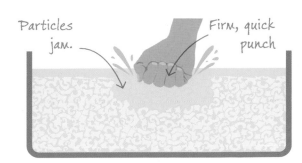

Particles jam.

Firm, quick punch

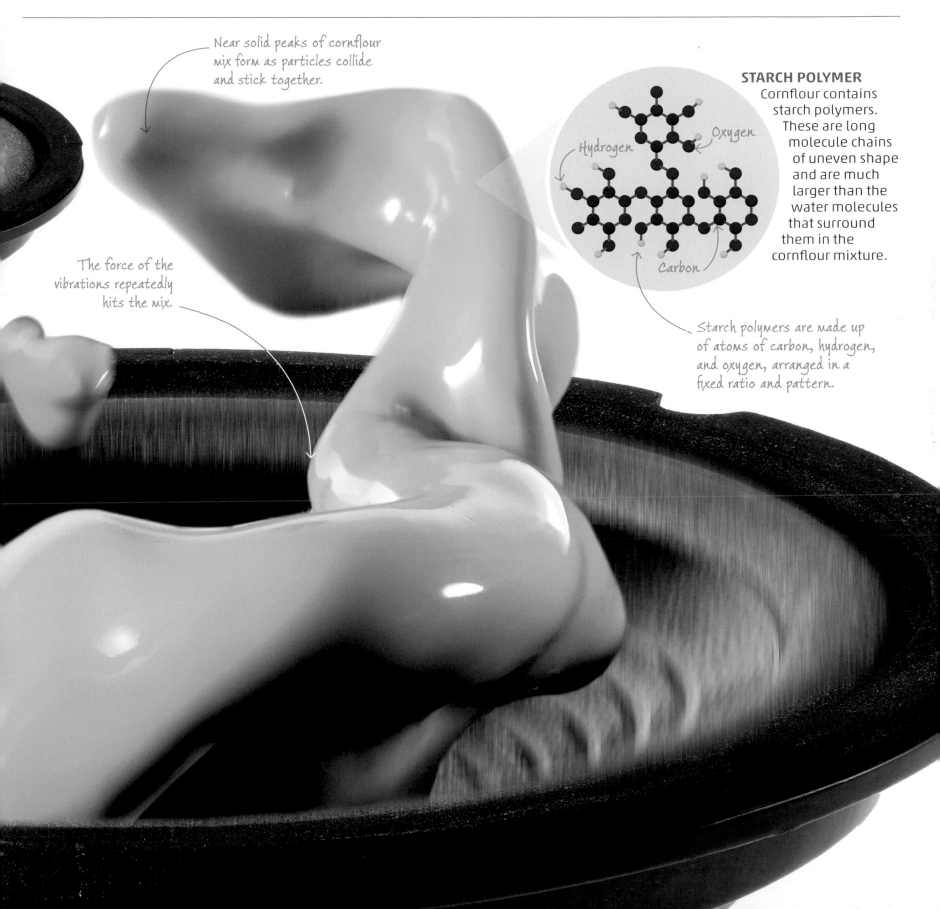

Near solid peaks of cornflour mix form as particles collide and stick together.

The force of the vibrations repeatedly hits the mix.

STARCH POLYMER

Cornflour contains starch polymers. These are long molecule chains of uneven shape and are much larger than the water molecules that surround them in the cornflour mixture.

Oxygen

Hydrogen

Carbon

Starch polymers are made up of atoms of carbon, hydrogen, and oxygen, arranged in a fixed ratio and pattern.

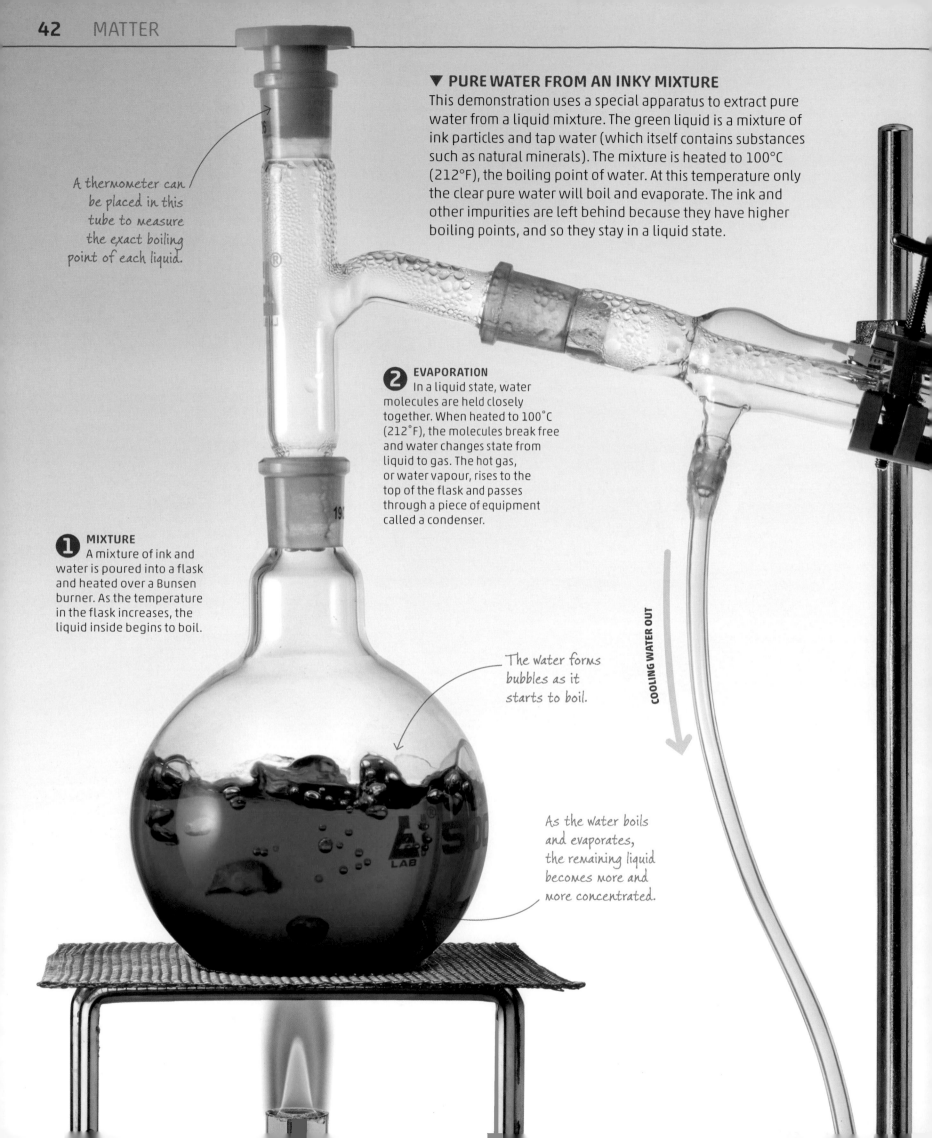

A thermometer can be placed in this tube to measure the exact boiling point of each liquid.

▼ PURE WATER FROM AN INKY MIXTURE
This demonstration uses a special apparatus to extract pure water from a liquid mixture. The green liquid is a mixture of ink particles and tap water (which itself contains substances such as natural minerals). The mixture is heated to 100°C (212°F), the boiling point of water. At this temperature only the clear pure water will boil and evaporate. The ink and other impurities are left behind because they have higher boiling points, and so they stay in a liquid state.

2 EVAPORATION
In a liquid state, water molecules are held closely together. When heated to 100°C (212°F), the molecules break free and water changes state from liquid to gas. The hot gas, or water vapour, rises to the top of the flask and passes through a piece of equipment called a condenser.

1 MIXTURE
A mixture of ink and water is poured into a flask and heated over a Bunsen burner. As the temperature in the flask increases, the liquid inside begins to boil.

The water forms bubbles as it starts to boil.

COOLING WATER OUT

As the water boils and evaporates, the remaining liquid becomes more and more concentrated.

HOW DISTILLATION WORKS

Distillation is a process used to separate liquid mixtures.
Liquids can be separated according to their boiling point.
When heated, the liquid with the lowest boiling point
evaporates first, and this evaporated gas can be collected
and cooled. As it cools, the gas condenses to form a pure,
distilled liquid. Other liquids in the mixture are left behind.

The condenser consists of a tube that runs through a glass chamber. Cool water is pumped through the chamber to cool the gas that passes through the tube and turn it into liquid.

Water starts dripping into the beaker.

COOLING WATER IN

❸ CONDENSATION
The condenser is used to change the state of a substance from gas to liquid. As the hot water vapour meets the cool surface of the glass condenser, it changes back into liquid and drips into the beaker placed below.

❹ PURE WATER
This clear liquid is pure water. The ink and other impurities have been left behind in the first flask because the temperature only reached 100°C (212°F). If the solution in the first flask was heated to above 100°C (212°F), other substances in the mixture might evaporate too.

Pure water has been separated from the ink and any other substances left in the flask.

OTHER METHODS OF SEPARATION
Different mixtures require different methods of separation. Sometimes, several methods of separation are needed to isolate a substance.

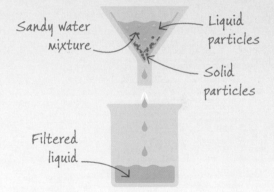

Sandy water mixture

Liquid particles

Solid particles

Filtered liquid

FILTRATION
A mixture of an insoluble solid and a liquid, such as sand in water, can be separated by filtration. Liquid particles can pass through the filter and be collected, while solid particles are held back.

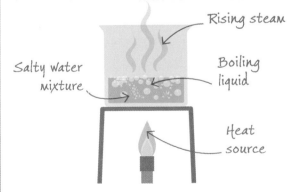

Rising steam

Salty water mixture

Boiling liquid

Heat source

EVAPORATION
A solid dissolved in a liquid, such as salt in water, can be separated by evaporation. Once the water has evaporated, solid crystals remain. At room temperature this takes time; heating speeds it up.

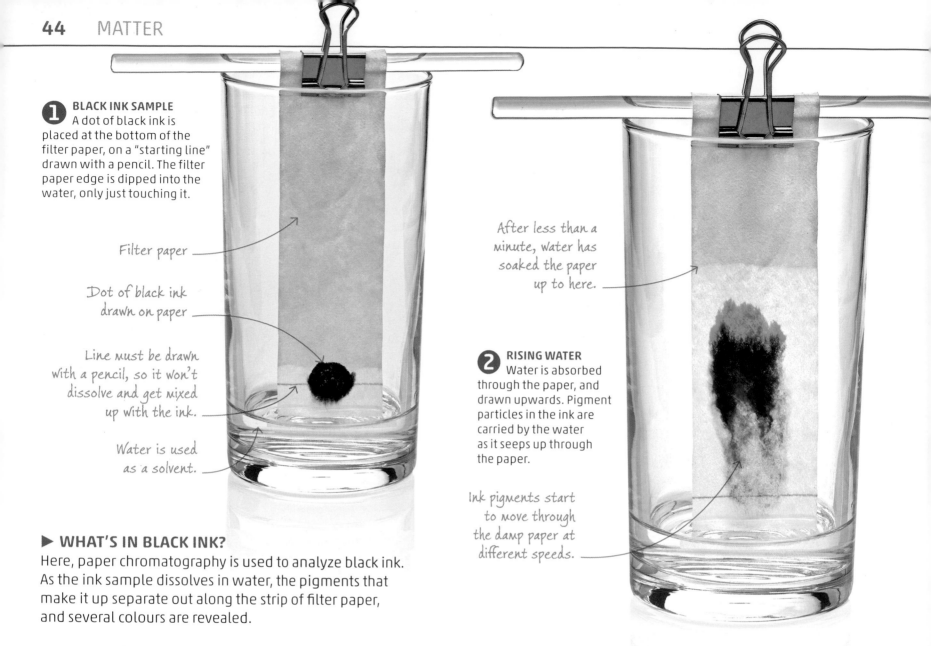

1 BLACK INK SAMPLE
A dot of black ink is placed at the bottom of the filter paper, on a "starting line" drawn with a pencil. The filter paper edge is dipped into the water, only just touching it.

Filter paper

Dot of black ink drawn on paper

Line must be drawn with a pencil, so it won't dissolve and get mixed up with the ink.

Water is used as a solvent.

After less than a minute, water has soaked the paper up to here.

2 RISING WATER
Water is absorbed through the paper, and drawn upwards. Pigment particles in the ink are carried by the water as it seeps up through the paper.

Ink pigments start to move through the damp paper at different speeds.

▶ WHAT'S IN BLACK INK?
Here, paper chromatography is used to analyze black ink. As the ink sample dissolves in water, the pigments that make it up separate out along the strip of filter paper, and several colours are revealed.

WHAT IS
CHROMATOGRAPHY?

Mixtures are made up of several ingredients and there are different ways to find out what these are. When only a small sample of a liquid is available, and it is important to find out exactly what's in it, scientists use chromatography. This method separates out each ingredient depending on how easily its particles dissolve in a solvent (such as water), and how long they spend travelling in that solvent. The simplest kind is known as paper chromatography, shown here.

GREEN INK TEST

This green ink contains red, yellow, and blue pigments.

USEFUL CHROMATOGRAPHY

Chromatography can be used to find out whether dangerous or illegal chemicals are present in a substance. It is used to test foods and cosmetics to make sure they are safe, and to test blood and urine samples from athletes and cyclists for evidence of doping. Chromatography is very sensitive and works with tiny samples. The process used to analyze these samples is more complex than in paper chromatography, but the principle is the same.

Blue pigment particles dissolved more easily in the water, and have travelled the fastest and furthest.

A tiny bit of yellow pigment is visible.

Red pigment particles were slower to dissolve, and didn't move up at the same rate as the water.

③ SEPARATED INK PIGMENTS

Particles in one pigment are different from those of another pigment – they vary in size, shape, and how easily they dissolve. This means that some travel faster than others along with the water. Each pigment separates out at a different point, and can be identified. The experiment shows that black ink contains blue, red, and yellow pigments.

WHAT'S IN OTHER COLOURS?

Most ink colours contain a mixture of pigments. Here, chromatography has proved that while blue and green ink both contain different pigment colours, this red ink does not.

RED INK TEST

This red ink contains only red pigments.

BLUE INK TEST

This blue ink has traces of red pigments.

HOW ATOMS WORK

All matter – you and everything you see around you – is made of atoms. In turn, an atom is made up of smaller particles called protons, neutrons, and electrons. Protons are positively charged particles and are balanced by negatively charged particles called electrons. Neutrons are neutral – they have no charge.

▶ CARBON ATOM

This model shows a carbon atom, with electrons circling the protons and neutrons in its nucleus. Carbon is an element – a pure substance that can't be broken down into simpler substances. Like all elements it has a unique number of protons in its nucleus: in carbon's case, there are six. An atom has the same number of negative electrons as it does positive protons, meaning that atoms are always neutral – they have no overall electric charge.

NUCLEUS

The protons and neutrons are found in the centre of the atom, known as the nucleus. Almost all the mass of an atom is here – more than 99.9 per cent. Electrons are so light that scientists only take account of the protons and neutrons when working out an atom's mass.

Proton

Six positive protons

Six neutral neutrons

The outer shell has four electrons out of a possible eight.

The inner shell has two electrons – the maximum amount for that shell.

C

ELECTRON SHELLS

Negatively charged electrons circle outside the nucleus, held in place by attraction to the positively charged protons. Their orbits are often pictured in a series of "energy levels", called shells. Each shell can hold a different number of electrons (see page 292).

Carbon is represented by the letter C.

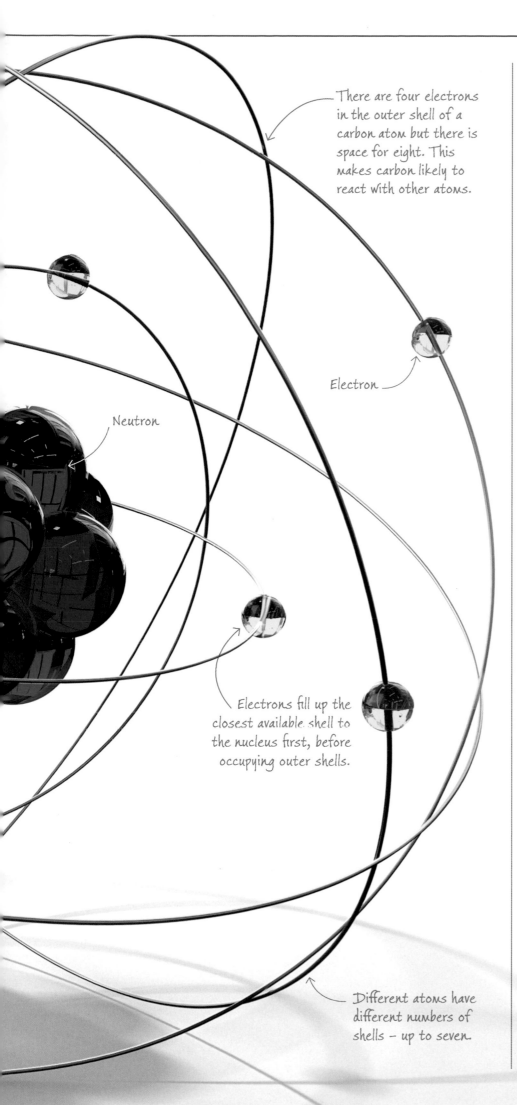

There are four electrons in the outer shell of a carbon atom but there is space for eight. This makes carbon likely to react with other atoms.

Electron

Neutron

Electrons fill up the closest available shell to the nucleus first, before occupying outer shells.

Different atoms have different numbers of shells – up to seven.

ATOMIC MODELS

Atoms are too tiny to see – about a million times smaller than the thickness of a human hair. But models can explain how they work. The planetary model, also called Bohr's model, is a common way of representing an atom. But its neat shells do not accurately show the paths of electrons. Models today – orbital models – instead show electrons in clouds around the nucleus.

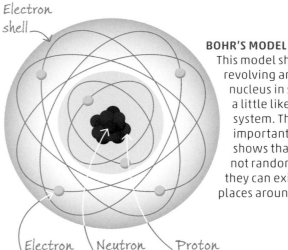

Electron shell

BOHR'S MODEL

This model shows electrons revolving around the nucleus in stable orbits, a little like a tiny solar system. The model is important because it shows that electrons are not randomly arranged: they can exist only in certain places around the nucleus.

Electron   Neutron   Proton

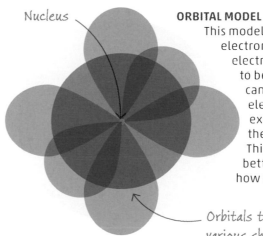

Nucleus

ORBITAL MODEL

This model shows orbitals, or electron clouds, where the electrons are most likely to be found. Each orbital can contain up to two electrons, but their exact location within the orbital is unknown. This model is much better at explaining how atoms behave.

Orbitals take various shapes.

ATOMIC PROPORTIONS

Atomic models are useful for summarizing how atoms work, but they are not to scale. The electrons are so far away from the atom's nucleus that if the nucleus were the size of a marble at the centre of a stadium, the electrons would be tiny specks around the outer wall.

Size of nucleus if atom was the size of a stadium

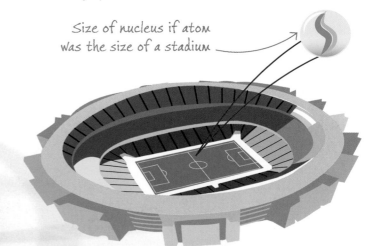

HOW ELEMENTS WORK

Elements are the building blocks of everything in the Universe. They are substances that cannot be broken down into simpler substances. The atoms of each element have a unique number of protons in their nucleus. The periodic table is used to arrange elements into groups according to their properties.

▶ **YELLOW SULFUR**
Sulfur is a soft and light non-metal that is solid at room temperature. Sulfur has a distinctive yellow colour and it is often found in volcanic rock. It reacts easily with hydrogen to produce hydrogen sulfide, a gas that smells of rotten eggs.

Each element has a unique number of protons in its nucleus. This is the element's atomic number.

16
S
SULFUR

Elements are marked on the periodic table with a symbol. Sulfur is marked with an "S".

The vertical columns are called groups.

Sulfur belongs to the oxygen group.

The horizontal rows are called periods.

Sulfur forms bright yellow crystals.

H																	He
Li	Be											B	C	N	O	F	Ne
Na	Mg											Al	Si	P	S	Cl	Ar
K	Ca	Sc	Ti	V	Cr	Mn	Fe	Co	Ni	Cu	Zn	Ga	Ge	As	Se	Br	Kr
Rb	Sr	Y	Zr	Nb	Mo	Tc	Ru	Rh	Pd	Ag	Cd	In	Sn	Sb	Te	I	Xe
Cs	Ba	La-Lu	Hf	Ta	W	Re	Os	Ir	Pt	Au	Hg	Tl	Pb	Bi	Po	At	Rn
Fr	Ra	Ac-Lr	Rf	Db	Sg	Bh	Hs	Mt	Ds	Rg	Cn	Nh	Fl	Mc	Lv	Ts	Og

	La	Ce	Pr	Nd	Pm	Sm	Eu	Gd	Tb	Dy	Ho	Er	Tm	Yb	Lu
	Ac	Th	Pa	U	Np	Pu	Am	Cm	Bk	Cf	Es	Fm	Md	No	Lr

PERIODIC TABLE
There are about 118 known elements in the periodic table (see pages 290–291). They are listed from left to right in order of their atomic number (the number of protons in their atoms), in rows known as periods. The chart's vertical columns group the elements according to their properties, such as how they react with other elements.

Sulfur can be found in volcanic mud and rock.

Individual sulfur crystals can be up to 4 cm (1½ inches) long.

SULFUR ATOM
A sulfur atom has 16 protons and 16 neutrons in its nucleus. There are three shells surrounding the nucleus with a total of 16 electrons. Sulfur is reactive because it has six electrons in its outer shell but there is room for eight.

Nucleus

Outer shell

Electron

ELEMENTS IN THE UNIVERSE
Hydrogen and helium are the most common elements, together comprising 98 per cent of the visible Universe. Stars contain large amounts of hydrogen. In their cores, nuclear reactions fuse hydrogen atoms together, creating other elements and releasing energy as heat and light.

ELEMENTS IN THE HUMAN BODY
Around 99 per cent of the human body is made of just six elements, but these are combined together to form thousands of different compounds. About two-thirds of the body is oxygen. Much of this is bonded with hydrogen to form water molecules.

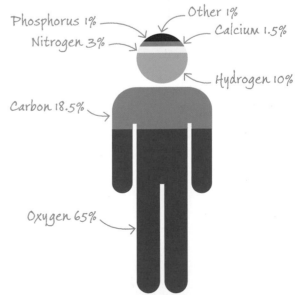

Phosphorus 1%

Other 1%

Nitrogen 3%

Calcium 1.5%

Hydrogen 10%

Carbon 18.5%

Oxygen 65%

CHAMPAGNE POOL

This bubbling pool in New Zealand is the result of volcanic activity, which causes hot water and carbon dioxide to rise from beneath the Earth's surface. The gas forms bubbles that make the water fizzy. The bright colours come from the many chemical elements in the volcanic rock – the orange is from compounds of arsenic and antimony. Although the Champagne Pool has an appealing name, it contains toxic sulfides (minerals made of sulfur) that smell like rotten eggs.

HOW ALKALI METALS WORK

The alkali metals, including lithium, sodium, and potassium, are highly reactive. They are not found in pure form in nature, but as compounds they are among the ten most common elements in Earth's crust. Sodium chloride makes up most of the salt in the oceans, while sodium and potassium are essential to keep our bodies functioning.

❶ CUT THE METAL
Potassium is taken out of a container of oil and a small piece is cut off. Potassium is soft and can be cut easily with a scalpel, revealing a shiny surface.

▼ ALKALI PRODUCERS
There are six alkali metals: lithium, sodium, potassium, rubidium, caesium, and francium. The group takes its name from the fact that all members produce acid-neutralizing compounds called alkalis when they react with water. The reaction, seen in this demonstration using potassium, is vigorous. To prevent them reacting with water vapour, alkali metals must be stored in oil.

Electron

Outer shell

POTASSIUM ATOM
Potassium, like all alkali metals, has just one electron in its outer shell. The outer electron is only weakly attracted to the nucleus of the atom, and is easily transferred to another element. This means the electron is easily lost when potassium reacts with hydrogen or oxygen.

LITHIUM
Lithium is the least reactive of the alkali metals but it does react with other elements. It also has the lightest atoms of any element that is a solid at room temperature. Lithium is used in lightweight batteries such as those in smartphones. Lithium also has many other uses: some lithium compounds are added to glass to make it stronger while others are used in certain medicines.

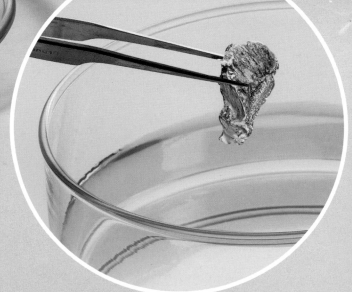

❷ ADD TO WATER
The piece of potassium is removed with tweezers and dropped into a dish of water. The reaction is violent so it has to be performed behind a safety screen.

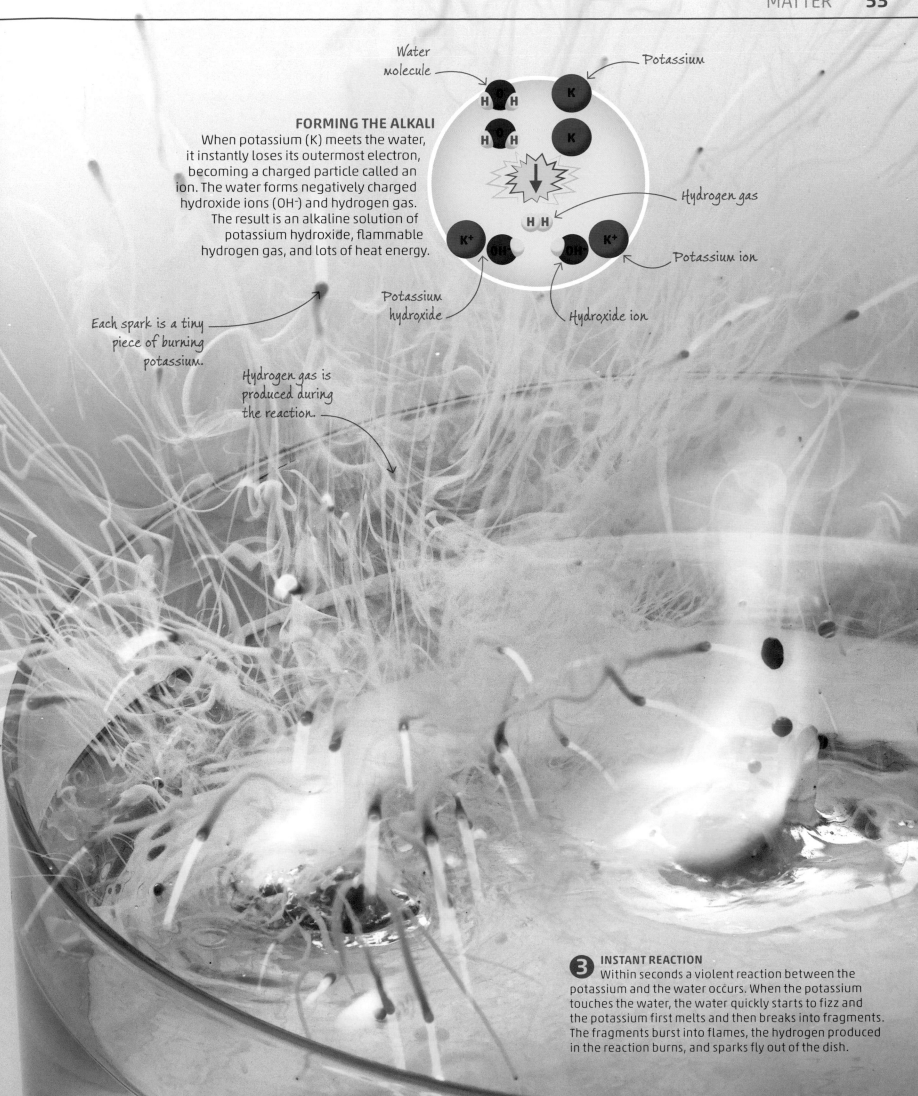

Water molecule

Potassium

FORMING THE ALKALI
When potassium (K) meets the water, it instantly loses its outermost electron, becoming a charged particle called an ion. The water forms negatively charged hydroxide ions (OH⁻) and hydrogen gas. The result is an alkaline solution of potassium hydroxide, flammable hydrogen gas, and lots of heat energy.

Hydrogen gas

Potassium ion

Each spark is a tiny piece of burning potassium.

Potassium hydroxide

Hydroxide ion

Hydrogen gas is produced during the reaction.

3 INSTANT REACTION
Within seconds a violent reaction between the potassium and the water occurs. When the potassium touches the water, the water quickly starts to fizz and the potassium first melts and then breaks into fragments. The fragments burst into flames, the hydrogen produced in the reaction burns, and sparks fly out of the dish.

ABUNDANT METALS

Transition metals are abundant in nature – Earth's core is made from iron, and many other metals, such as titanium, are present in Earth's crust. Iron is one of the easiest metals to extract from its ore, so it has been used for making tools for thousands of years.

This iron cutting tool dates from the Iron Age, which began around 1,200 BCE.

CONDUCTING ELECTRICITY

Many of the transition metals are good conductors of electricity. Copper is one of the best conductors and it is ductile, meaning it can be easily drawn into long, thin electrical wires for buildings, motors, and generators. Gold is also a good conductor and is sometimes used in electrical coating.

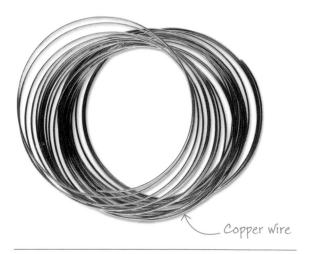

Copper wire

SUPER STRENGTH

Typically strong, the transition metals are often combined to make even stronger metals. Titanium is known for being strong, light, and unreactive, making it ideal for use in spectacle frames and artificial body parts, such as replacement hip joints.

Titanium-framed spectacles

WHAT IS A TRANSITION METAL?

Metals in the middle of the periodic table, such as iron, copper, gold, and silver, are known as transition metals. They can be found all around us, from the steel that supports skyscrapers to the coins used across the globe. As many are easily worked and bent into shape, transition metals have been used for millennia by people who have taken advantage of their many useful properties.

▶ VERSATILE METALS

Consisting of more than 30 elements, the transition metals make up the largest set of elements in the periodic table. While their properties vary, transition metals are typically hard and shiny, are good conductors of heat and electricity, and have high melting and boiling points.

Silver is very shiny, easy to mould, and does not react with skin, making it a common material for jewellery.

SILVER

This vanadium has been extracted from its ore and allowed to form crystals.

VANADIUM

IRON ORE

Some metals are found as compounds within rocks. This iron ore is a rock from which iron can be extracted.

This pellet of pure osmium, one of the rarest and densest metals, has been refined in a laboratory.

OSMIUM

COPPER

People first used copper 10,000 years ago to make weapons and jewellery.

The nucleus is made up of 79 protons and 118 neutrons.

GOLD

GOLD ATOM

The nucleus of a gold atom contains 79 protons and 118 neutrons, surrounded by 79 electrons arranged in shells. These electrons are moving extremely fast, and as a result the lone, negatively charged electron in the outermost shell is more strongly attracted to the heavy, positively charged nucleus, making gold unreactive.

Gold has 79 electrons.

Gold has been prized for centuries because it is unreactive and is found in its pure state.

▶ A DENSE METAL

Several metals, including iron and silver, float on mercury despite being heavy solids. This is because mercury atoms are large and contain a lot of matter, making them more dense than many other metals. Mercury is 13 times denser than water, so objects that would sink in water, such as an iron bolt, can float in mercury.

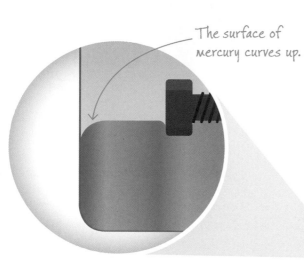

The surface of mercury curves up.

CURVED MENISCUS

The upper surface of most liquids, known as the meniscus, curves slightly down when settled in a beaker. Mercury's meniscus is different because it curves up. This is because mercury's atoms are more attracted to each other than to the atoms in the container.

CINNABAR

This bright red mineral, called cinnabar, is the source of much of the world's mercury. Liquid mercury is extracted from it by heating the rock. It has been mined since Neolithic times (8000–4500 BCE) and it has also been used as a red paint pigment, known as vermilion, for thousands of years.

Iron is less dense than mercury so the bolt floats on the surface.

Unlike water, mercury does not cling to glass.

HOW **MERCURY** WORKS

Mercury is a transition metal, but it is unlike other metals in the group. Mercury is the only metal that is liquid at room temperature and it is very toxic. It was once commonly used in thermometers, dental fillings, and light bulbs, but its use is now carefully monitored because it is so hazardous to human health. It poisons human cells and can damage organs and nerves if inhaled or swallowed.

Mercury's outermost electrons are strongly attracted to the nucleus.

LIQUID METAL
Mercury has a very low melting point of -39°C (-38°F). This is due to the way its electrons are arranged. In an atom, the negative electrons are held in place by their attraction to the positive protons in the nucleus. In mercury atoms, this attraction is particularly strong. As a result, pure mercury does not have as many free electrons in its structure as other metals, so its metallic bonds are weak (see page 73), leaving the atoms free to move around in a liquid state.

The nucleus is densely packed, with 80 protons and, usually, 121 neutrons.

Mercury is silver coloured and flows quickly, which is why it is sometimes called quicksilver.

CARBON COMPOUNDS

Carbon atoms have four electrons in their outer shell, meaning they can bond with up to four other atoms and form an incredible variety of molecular shapes. Long chains of carbon atoms that include hydrogen, oxygen, and nitrogen are common in nature. Compounds containing only hydrogen and carbon are called hydrocarbons. The simplest of these is methane, found in natural gas, in which four hydrogen atoms are bonded to one carbon atom.

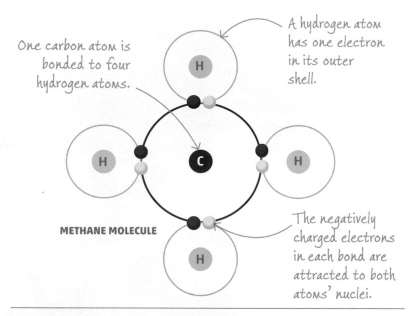

One carbon atom is bonded to four hydrogen atoms.

A hydrogen atom has one electron in its outer shell.

METHANE MOLECULE

The negatively charged electrons in each bond are attracted to both atoms' nuclei.

ESSENTIAL ELEMENT
All life on Earth is based on carbon. It is a key part of sugars, fats, and proteins in the food we eat. People, animals, and plants all contain carbon in their DNA. Carbon is abundant on Earth with plants alone containing an estimated 450 billion tonnes of carbon worldwide.

GRAPHITE
The carbon atoms in graphite are arranged in layers which slide over each other. Each atom is joined to three others by covalent bonds, leaving one electron free to conduct electricity. This structure makes graphite soft and able to flake apart.

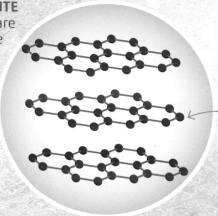

Graphite atoms form layers that separate easily.

Graphite can easily be cut and peeled with a pencil sharpener.

Thin layers of carbon flake off when graphite is rubbed on paper.

HOW **CARBON** WORKS

Carbon is the fourth most abundant element in the Universe. Its atoms can bond together in different ways to form substances with very different properties. Diamond and graphite are both forms of carbon – diamond is the world's hardest naturally occurring material while graphite is one of the softest.

▶ FORMS OF CARBON

When the atoms of an element can be arranged in molecules of different shapes, each shape is known as an allotrope. Graphite and diamond are both allotropes of carbon. Although both are made from carbon atoms, they have very different qualities. Graphite is used as the "lead" in pencils because it is soft and crumbly, while diamond is hard and used in industry for cutting.

Many small facets are cut into diamond to make it sparkle.

This diamond has been cut and polished to reflect light.

DIAMOND

Each carbon atom of diamond is joined to four other carbon atoms by covalent bonds (where atoms share electrons; see page 73). This creates a very strong structure and is what makes diamond so hard. There are no free electrons so diamond does not conduct electricity.

Each carbon atom is joined to four others.

HOW OXYGEN WORKS

Oxygen is the third most abundant element in the Universe after hydrogen and helium. This highly reactive element forms many compounds, including water, and is found in many of the minerals in Earth's crust. As a transparent gas it makes up one-fifth of our atmosphere and is vital to life on Earth.

▶ THIN BLUE LINE

Seen from space, Earth's atmosphere looks like a thin blue line fading into black. This blanket of gases, held in place by Earth's gravity, is roughly 21 per cent oxygen, 78 per cent nitrogen, and around 1 per cent other gases.

EARTH'S ATMOSPHERE

The atmosphere has five distinct layers. The troposphere is the layer closest to the surface. It contains the oxygen we breathe, and is where all weather occurs. Further from Earth, each layer becomes thinner. In the stratosphere a layer of oxygen molecules, called ozone, protects Earth from harmful ultraviolet rays. The outermost layer of the atmosphere, the exosphere, thins into space.

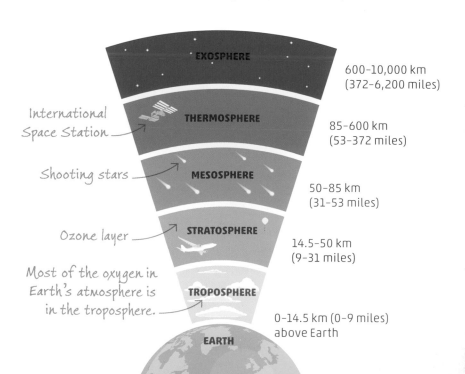

EXOSPHERE — 600–10,000 km (372–6,200 miles)

International Space Station

THERMOSPHERE — 85–600 km (53–372 miles)

Shooting stars

MESOSPHERE — 50–85 km (31–53 miles)

Ozone layer

STRATOSPHERE — 14.5–50 km (9–31 miles)

Most of the oxygen in Earth's atmosphere is in the troposphere.

TROPOSPHERE — 0–14.5 km (0–9 miles) above Earth

EARTH

OXYGEN ATOM

An oxygen atom has eight protons and eight neutrons, which are balanced by eight electrons in its shells. Six electrons are in the outer shell, so oxygen reacts with other atoms to achieve a full outer shell of eight electrons. Pure oxygen gas occurs as molecules, not single atoms, because oxygen atoms join together to complete each atom's outer shell.

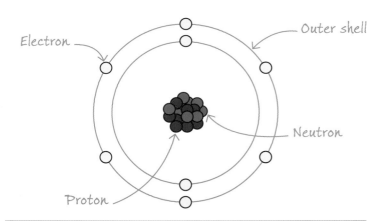

Electron

Outer shell

Neutron

Proton

OXYGEN ON EARTH

Oxygen exists in two pure forms and many different compounds. The oxygen we breathe, O_2, is made of two oxygen atoms bonded together. Ozone, O_3, is made of three bonded oxygen atoms. Water, H_2O, is a compound of one oxygen atom and two hydrogen atoms.

OXYGEN GAS

Oxygen molecules contain two oxygen atoms joined by a strong bond. Oxygen has low melting and boiling points, so it is a gas at room temperature. O_2 molecules react with almost all elements to produce compounds called oxides.

The oxygen gas we breathe in the air is composed of O_2 molecules.

OZONE

Ozone is created when a molecule of two oxygen atoms is split by sunlight. Each of the single atoms then bond with other oxygen molecules to make O_3. The ozone layer absorbs dangerous rays from the Sun, but ozone itself is a toxic gas which would cause lung problems if breathed in.

O_3 molecules mostly exist in the ozone layer but are also thinly spread in ground level air too.

WATER

Water molecules contain one oxygen atom and two hydrogen atoms. Each hydrogen atom is bonded to the oxygen atom by a shared pair of electrons. Water is found on Earth as a solid, a liquid, or a gas.

Water is about 88 per cent oxygen because oxygen atoms are much bigger than hydrogen.

1 BROMINE AND METAL
A small amount of liquid bromine is poured into a beaker. At room temperature some of the liquid evaporates, turning to a toxic orange gas.

2 EXPLOSIVE REACTION
A piece of aluminium foil is dropped into the beaker and gently swirled around. Within seconds, sparks indicate that a chemical reaction is under way.

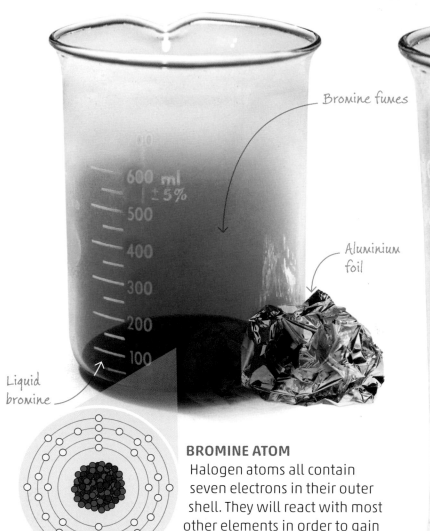

Bromine fumes

Aluminium foil

Liquid bromine

BROMINE ATOM
Halogen atoms all contain seven electrons in their outer shell. They will react with most other elements in order to gain an eighth electron and stabilize.

▶ **SALT PRODUCERS**
The name halogen means "salt forming". The elements in this group produce salts when they react with metals. Table salt is produced when chlorine reacts with the metal sodium (see pages 74–75). In this experiment, bromine reacts with aluminium to produce the salt aluminium bromide.

Halogen reactions are often lively and this reaction quickly produces sparks.

HOW **HALOGENS** WORK

The halogens are a group of very reactive non-metallic elements.
There are six elements in this group: fluorine, chlorine, bromine, iodine, astatine, and tennessine. They are corrosive, highly toxic, and so reactive that none is found in nature in pure form.

③ SALT FUMES
The reaction takes only 30 seconds, emits a lot of heat, and produces a white vapour. The reaction ends when either the aluminium foil or bromine has been used up. As the vapour cools, it leaves a residue of salt, called aluminium bromide, on the glass beaker.

Vapour fumes of aluminium bromide are produced by the heat of the reaction.

UNIQUE GROUP
The halogen group is the only group in the periodic table to contain elements in all three states of matter at room temperature and pressure.

GASES
Chlorine and fluorine are both gases at room temperature. Chlorine is green-yellow and fluorine is pale yellow in colour.

LIQUID
Bromine is a red-brown liquid and one of just two elements that are liquid at room temperature (the other is mercury).

SOLID
Iodine is a black solid that sublimes (turns directly into a gas) just above room temperature.

UNUSUAL HALOGENS
Astatine, a solid halogen, is a very rare, naturally occurring element that is highly radioactive. It is found in minerals brought to Earth's surface through volcanic eruptions. Tennessine is a synthetic element – it was produced in a laboratory and does not exist in nature. Discovered in 2010, it was named after the US state of Tennessee. Little is known about its properties.

ALUMINIUM BROMIDE
The product of the reaction is a compound called aluminium bromide. It is a gas at the high temperatures generated in the experiment, but as it cools to room temperature it becomes a solid.

The vapour leaves a salt residue on the side of the beaker.

Aluminium

Bromide

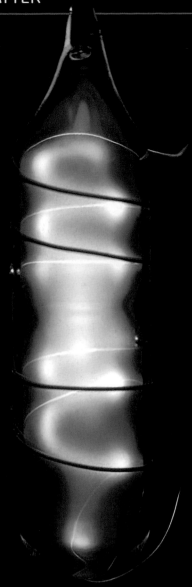

HELIUM
Helium is the second lightest element after hydrogen. It is used to fill weather balloons and airships because it is so much lighter than air but unlike hydrogen will not cause explosion or fire.

NEON
Tubes of bright red-orange neon are used to make glowing signs. Signs in different colours are often referred to as neon but in fact contain other gases.

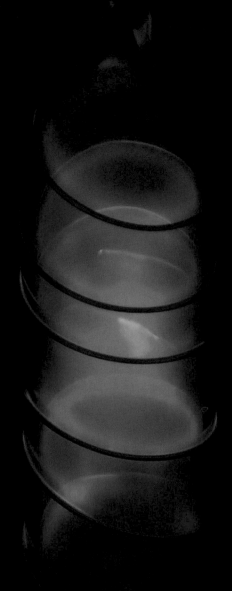

ARGON
Argon is sometimes used to fill the gaps in double-glazed windows because it is a good, cheap insulator. Its name is from the Greek word *argos*, meaning idle.

HOW
NOBLE GASES
WORK

There are six noble gases: helium, neon, argon, krypton, xenon, and radon. They are invisible, they have no smell or taste, and in nature they never react with other elements – they are named "noble" because they are so unreactive. However, when an electric current passes through them they glow brightly.

▲ GLOWING GASES
Each of these sealed glass tubes contains a sample of gas. When an electric current is passed through a wire wrapped around each tube, the gas inside glows. Each gas produces a different coloured light.

STABLE ATOMS

Most noble gas atoms, like the neon atom below, have eight electrons in their outer shell. This makes them stable and unlikely to react with other atoms. Helium atoms, however, are stable with only two electrons in their outer shells as they are very small.

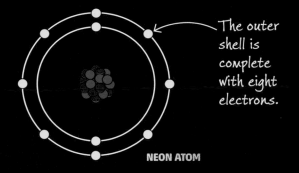

The outer shell is complete with eight electrons.

NEON ATOM

RADON

Radon is a radioactive gas contained in minerals deep underground. Volcanic eruptions bring the minerals to the surface, so the mud around volcanic springs such as this one in California, USA, contains radon.

EXCITED ELECTRONS

When an electric current is passed through the wire, the gas atoms are pulled apart – negative electrons break away leaving positively charged ions. The electrons and ions move excitedly around the tube, crashing into each other. When an electron combines with an ion to reform an atom, the energized electron loses some energy. This is released as light, causing the gas to glow.

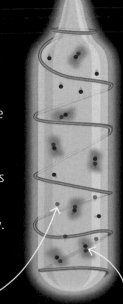

Separated electrons and ions crash around the tube.

Light is produced when the electrons and ions recombine.

KRYPTON

The brilliant white light produced by krypton is useful in flash bulbs. Like all the noble gases, it is very rare in nature, only found in trace amounts in the atmosphere.

XENON

The bright blue glow of xenon makes it ideal for use in powerful lamps such as car headlights, search lights, and camera bulbs.

In a **chemical reaction**, atoms are rearranged and **new substances form**. Some reactions are sudden, violent, and **explosive**, while others happen so slowly you might barely notice. Chemical reactions happen **all around us** – from **rust forming** on a metal to the **spark** that flares when you strike a match.

HOW CHEMICAL REACTIONS WORK

A chemical reaction happens when atoms from different elements react with each other and new compounds are formed. There are many different kinds – some reactions are slow, others are explosive. Some produce gases, heat, or changes in colour. What happens depends on how reactive the elements are, and what type of bonds their atoms form.

REACTANTS AND PRODUCTS

The substances that take part in a reaction are called reactants. These can be elements (containing the same type of atom) or compounds (atoms from different elements that are bonded together). When the atoms from two or more reactants meet, a reaction takes place as bonds break and form. The result is at least one new substance, known as the product.

REACTANTS
Whether the reactants are gases, liquids, or solids, pure elements or compounds, each reactant has a certain number of atoms, arranged in specific ways.

REACTANT 1   **REACTANT 2**

REACTION
Chemical reactions can occur when different substances come into contact. Energy is used as existing bonds between atoms break, and released as new bonds form.

REACTION

PRODUCT
No atoms are destroyed or created in a reaction. All atoms from the reactants are present in the product, but have been rearranged into one or more new compounds, which look different from the reactants and have very different properties.

PRODUCT

▼ **TWO SUBSTANCES BECOME ONE**
In this experiment, a metal called lithium reacts with oxygen, one of the gases present in air. The result is a compound called lithium oxide. This reaction gives out a lot of heat energy.

The metal glows red because it is very hot.

❸ **REACTION**
As the metal burns (combusts) more heat is released and the reaction keeps going. The metal looks as if it melts away, while brightly glowing clusters pop up all over it – a new substance is forming.

❷ **HEAT TRIGGER**
The lithium is heated with a blow torch until it glows red. The heat triggers the reaction between the lithium and oxygen in the air around it. The two elements begin to react violently with each other.

Piece of lithium metal

❶ **PURE LITHIUM**
A shiny, silvery metal, lithium is very reactive and has to be stored in oil. As soon as it comes into contact with moisture in the air, it turns a dull grey.

4 EXCESS ENERGY
In the reaction, as the lithium atoms continue to bond with the oxygen atoms, a lot of energy is released as heat and light. The bright white glow soon engulfs the lump.

5 A NEW COMPOUND
When the reaction comes to an end, the product becomes visible as it starts to cool down. It is a white, solid substance called lithium oxide.

Heat and light are signs that a chemical reaction is taking place.

HOW COMPOUNDS WORK

Compounds are substances which contain two or more elements that are joined by chemical bonds. Forming a new compound requires existing bonds between atoms to break and new bonds to form. The new compound formed will usually have different properties to the elements that went in to it.

1 IRON AND SULFUR
Iron and sulfur are elements: they contain only one type of atom. They look very different and have different properties. Iron, a metal, is magnetic and a good conductor of heat; sulfur, a yellow non-metal, is neither of those.

Powdered sulfur (S)

Some of the unreacted sulfur turns to gas in the heat. The yellow vapours rise out of the boiling tube.

2 MIXED ELEMENTS
The iron powder is added to the sulfur powder. They are stirred together evenly. When iron and sulfur are placed together they don't start to react by themselves. Instead they make up a mixture, which still looks quite similar to the reactants that went in. The mixture is poured into a test tube.

Powdered iron (Fe)

Mixture of sulfur and iron

Magnet

MIXTURE OR COMPOUND?
In a mixture, the substances are not chemically bonded to each other, which means that they can easily be separated. The iron, which is magnetic, can be removed from the powdered sulfur with a magnet.

Iron particles are attracted by the magnet.

Sulfur powder is not magnetic so it remains on the plate.

IRON SULFIDE (FeS)

4 IRON SULFIDE
Iron sulfide is a black solid that doesn't dissolve in water. It is not magnetic in the same way that pure iron is. Like many compounds, it is a naturally occurring mineral. It is rarely found on Earth, however, but is more common in meteorites, especially those from the Moon and Mars.

The sulfur melts when the temperature reaches 115°C (239°F), so droplets of liquid sulfur appear in the tube as it gets hot.

3 CHEMICAL BONDING
The mixture is placed in a boiling tube and heated over a Bunsen flame to start the reaction. As the two substances react with each other, the contents of the tube give off a brilliant orange glow. The reaction generates its own heat, so the Bunsen burner can soon be turned off. The new compound starts to form at the bottom of the tube.

▲ FORMING A COMPOUND
In this experiment, two elements react to form a compound. The reactants, iron and sulfur, are mixed together and heated. The heat causes a chemical reaction to take place. During the reaction, new bonds form between the iron and the sulfur. The product is a compound called iron sulfide. It looks very different from the reactants, and has different properties. It cannot easily be separated back into pure iron and pure sulfur.

Solid iron sulfide begins to form at the bottom of the tube.

IONIC BONDING

Ionic bonding occurs when metals transfer electrons to non-metal elements. Electrons have a negative charge, so if an atom loses an electron it becomes a positively charged ion, and if it gains one it becomes a negatively charged ion. In a solid ionic compound, the ions are held together by the attractions between these charges, forming a repeating 3D lattice structure.

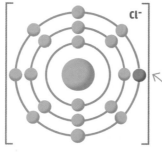
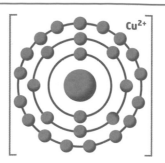
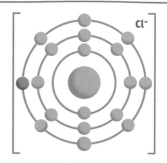

Each chlorine atom gains an electron from the copper. All atoms are now ions.

TRANSFERRING ELECTRONS

Copper chloride forms from the elements copper and chlorine as electrons are transferred between their atoms, creating ions. The ions are attracted to each other and stay close together.

Blue copper chloride crystals contain water. If heated, the water escapes from the structure, leaving behind a repeating pattern of copper and chlorine ions.

IONICALLY BONDED copper chloride (CuCl₂)

COPPER CHLORIDE CRYSTALS

These blue-green crystals are called hydrated copper chloride. They form when water molecules are trapped in the copper chloride structure. Ordinarily copper chloride is a powdery brown substance.

HOW **BONDING** WORKS

Atoms bond with other atoms to fill their outer electron shell, in order to become stable. If the atoms are from different elements, chemical compounds form. Elements in a compound are connected by chemical bonds. There are three types: ionic, covalent, and metallic.

WATER
Water is a simple molecular substance: it is made up of individual water molecules.

COVALENT BONDING

Covalent bonds form between atoms when they share electrons to get full outer shells. The number of electrons needed to form a full outer shell varies between elements (see page 292). Elements joined by covalent bonds form molecules.

Water **MOLECULE** (H_2O)

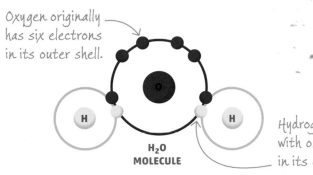

Oxygen originally has six electrons in its outer shell.

H_2O MOLECULE

Hydrogen starts with one electron in its outer shell.

SHARING ELECTRONS
In a water molecule, the hydrogen atoms share their single electron with the oxygen atom. Now, the outermost shell of each is full: oxygen has eight electrons, and hydrogen two.

METALLIC BONDING

Metallic bonding is found in metals, both pure metals and alloys (mixtures of metals). Metal ions, surrounded by free electrons, form a regular, repeating 3D structure. These mobile electrons conduct electricity, so metals are good conductors.

Ions arranged in layers

METALLICALLY BONDED magnesium (Mg)

MAGNESIUM RIBBON
Magnesium, like almost all metals, is malleable: it can be bent into different shapes, because metallic bonding allows layers of ions to slide over each other.

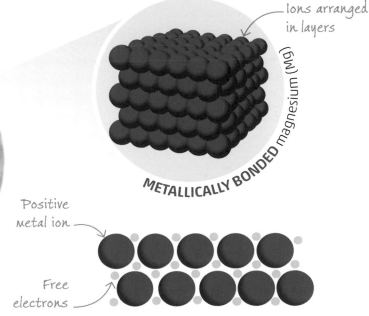

Positive metal ion

Free electrons

FREE ELECTRONS
Atoms of metals become positively charged ions by giving up their electrons. The electrons move freely, and are often described as forming a "sea" of electrons.

HOW SALT WORKS

In chemistry, the word "salt" is used to describe a whole group of ionic compounds that form when acids react with bases. However, the most familiar salt – sodium chloride, or table salt – can be produced by reacting two elements (a gas and a metal) together.

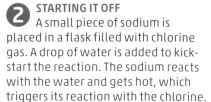

A pipette is used to add a drop of water to the sodium in the flask.

▶ MAKING SODIUM CHLORIDE

In this reaction, sodium metal reacts violently with chlorine gas. The product is a salt called sodium chloride (also known as table salt). This white solid compound is stable and edible, properties that are completely different from those of its very reactive, dangerous ingredients – sodium and chlorine.

The **REACTANTS**

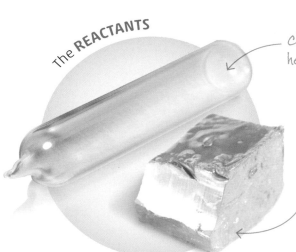

Chlorine gas, held in a sealed vial

This shiny piece of sodium will soon react with oxygen in the air and turn a dull grey.

2 STARTING IT OFF
A small piece of sodium is placed in a flask filled with chlorine gas. A drop of water is added to kick-start the reaction. The sodium reacts with the water and gets hot, which triggers its reaction with the chlorine.

Chlorine gas is pale yellow-green in colour.

Sand absorbs some of the heat produced, and prevents the glass from cracking.

1 A GAS AND A METAL
These reactants are two very different elements. Chlorine is a poisonous yellow-green gas. Sodium is a soft, shiny metal. Sodium is stored in oil to prevent it reacting with moisture in the air. When exposed to oxygen, its surface turns a dull grey as it tarnishes.

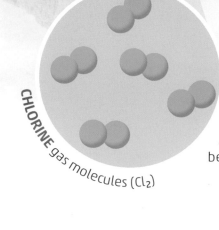

SODIUM
Like most metals, at room temperature sodium is a silvery-grey solid. It is extremely reactive, and bursts into flames on contact with water.

Solid **SODIUM** (Na)

CHLORINE
Pure chlorine is a gas at room temperature. It is made up of chlorine molecules, consisting of two atoms each. Chlorine is very reactive and poisonous, so must be handled carefully.

CHLORINE gas molecules (Cl_2)

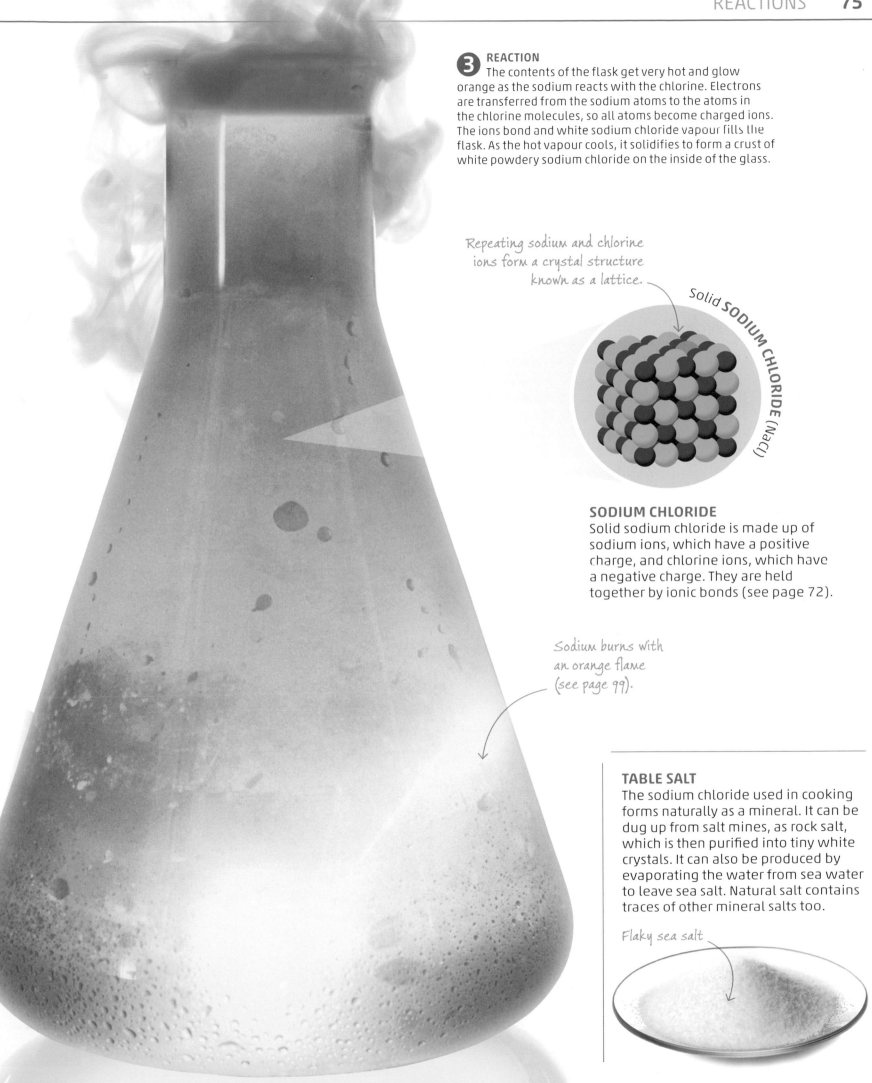

3 REACTION

The contents of the flask get very hot and glow orange as the sodium reacts with the chlorine. Electrons are transferred from the sodium atoms to the atoms in the chlorine molecules, so all atoms become charged ions. The ions bond and white sodium chloride vapour fills the flask. As the hot vapour cools, it solidifies to form a crust of white powdery sodium chloride on the inside of the glass.

Repeating sodium and chlorine ions form a crystal structure known as a lattice.

Solid SODIUM CHLORIDE (NaCl)

SODIUM CHLORIDE

Solid sodium chloride is made up of sodium ions, which have a positive charge, and chlorine ions, which have a negative charge. They are held together by ionic bonds (see page 72).

Sodium burns with an orange flame (see page 99).

TABLE SALT

The sodium chloride used in cooking forms naturally as a mineral. It can be dug up from salt mines, as rock salt, which is then purified into tiny white crystals. It can also be produced by evaporating the water from sea water to leave sea salt. Natural salt contains traces of other mineral salts too.

Flaky sea salt

HOW
COMBUSTION
WORKS

When something catches fire and burns a chemical reaction is taking place. Known as combustion, it happens when a fuel reacts with oxygen. The fuel may be a fossil fuel such as wood, coal, oil, or a natural gas such as methane.

▶ BURNING METHANE BUBBLES

Methane gas is a hydrocarbon, meaning it contains only carbon and hydrogen. Compounds like methane give out lots of energy when they react with oxygen. Methane is very flammable – it is the gas used in gas cookers. In this demonstration, methane gas has been blown into washing-up liquid so that the soap bubbles on the plate are full of gas. When ignited by a match, the mixture combusts immediately and flames shoot up.

A methane molecule contains one carbon atom and four hydrogen atoms.

Oxygen

CH_4

O_2

COMBUSTION OF METHANE

Methane consists of carbon and hydrogen. When it reacts with a good supply of oxygen, the products are carbon dioxide and water. Lots of energy is released as heat and light, and the water evaporates as steam.

CO_2

H_2O

Carbon dioxide

Water

FIRE TRIANGLE

Fuel, oxygen, and heat are the three factors necessary for combustion – as long as all three are present, the reaction will continue. But if one of these is removed, the reaction stops, and the fire goes out. The fire triangle is used to explain this in a simple way and increase awareness of fire safety.

OXYGEN   HEAT

FUEL

ESSENTIAL OXYGEN
When there is plenty of oxygen reacting with the fuel, the combustion is complete, forming water and carbon dioxide. But if less oxygen is available, incomplete combustion occurs and other products form, including soot and carbon monoxide. The flame of a Bunsen burner, which can be adjusted, clearly shows the difference in colour.

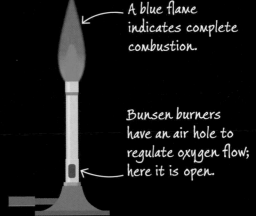

A blue flame indicates complete combustion.

Bunsen burners have an air hole to regulate oxygen flow; here it is open.

COMPLETE COMBUSTION
A blue, nearly see-through flame shows that there is plenty of oxygen. In the reaction, all carbon atoms in the fuel bond with oxygen atoms to form carbon dioxide, which is not harmful in low concentrations. The hot blue flame of a Bunsen burner is the one used in experiments, but it can be hard to see.

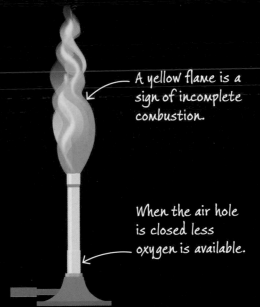

A yellow flame is a sign of incomplete combustion.

When the air hole is closed less oxygen is available.

INCOMPLETE COMBUSTION
A yellow flame is a sign that combustion is incomplete. This means that soot and carbon monoxide, a harmful substance, are produced. The Bunsen burner was designed to have a yellow flame when the air hole is closed, in order to make the flame easier to see when the Bunsen burner is not in use.

This flame is yellow because it contains soot particles.

These soap bubbles are full of flammable methane gas.

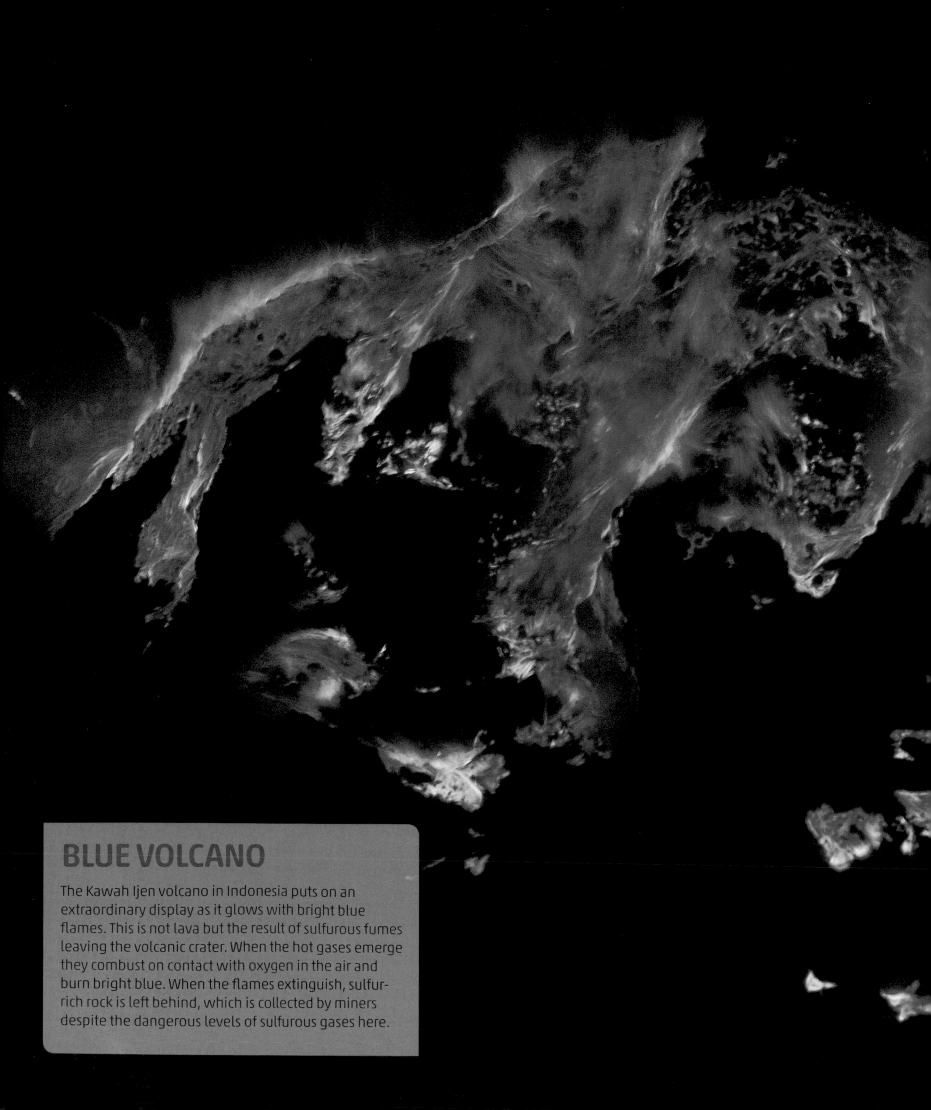

BLUE VOLCANO

The Kawah Ijen volcano in Indonesia puts on an extraordinary display as it glows with bright blue flames. This is not lava but the result of sulfurous fumes leaving the volcanic crater. When the hot gases emerge they combust on contact with oxygen in the air and burn bright blue. When the flames extinguish, sulfur-rich rock is left behind, which is collected by miners despite the dangerous levels of sulfurous gases here.

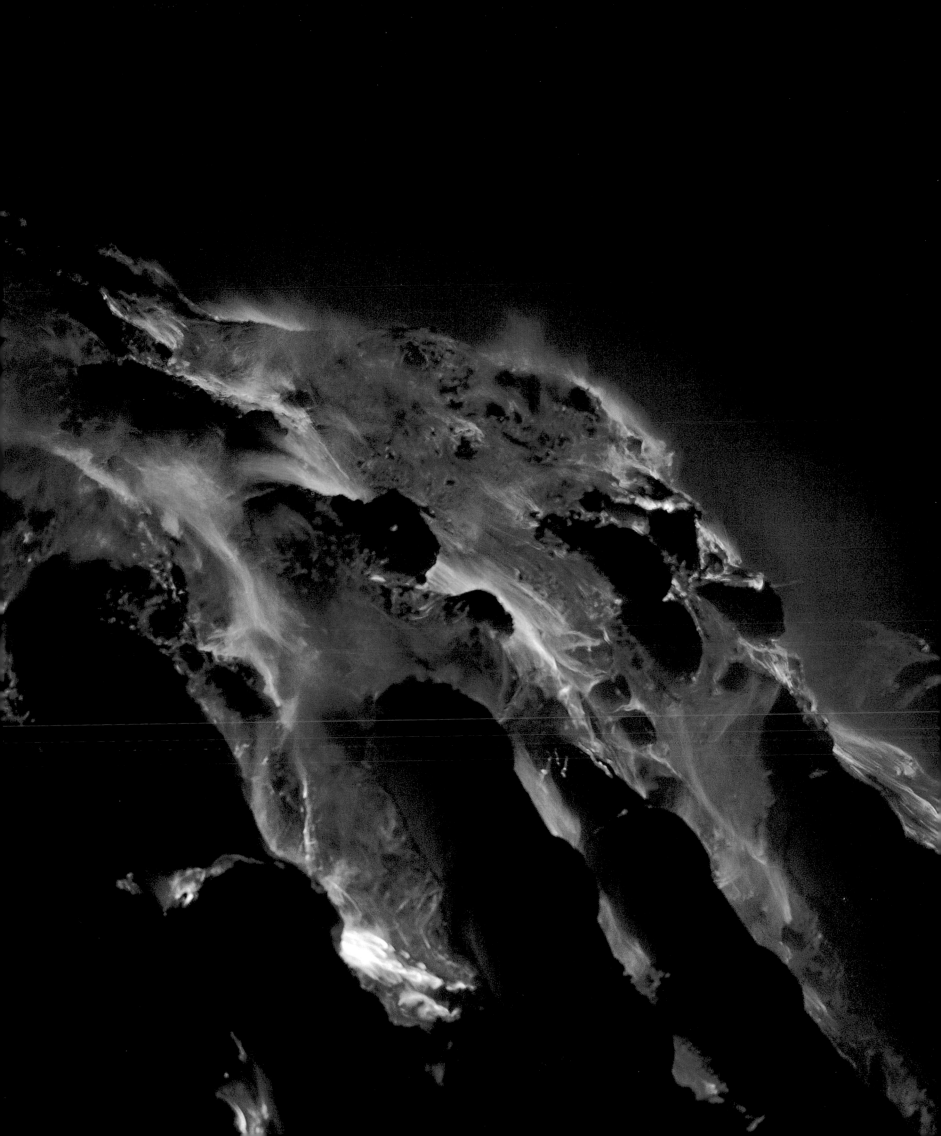

HOW REACTIONS
RELEASE ENERGY

All chemical reactions involve energy changes:
energy goes in, and energy is released. In some
reactions, a lot more energy is released than goes in.
That energy appears as heat and light. Such reactions
are called exothermic, which means "outside heat".
This demonstration, nicknamed "the screaming jelly baby",
is a well-known example of an exothermic reaction.

*The lilac flame
colour is due to
the potassium in the
potassium chlorate.*

1 PREPARING THE REACTANTS
Potassium chlorate, a white crystalline
compound, is used as the source of oxygen
for this reaction. It has to be molten to react,
so it is heated with a Bunsen flame until it
melts, at 356°C (673°F). The heat source is
removed and the jelly baby is dropped into
the tube with tongs. The high temperature
of the potassium chlorate makes the reaction
with the glucose happen very quickly.

*Jelly baby
sweets contain a
lot of the simple
sugar glucose.*

*Molten
potassium chlorate*

*A boiling tube is made
of strong glass that
can withstand high
temperatures.*

▶ **THE SCREAMING JELLY BABY**
In this experiment a jelly baby, containing large
amounts of the sugar glucose, is dropped into molten
potassium chlorate, a source of oxygen. The glucose
reacts with the oxygen in spectacular fashion,
producing heat, colourful smoke, and an eerie noise.

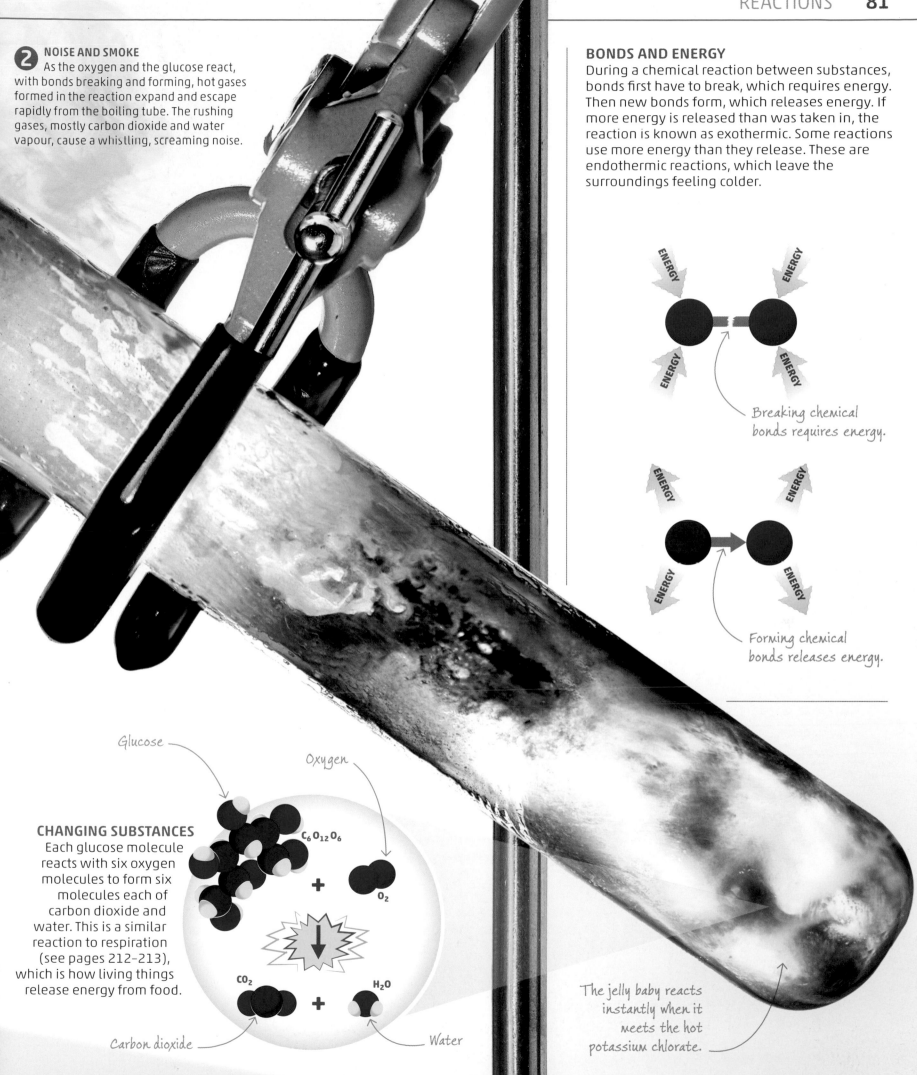

2 NOISE AND SMOKE

As the oxygen and the glucose react, with bonds breaking and forming, hot gases formed in the reaction expand and escape rapidly from the boiling tube. The rushing gases, mostly carbon dioxide and water vapour, cause a whistling, screaming noise.

BONDS AND ENERGY

During a chemical reaction between substances, bonds first have to break, which requires energy. Then new bonds form, which releases energy. If more energy is released than was taken in, the reaction is known as exothermic. Some reactions use more energy than they release. These are endothermic reactions, which leave the surroundings feeling colder.

ENERGY ENERGY
ENERGY ENERGY

Breaking chemical bonds requires energy.

ENERGY ENERGY
ENERGY ENERGY

Forming chemical bonds releases energy.

CHANGING SUBSTANCES

Each glucose molecule reacts with six oxygen molecules to form six molecules each of carbon dioxide and water. This is a similar reaction to respiration (see pages 212–213), which is how living things release energy from food.

Glucose

Oxygen

$C_6O_{12}O_6$

O_2

CO_2

H_2O

Carbon dioxide

Water

The jelly baby reacts instantly when it meets the hot potassium chlorate.

HOW A REACTION PRODUCES
MOLTEN IRON

Many reactions give out heat, but some are more powerful than others. When thermite (a mixture of iron oxide and aluminium powder) is ignited by a simple sparkler, it produces staggering amounts of heat. The reaction becomes hot enough to melt iron, something usually only achieved in the high temperatures of purpose-built furnaces.

▶ **SUPER-HOT REACTION**
In this highly exothermic reaction, thermite powder is placed in a paper cone. A hot sparkler ignites the mixture, and from that point onwards the reaction generates its own heat – getting so hot that it passes the melting point of iron at 1,535°C (2,795°F). Glowing blobs of liquid iron are produced, and collected in the beaker below.

THERMITE MIXTURE
The thermite mixture is finely powdered aluminium metal mixed with iron oxide powder, in a ratio of about three parts aluminium to eight parts iron oxide. The mixture has to be very dry, as any moisture makes it hard to ignite.

The long sparkler acts as a fuse, allowing the person who lights it time to move away before the reaction begins.

The thermite mixture is placed in the cone.

1 SETTING UP
The highly reactive thermite mixture is carefully prepared, and placed in a cone made of filter paper. A magnesium sparkler is used to ignite the mixture. This can reach higher temperatures than an ordinary taper or match, and so provides the large amount of heat needed to start the reaction. A beaker filled with water and sand is placed beneath the cone to collect the molten iron.

The beaker contains both water and sand, which will absorb and disperse the heat energy produced by the reaction and prevent the beaker from breaking.

A tripod holds the cone and sparkler in place.

Sparks fly in all directions
as the reaction reaches
temperatures of 2,000°C
(3,632°F) and some of
the thermite powder
shoots into the air.

2 EXPLOSIVE THERMITE

Once the mixture is ignited, it reacts
very quickly, producing a dramatic burst
of heat and light as the bonds in the iron
oxide compound are broken and new
bonds are formed. Aluminium is a more
reactive metal than iron (see pages 88–
89), so the released oxygen reacts with
the aluminium to form a new compound,
aluminium oxide. The released iron melts
and drops as a glowing liquid blob into
the beaker below.

LUMP OF IRON

Once the molten iron
has cooled down, it forms
a rough lump that is quite
brittle. This sort of iron is called
pig iron, or crude iron.

The hot iron drops into the water as
a glowing liquid, but will eventually
cool to form a hard solid.

HOW **RUST** WORKS

Objects made from iron or steel will rust if left exposed to water and air. Rusting is a form of chemical reaction known as corrosion, which happens when iron comes into contact with both oxygen and water. The product, rust, is a combination of different iron compounds, which produce rust of different colours, the most common being red rust.

Seen through a powerful microscope, rust has a crystal-like appearance.

EXTREME CLOSE-UP of rust

▶ RUSTY WRECK

The harsh impact of rust on iron is clearly visible in this photo of the wreck of the SS *Maheno*, which ran aground off the coast of Fraser Island, Australia, in 1935. Its hull is made of steel, an alloy of iron. Over the decades, rust has spread all over its hull, making the steel brittle to the point where it has crumbled apart.

COLOURFUL CORROSION

Rust consists of iron compounds, including iron hydroxides and iron oxides. Depending on which other elements are present in the compounds, rust comes in different colours, from blue-green to orange and red.

RUST CHEMISTRY

When water and oxygen come into contact with iron, the iron atoms lose electrons and form ions with a positive charge. At the same time, oxygen reacts with water and gains electrons to form negatively charged hydroxide ions. These ions react with each other, and with oxygen atoms, to form rust. This type of reaction, in which electrons are lost and gained, is called a redox reaction (see page 293).

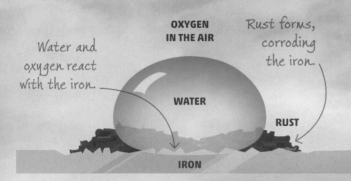

Water and oxygen react with the iron.

OXYGEN IN THE AIR

Rust forms, corroding the iron.

WATER

RUST

IRON

PREVENTING RUST

If the surface of iron or steel is protected from oxygen and water, it won't rust. One simple way to protect it is to paint it. Another is to use a process called galvanizing, in which the metal is coated with a layer of zinc. Stainless steel is an alloy of iron to which others elements, such as chromium, have been added to increase its resistance to corrosion. It is used in bridges as well as in cutlery.

Uncoated, newly made steel is shiny.

Steel rusts over time when exposed to oxygen and water.

A coating of zinc protects the metal.

NEW STEEL BOLT AND WASHERS   **RUSTY BOLT**   **GALVANIZED STEEL BOLT**

Rust has weakened the structure.

Rust is brittle. Once a layer has formed it flakes off, leaving more of the original metal open to the elements. Eventually, rust eats through the metal, weakening it until it finally crumbles.

Sea water contains salt (sodium chloride). The salt ions speed up the corrosion reaction, so iron or steel exposed to sea water rusts quicker than if exposed to just rain or fresh water.

▶ THE "BLACK SNAKE" EXPERIMENT

If it is heated in plenty of oxygen, sugar (sucrose) burns to produce carbon dioxide and water. Most of the sugar in this experiment doesn't come into contact with much oxygen. Instead of burning, the sugar decomposes into water and carbon. The baking soda (sodium hydrogen carbonate) forms carbon dioxide, water, and sodium carbonate.

❶ REACTANTS
Sugar is mixed with baking soda and placed on some sand. A little bit of lighter fuel is added and the mixture is ignited.

Mixture of sugar and baking soda

❷ BURNING SUGAR
The sugar around the edges of the heap is surrounded by oxygen in the air. It burns (combusts) to form carbon dioxide and water. This reaction gives out a lot of heat.

1 MINUTE

The fuel and the outer layer of sugar combusts.

❸ SUGAR BREAKS APART
The sugar in the middle of the heap gets hot. It breaks down (decomposes) into pure carbon and water vapour. The baking soda decomposes, too, to produce the carbon dioxide that causes the snake to grow.

A black carbon snake starts growing out of the burning mixture.

5 MINUTES

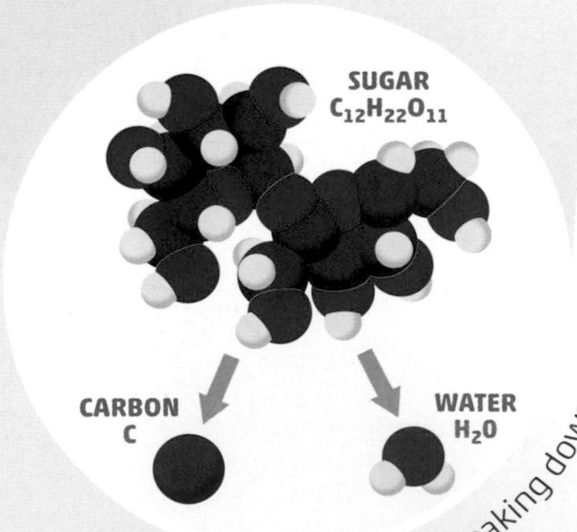

SUGAR
$C_{12}H_{22}O_{11}$

CARBON
C

WATER
H_2O

SUGAR breaking down

The sand stops the heat and flames spreading beyond the plate.

15 MINUTES

HOW **SUGAR** BREAKS DOWN

When some compounds are heated, they break down into smaller, simpler substances. This process is known as decomposition. In this experiment, sugar and baking soda decompose to form carbon dioxide gas, solid carbon, and water vapour. Together, they produce a writhing carbon snake.

Once the reaction is complete the structure left behind is rigid, but full of holes. It feels hard and crumbly, like a meringue.

Bubbles of carbon dioxide and water vapour

CARBON DIOXIDE
As the reaction takes place, carbon dioxide gas and water vapour bubble through the mixture, creating holes. The same happens in baking, when baking soda is used to make cakes rise to be light and airy.

4 GROWING SNAKE
The snake is mostly solid carbon, with a little sodium carbonate. It expands as it grows, pushed outwards by bubbles of gas. Twisting, it often curls over itself. The mixture can keep burning for more than 20 minutes.

The copper wire is made of atoms.

The silver dissolved in the solution takes the form of charged ions.

1 COPPER IN SILVER NITRATE
A coil of copper wire is placed in a solution of silver nitrate and water. Silver nitrate is an ionic compound, so it contains charged ions. It readily dissolves in water to form a colourless solution.

Silver crystals begin to form on the surface of the copper wire.

The silver ions gain electrons and become atoms.

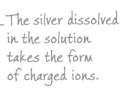

CHANGING PLACES
During the reaction, the copper atoms (Cu) in the wire each give up two electrons to become positively charged copper ions (Cu^{2+}) and enter the solution. The silver ions (Ag^+) each gain an electron to become silver atoms (Ag) that form solid crystals.

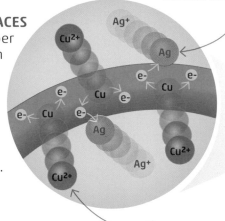

The copper atoms lose electrons and become ions.

2 REACTION BEGINS
Crystals of silver metal start to form on the copper wire. As copper ions form in the clear solution, it starts changing colour – a sign that a chemical reaction is happening.

HOW ONE METAL DISPLACES ANOTHER

Some elements are more chemically reactive than others. When a more reactive metal takes the place of a less reactive one in a compound, this is known as a displacement reaction. In this experiment, the more reactive copper pushes silver out of its compound.

▲ COPPER REACTING WITH SILVER
When a piece of copper wire is placed in a solution containing a silver nitrate compound, silver crystals form on the wire and the liquid turns blue. The copper has displaced the silver: the copper becomes part of the compound in the solution, and the silver leaves the solution, forming solid silver crystals on the wire.

3 SOLID SILVER CRYSTALS
Left overnight, the copper wire is now covered in crystals of solid silver metal. The solution has become copper nitrate, getting its blue colour from the copper ions.

REACTIVITY SERIES
Different metals (and sometimes non-metals, such as carbon) can be placed in a list according to how reactive they are. Known as a reactivity series, it is a useful tool to compare elements, and predict how each one might react with other elements. The one below compares 10 metals.

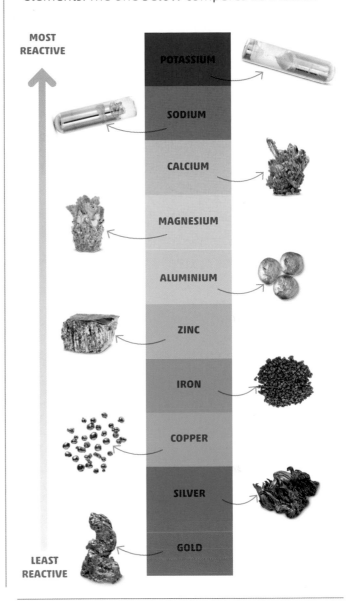

MOST REACTIVE

POTASSIUM
SODIUM
CALCIUM
MAGNESIUM
ALUMINIUM
ZINC
IRON
COPPER
SILVER
GOLD

LEAST REACTIVE

SILVER-COATED WIRE
Once all the silver ions in the solution have become silver atoms, the reaction stops. There was more copper than silver to begin with, so some copper wire remains underneath the thick layer of silver.

HOW A
SOLID
CAN FORM IN A SOLUTION

Sometimes a solid forms when two solutions are mixed, in a reaction called precipitation. In the most dramatic examples, the solid that forms is a very different colour to that of the solutions being mixed, as seen in this reaction where two colourless solutions combine to form a bright yellow solid, as if by magic.

▶ **MAKING A PRECIPITATE**
In this demonstration, two colourless solutions, lead nitrate and potassium iodide, are mixed, resulting in the formation of a startling yellow solid called lead iodide. A solid that forms like this out of a solution is called a precipitate.

1 **TWO COLOURLESS SOLUTIONS**
Both potassium iodide and lead nitrate form colourless solutions when dissolved in water. They are both made up of charged particles, called ions, which move freely amongst the water molecules. It is almost impossible to tell just by looking that the solutions are any different from plain water.

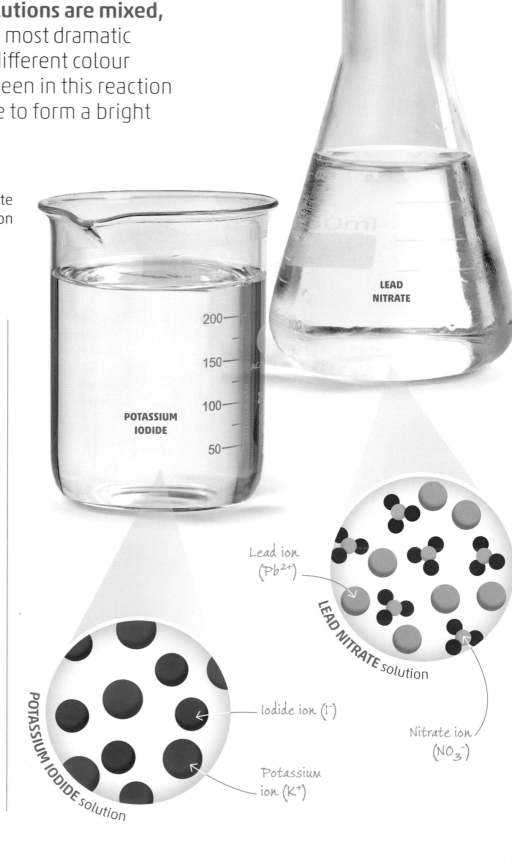

LEAD
NITRATE

200
150
100
50

POTASSIUM
IODIDE

Lead ion
(Pb²⁺)

LEAD NITRATE solution

Limescale
crystals

Heating
element from
a kettle

LIMESCALE
One of the most familiar examples of precipitation is found in many kitchens on the inside of a kettle in the form of limescale. When water containing calcium ions (called "hard" water) is heated, calcium carbonate precipitates out of the water. This precipitate, also called limescale, sticks to the heating element of the kettle.

POTASSIUM IODIDE solution

Iodide ion (I⁻)

Nitrate ion
(NO₃⁻)

Potassium
ion (K⁺)

2 A SOLID POWDER
When the two solutions are combined, the iodide ions from the potassium iodide join up with the lead ions from the lead nitrate to form lead iodide. Unlike lead nitrate, lead iodide is insoluble – it does not dissolve in water. As a result, when it forms it immediately "falls out" of solution, and we see a yellow powder.

AN IONIC SOLID
The lead iodide is made up of positively charged lead ions and negatively charged iodide ions, so it is called an ionic solid. These charges attract, holding the ions together in a regular, repeating pattern. There are two iodide ions for each lead ion.

Solid **LEAD IODIDE** (PbI_2)

Lead ion (Pb^{2+})

Iodide ion (I^-)

Potassium iodide is poured directly into the flask.

Potassium iodide precipitates as soon as it comes into contact with lead nitrate.

POTASSIUM NITRATE SOLUTION
The formation of lead iodide removes all the lead and iodide ions from the solution, leaving potassium ions and nitrate ions behind. These remaining ions are still able to mix with the water molecules and form a colourless potassium nitrate solution.

POTASSIUM NITRATE solution

Nitrate ion (NO_3^-)

Potassium ion (K^+)

▶ **SPLITTING WATER**

In this experiment, an electric current is run through water, using a battery and two electrodes attached to a beaker. The water molecules (H_2O) split up into electrically charged ions, which in turn form hydrogen gas (H_2) and oxygen gas (O_2). There is twice as much hydrogen as oxygen, because each water molecule contains two hydrogen atoms and one oxygen atom.

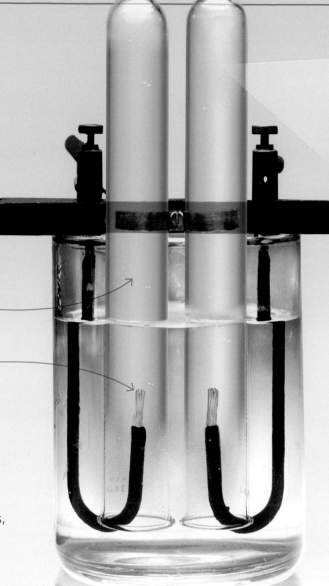

Inverted test tubes full of water

The electrodes are encased in an insulating material. A stump of bare wire sticks out at the end of each electrode.

① THE APPARATUS
A beaker is filled with water. A specially designed clamp is used to secure the electrodes in place, and to support two upturned test tubes, full of water, over the electrodes. The water serves as electrolyte, the liquid substance needed for electrolysis to work.

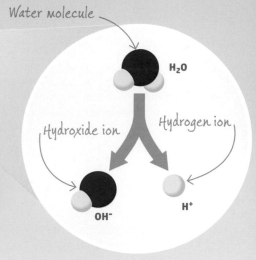

Water molecule

H_2O

Hydroxide ion   Hydrogen ion

OH^- H^+

WATER AS ELECTROLYTE
An electrolyte is a liquid that conducts electricity because it contains charged ions. It could be a molten metal or a dissolved compound. Water is an electrolyte because a tiny number of its molecules naturally split up into negatively charged hydroxide ions and positively charged hydrogen ions.

② CONNECT THE BATTERY
When the battery is connected to the electrodes, electrons flow through the wires. This causes one electrode to become positively charged – this is the anode. The other electrode becomes negatively charged – this is the cathode.

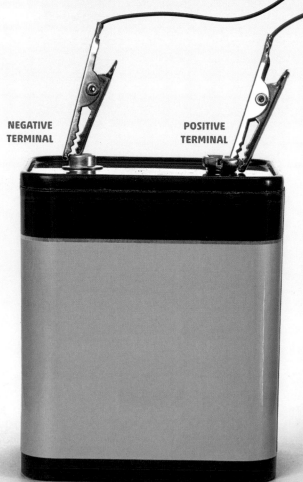

NEGATIVE TERMINAL   **POSITIVE TERMINAL**

HOW ELECTROLYSIS WORKS

It is possible to split up some compounds into pure substances by passing an electric current through them. Known as electrolysis, this method is used in industry, for example to extract pure aluminium from molten rock containing aluminium and other elements. Electrolysis can also be used to separate the elements that make up water.

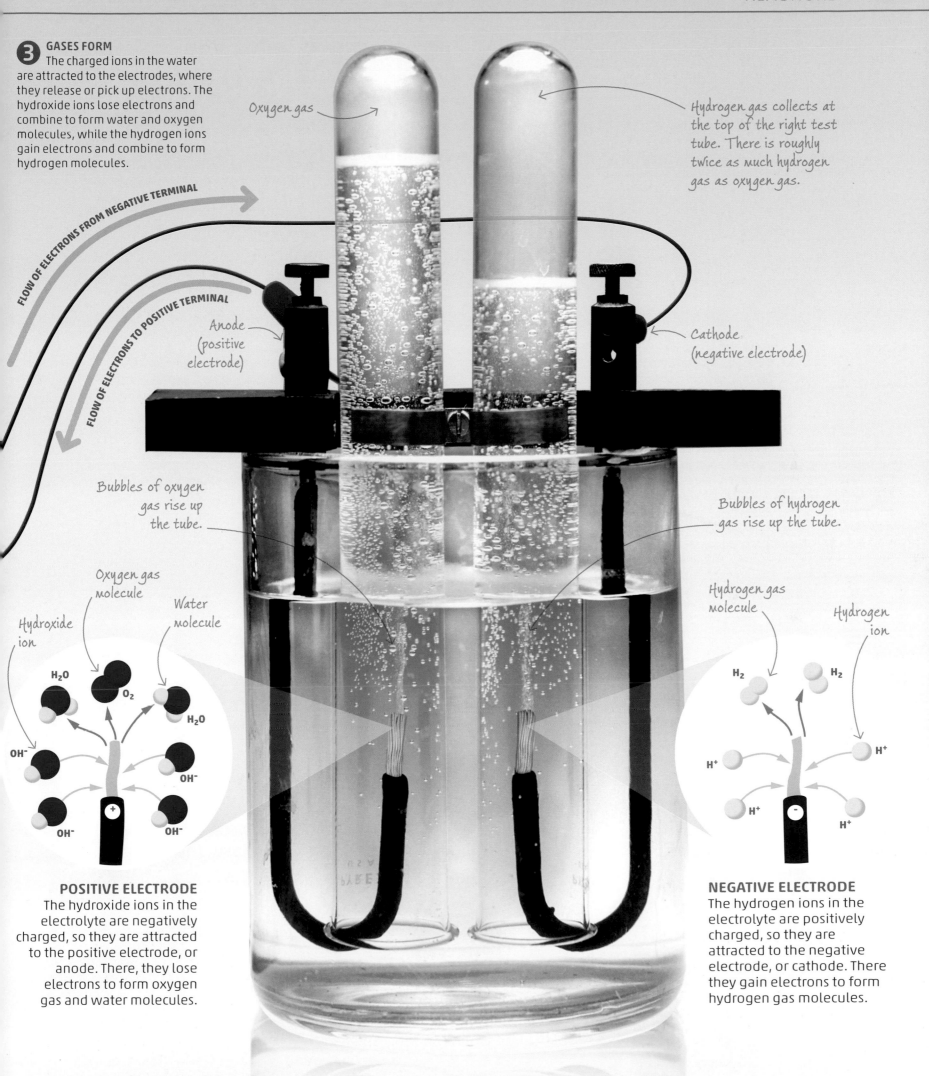

3 GASES FORM
The charged ions in the water are attracted to the electrodes, where they release or pick up electrons. The hydroxide ions lose electrons and combine to form water and oxygen molecules, while the hydrogen ions gain electrons and combine to form hydrogen molecules.

FLOW OF ELECTRONS FROM NEGATIVE TERMINAL

FLOW OF ELECTRONS TO POSITIVE TERMINAL

Oxygen gas

Hydrogen gas collects at the top of the right test tube. There is roughly twice as much hydrogen gas as oxygen gas.

Anode (positive electrode)

Cathode (negative electrode)

Bubbles of oxygen gas rise up the tube.

Bubbles of hydrogen gas rise up the tube.

Oxygen gas molecule

Water molecule

Hydrogen gas molecule

Hydrogen ion

Hydroxide ion

H_2O

O_2

H_2O

OH^-

OH^-

OH^-

OH^-

H_2

H_2

H^+

H^+

H^+

H^+

POSITIVE ELECTRODE
The hydroxide ions in the electrolyte are negatively charged, so they are attracted to the positive electrode, or anode. There, they lose electrons to form oxygen gas and water molecules.

NEGATIVE ELECTRODE
The hydrogen ions in the electrolyte are positively charged, so they are attracted to the negative electrode, or cathode. There they gain electrons to form hydrogen gas molecules.

ACID, BASE, OR NEUTRAL

A base is a substance that reacts with an acid and neutralizes it. Alkalis are bases that dissolve in water and produce hydroxide ions (OH⁻). Acids added to water produce hydrogen ions (H⁺). A solution with more H⁺ ions is an acid, and one with more OH⁻ ions is an alkali. A neutral solution, such as water, has equal amounts of both. The pH value of a substance (see pages 96–97) tells how acidic it is.

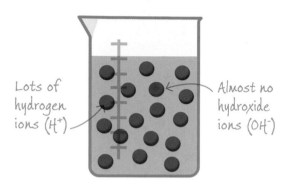

Lots of hydrogen ions (H^+)

Almost no hydroxide ions (OH^-)

ACID

When added to water, acids break apart to form hydrogen ions (H⁺). Acids that break apart easily to form lots of hydrogen ions are called strong acids, while those that don't are called weak acids. Hydrochloric acid is an example of a strong acid, while ethanoic acid, in vinegar, is a weak acid. Strong acids generally have lower pHs than weak acids.

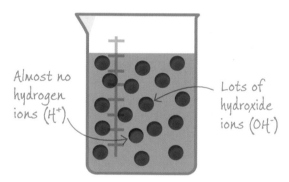

Almost no hydrogen ions (H^+)

Lots of hydroxide ions (OH^-)

ALKALI

Alkalis are substances that release hydroxide ions (OH⁻) when added to water. In a very alkaline solution, such as powerful drain cleaners (with a pH of around 14), there are almost no hydrogen ions present.

CORROSIVE LIQUIDS

Both acids and alkalis can be corrosive, which means they can damage surfaces they come into contact with. Depending on how concentrated they are, they may be ableto burn through skin or metal.

HAZARD SYMBOL WARNS OF RISK OF CORROSION

HOW ACIDS WORK

Chemical compounds can be either acids, bases, or neutral. Acids are compounds that break up in water to produce hydrogen ions (H⁺). There are strong acids, which can be very corrosive, and weak acids, such as those in lemon juice and vinegar, which can be edible. When acids react with bases, they always produce salts.

1 REACTANTS
The acid used in this demonstration is hydrochloric acid. It is strong and has to be handled very carefully, as it can burn through skin. This is the acid that helps to digest food in the stomach. The metal is zinc. Not all metals react readily with acids, but zinc is reactive enough to do so.

Hydrochloric acid is a solution of hydrogen chloride dissolved in water.

Pieces of pure zinc, refined in a laboratory

▶ **ACID REACTING WITH METAL**
This experiment shows how hydrochloric acid reacts with a metal. Lumps of solid zinc are placed in a petri dish, and hydrochloric acid is carefully poured over the metal. In the reaction, the solid metal is dissolved and a salt and hydrogen gas are produced.

The test tube contains hydrochloric acid.

Zinc

Hydrochloric acid (HCl)

Zn + H+ Cl⁻

H+ Cl⁻

↓

Cl⁻ Zn²⁺ Cl⁻ + H₂

Zinc chloride (ZnCl₂)

Hydrogen gas

2 FIZZY REACTION
When hydrochloric acid is poured carefully onto the zinc, the two substances react to form two new products: hydrogen gas and zinc chloride, a salt. The mixture fizzes as the hydrogen gas forms. The fizzing, known as effervescence, is a sign that a chemical reaction is occurring.

Zinc and chloride ions form a colourless solution of zinc chloride.

Hydrogen gas is always produced when an acid reacts with a metal.

1 **ALKALINE SOLUTION**
A small amount of sodium bicarbonate (baking soda) is dissolved in water. Adding a few drops of universal indicator turns the colourless liquid violet, signalling that the pH is 13, an alkaline solution.

An ALKALINE SOLUTION of pH 13

HOW THE
pH SCALE
WORKS

The pH scale measures acidity and goes from 0 to 14. When mixed with water, acids form particles called hydrogen ions. The pH scale measures the number of these ions. Acids contain many hydrogen ions and have a low pH, while alkalis have almost none and a high pH. Each step up the scale represents a concentration of hydrogen ions 10 times lower than the one before.

Chips of dry ice (carbon dioxide) make the solution more acidic.

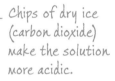

▶ FROM ALKALI TO ACID
Universal indicator is a chemical that can be used to signal the pH of a solution. In this demonstration, solid carbon dioxide (dry ice) is added to an alkaline solution of sodium bicarbonate and water, which is gradually neutralized before becoming acidic.

3 **NEUTRAL SOLUTION**
As the dry ice continues to react and more acid forms, enough hydrogen ions form to completely neutralize the solution. It turns green, indicating the pH is about 7.

A LESS ALKALINE solution of pH 9

2 **ADDING DRY ICE**
Chips of frozen carbon dioxide, known as dry ice, are added to the liquid. Carbon dioxide is a gas at room temperature, but below -78.5°C (-109.3°F) it freezes. When the frozen carbon dioxide is added to the alkaline liquid, it reacts with the water to form carbonic acid. As more of this acid forms, it begins to neutralize the solution, which becomes less alkaline and turns blue.

The solution NEUTRALIZES to pH 7

Green colour indicates a neutral solution.

Water vapour in the air becomes condensed by the very cold carbon dioxide, forming a smoky mist.

4 ACIDIC SOLUTION
The dry ice continues to react with the water in the solution, making it acidic. The universal indicator turns a dark yellow colour, signalling that the pH is between 4 and 5.

Yellow colour indicates the pH is about 4.5

pH INDICATORS

Scientists use a variety of indicators to identify the pH of substances. Most pH indicators only change between two or three colours. For example, litmus paper turns red when exposed to a substance below about pH 4.5, blue above about pH 8.3, and purple in between.

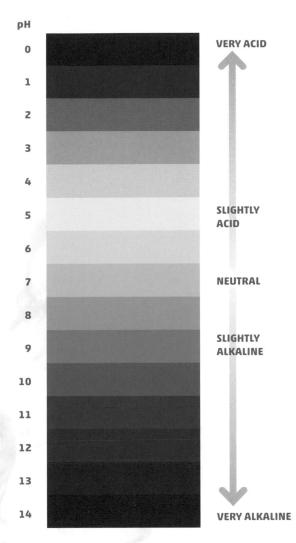

pH	
0	VERY ACID
1	
2	
3	
4	
5	SLIGHTLY ACID
6	
7	NEUTRAL
8	
9	SLIGHTLY ALKALINE
10	
11	
12	
13	
14	VERY ALKALINE

UNIVERSAL INDICATOR COLOURS

Universal indicator is actually a mixture of several different indicators that change colour to indicate a broad range of pHs. This chart shows the colours that universal indicator will become when mixed with solutions of different pH values.

NATURAL pH INDICATORS

Many plants contain chemicals which are natural pH indicators. Hydrangea flowers are blue if the plant is grown in more acidic soil, but pink if soil is more alkaline.

HOW FLAME TESTS WORK

Scientists use flame tests to identify which elements are present in a sample. The samples are usually of metal salts, which are compounds formed when a metal reacts with an acid. The metal in the salt is in the form of charged particles, called ions, which give out different colours of light when they are burned. As each metal always burns with the same colour flame, scientists can use this property to work out which metal is in the salt.

▼ RAINBOW SALTS

In this demonstration, six common metal salts are burned with a small amount of alcohol. As the alcohol burns, its flame turns a different colour according to which metal salt is present in the sample. Different colours occur because when heated an electron in a metal ion can become "excited" and jump to a higher energy level. When the electron returns to its original state, energy is released as light (see page 142). The wavelength of this light varies between elements, so their colours vary.

Apple-green flame

Red-orange flame

Bright red flame

BARIUM
Barium ions produce an apple-green flame. Barium, strontium, and calcium are part of a group of elements called alkaline earth metals. They have two electrons in their outer shell.

STRONTIUM
Strontium ions produce a bright red flame. Like the other alkaline earth metals, strontium is a shiny, silvery-white metal. These metals form alkalis when they react with water.

CALCIUM
Calcium ions turn a flame red-orange. The fifth most abundant element in Earth's crust, calcium is vital to life – it is a major component of the bones, shells, and teeth of animals.

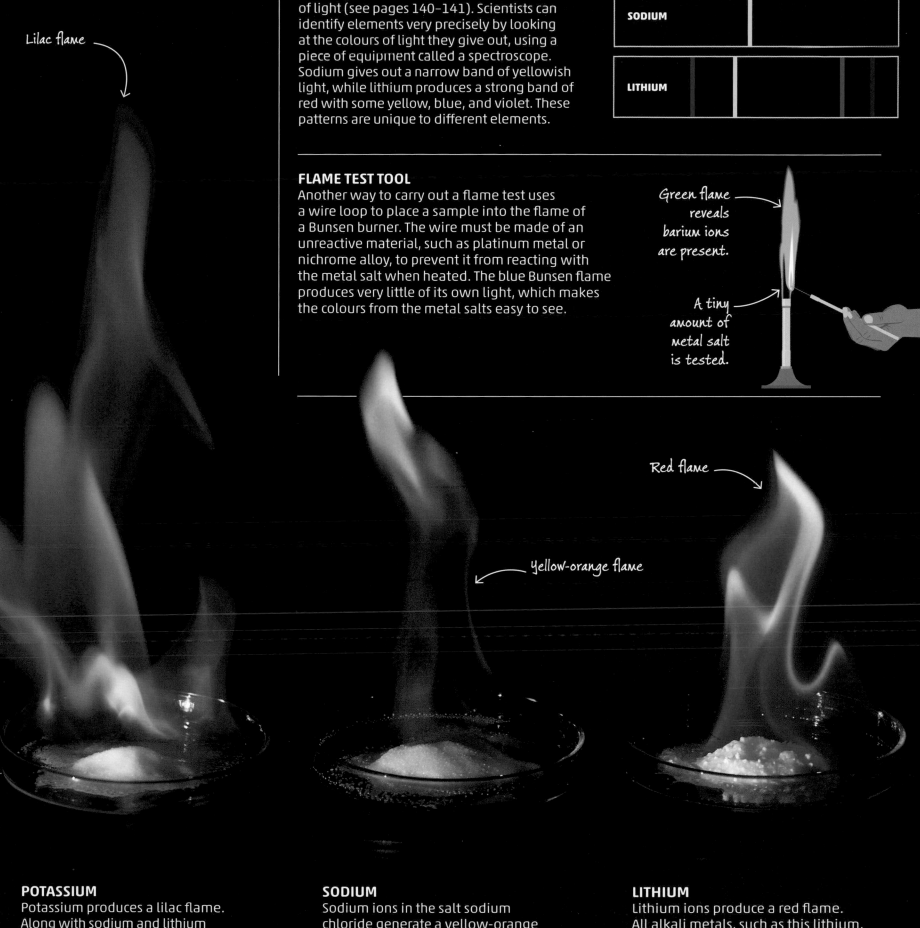

Lilac flame

White light is made up of different colours of light (see pages 140–141). Scientists can identify elements very precisely by looking at the colours of light they give out, using a piece of equipment called a spectroscope. Sodium gives out a narrow band of yellowish light, while lithium produces a strong band of red with some yellow, blue, and violet. These patterns are unique to different elements.

| SODIUM | |
| LITHIUM | |

FLAME TEST TOOL
Another way to carry out a flame test uses a wire loop to place a sample into the flame of a Bunsen burner. The wire must be made of an unreactive material, such as platinum metal or nichrome alloy, to prevent it from reacting with the metal salt when heated. The blue Bunsen flame produces very little of its own light, which makes the colours from the metal salts easy to see.

Green flame reveals barium ions are present.

A tiny amount of metal salt is tested.

Red flame

Yellow-orange flame

POTASSIUM
Potassium produces a lilac flame. Along with sodium and lithium it belongs to a different group of elements called the alkali metals (see pages 52–53).

SODIUM
Sodium ions in the salt sodium chloride generate a yellow-orange flame. Sodium is the most abundant alkali metal and the sixth most abundant element on Earth.

LITHIUM
Lithium ions produce a red flame. All alkali metals, such as this lithium, are very soft and have low melting points. They each have one electron in their outermost shell.

FIREWORK DISPLAY

The colours, lights, and sounds of a firework display result from reactions between explosive chemicals stored in a shell inside each firework. These contain a mixture of gunpowder and "stars" made from metal salts. Different salts produce different colours: sodium salts burn yellow, strontium looks red, barium makes green. When the gunpowder ignites it propels the rocket skyward. Then the airborne stars explode, creating their beautiful display.

HOW CATALYSTS WORK

Some reactions are fast, while others happen much more slowly. Sometimes slow reactions can be speeded up by adding another substance called a catalyst. A catalyst makes a reaction quicker, but is not itself used up or changed by the reaction. It can be collected and used again afterwards.

This experiment is known as "elephant's toothpaste" thanks to the gigantic squirt of foam pushing out.

1 ADDING THE CATALYST
The hydrogen peroxide is gently mixed with a small amount of water and washing up liquid. The catalyst – a chemical called potassium iodide – is carefully added.

The catalyst is poured into the flask.

2 REACTION STARTS
As soon as the catalyst hits the solution, the hydrogen peroxide begins to break down. Oxygen gas is released and trapped by the washing up liquid, creating a large amount of foam.

Dye is added to colour the foam green.

3 BURSTING OUT
After seconds, so much foam is produced so quickly that it shoots up out of the flask high into the air. The foam is hot because the reaction releases energy.

Bubbles of oxygen gas

A mass of foam is produced from a small amount of hydrogen peroxide. The foam also contains water produced in the reaction

Foam quickly fills the flask and rushes up out of the neck. It will continue to be produced until all the hydrogen peroxide is used up.

▶ FOAM FOUNTAIN

In this experiment, a small amount of hydrogen peroxide is placed in a conical flask, with a few drops of water and washing up liquid. Hydrogen peroxide naturally breaks down into water and oxygen gas. Usually, this happens so slowly as to be barely noticeable. But adding a catalyst makes it happen very quickly indeed – a huge quantity of oxygen-rich foam is produced and shoots up out of the flask.

SPEEDING UP A REACTION

A certain amount of energy is needed for a reaction to start. This is the activation energy. Catalysts work by lowering the energy required to get a reaction going, by providing a kind of short cut. Many catalysts do this by temporarily combining with the reactants, making it easier for them to react with each other.

REACTANT

REACTANT   REACTANT

PRODUCT

CATALYST

CATALYST

CATALYST

1 SEPARATE
Away from the catalyst, the reactants do not have enough energy to react.

2 TOGETHER
The reactants temporarily stick to the catalyst, which enables a reaction.

3 CATALYZED
A reaction has taken place. The reactants have bonded but the catalyst remains unchanged.

The word **materials** describes the matter that forms the **objects** around us. Materials can be strong or weak, hard or soft, flexible or rigid, and lightweight or heavy – they are chosen for **different uses** depending on their **properties**. Inspired by materials found in nature, scientists have developed new **synthetic materials** with incredible properties to improve upon those of **natural materials.**

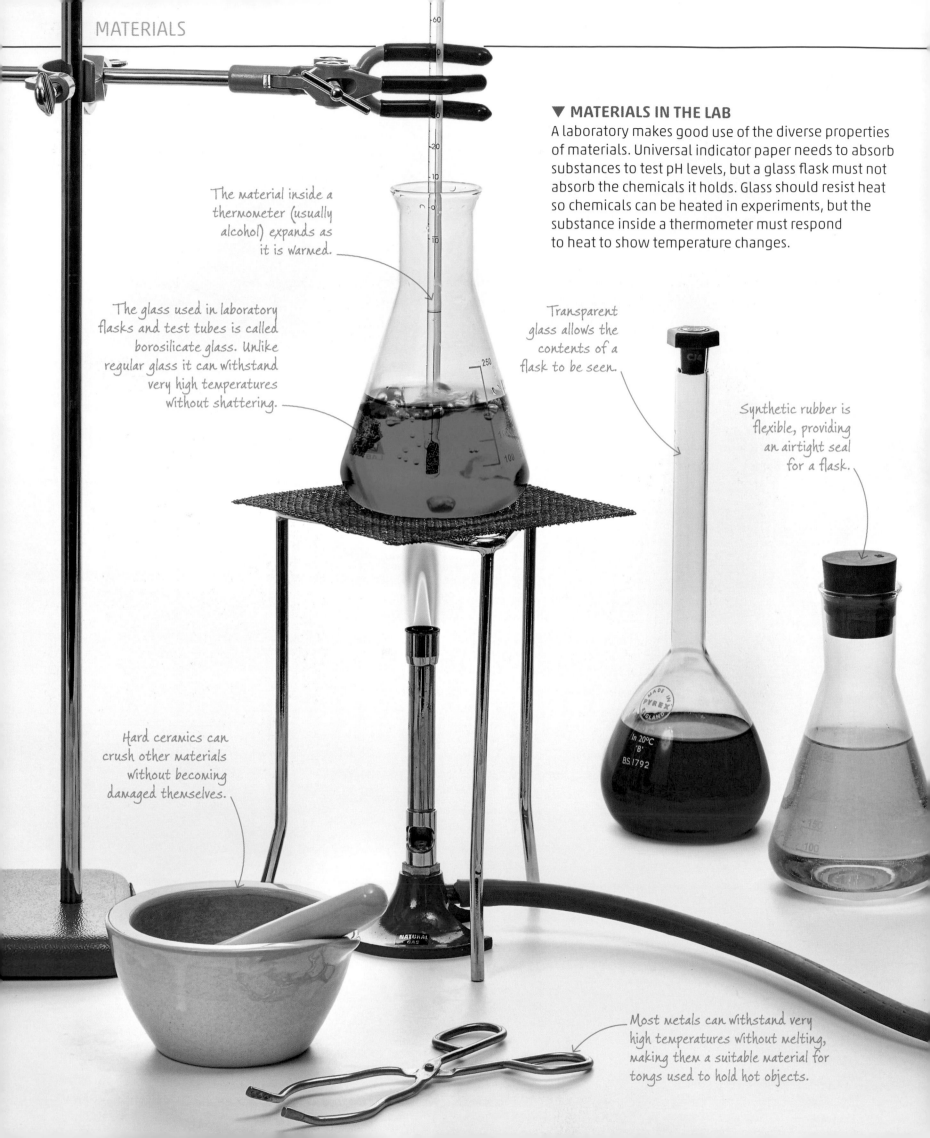

The material inside a thermometer (usually alcohol) expands as it is warmed.

The glass used in laboratory flasks and test tubes is called borosilicate glass. Unlike regular glass it can withstand very high temperatures without shattering.

Hard ceramics can crush other materials without becoming damaged themselves.

▼ **MATERIALS IN THE LAB**
A laboratory makes good use of the diverse properties of materials. Universal indicator paper needs to absorb substances to test pH levels, but a glass flask must not absorb the chemicals it holds. Glass should resist heat so chemicals can be heated in experiments, but the substance inside a thermometer must respond to heat to show temperature changes.

Transparent glass allows the contents of a flask to be seen.

Synthetic rubber is flexible, providing an airtight seal for a flask.

Most metals can withstand very high temperatures without melting, making them a suitable material for tongs used to hold hot objects.

HOW MATERIALS WORK

Everything that is made, built, or grown is made of materials. Materials can be natural, such as wood, or synthetic, like nylon. Since ancient times, people have sought materials for different needs, such as building and clothing. Now, materials scientists can create brand new materials with amazing properties that suit almost any purpose, from super-strong synthetic silk to tiny nanoparticles used in medicine.

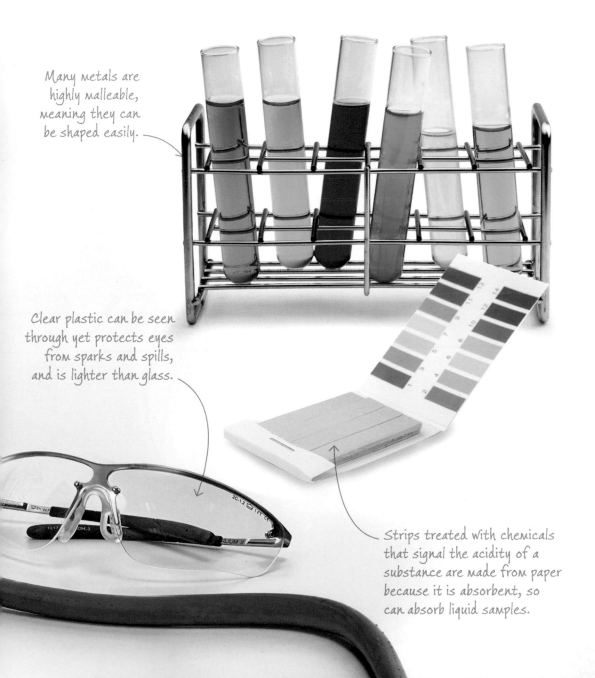

Many metals are highly malleable, meaning they can be shaped easily.

Clear plastic can be seen through yet protects eyes from sparks and spills, and is lighter than glass.

Strips treated with chemicals that signal the acidity of a substance are made from paper because it is absorbent, so can absorb liquid samples.

MATERIAL WORLD
Some of the best materials in use today have their origins in nature, such as wood, metals, and ceramics. Synthetic materials made by scientists and engineers can offer different properties than natural materials.

CERAMIC
From ancient pottery to electrical insulation for power cables (shown above), ceramics have wide-ranging uses because of their heat resistance and insulating properties.

METAL
Used for car parts, construction materials, and tools, metals have a range of properties. Some are used for their strength, while others are used for their ability to conduct heat and electricity.

WOOD
Obtained from tree stems and roots, wood has been used for millennia for building, tools, and fuel. Its strength means it is still used for building around the world.

POLYMERS
While common in nature, the best known polymers are plastics, such as polythene and Lycra. These synthetic polymers were created to find materials with new properties.

HOW PLASTICS WORK

Plastics are synthetic, or partly synthetic, materials formed from long chain-like particles called polymers. Their flexibility and strength give plastics countless uses. While many polymers are synthetic, they can also be found in nature, from the cellulose that makes up plants to the DNA in living cells.

Low density polyethene (LDPE) has many useful properties – it is resistant to water, transparent, light, and strong.

WHAT IS A POLYMER?

Polymers are made when strings of small identical molecules, called monomers, join together in a process called polymerization. To make the polymer that forms this plastic bag, a double bond in the monomer ethene is broken so it can bond with other ethene monomers, creating long polymer chains.

1 MONOMER
Ethene (or ethylene) contains two carbon atoms, joined by a double bond, and four hydrogen atoms.

Double bond

Hydrogen atom

Carbon atom

Single bond

2 POLYMER
When the double bond is broken, ethene monomers join to make a polymer called polyethene.

NATURAL POLYMERS

Nature is full of polymers, and many of them are harvested for their useful properties. Some, like wood, are commonly used in construction. Others, such as cotton and wool, can be used to make clothing.

Silk cocoon

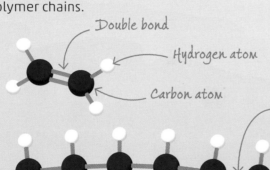

SILK
One silkworm produces about 500 m (1,640 ft) of silk, a natural polymer, to build its cocoon.

RUBBER
The white sap of a rubber tree contains the polymer latex, which can be treated to make rubber for car tyres.

The strong, flexible plastic hugs the pencil.

The polymer molecules form a seal around the pencil.

A sharp pencil easily squeezes between the polymer chains.

WATERTIGHT
Polymer chains are flexible, so allow the pencil to pass through them then close tightly around it. Water molecules also have forces that make them stick together, helping to keep the water inside the bag.

▲ MAGIC BAG
Bags like this one are made of a plastic called low density polyethene (LDPE). The polymer chains hold the water in, but a sharp pencil is able to push the polymer molecules apart and slide through. A temporary seal forms around the edge of the pencil, keeping the water in the bag – until the pencil is pulled out!

Long rows of polymer molecules slide over each other.

POLYMER CHAINS
Polyethene polymers are long chains arranged in rows. The pencil increases the gap between the chains without breaking the forces that hold them together, so they grip the pencil tightly.

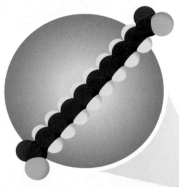

TOP LAYER
The monomer in the top liquid layer is made of ten carbon atoms (black) with an oxygen (red) and chlorine (green) atom at each end. The remaining atoms are hydrogen (white). This molecule is called decanedioyl dichloride, or sebacoyl dichloride.

1 LAYERED LIQUIDS
The two liquids are poured into one beaker. Care must be taken to avoid mixing the liquids too much – the second is allowed to flow slowly down the side of the glass so it sits on top of the first.

2 POLYMERIZATION
The point at which the two liquids meet is called the interface. Here, the two monomers react with each other to form nylon polymer chains in a process called polymerization. The nylon appears as a thin film that can be pulled up with a pair of tweezers.

Polymerization has created nylon.

BOTTOM LAYER
The monomer in the bottom liquid layer is a chain made of six carbon atoms (black), with a nitrogen atom (blue) at each end. The remaining atoms are hydrogen (white). The molecule is called 1,6-diaminohexane.

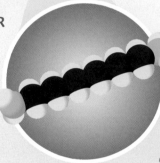

An indicator has been added, which colours the alkaline bottom layer pink.

HOW NYLON WORKS

First created more than 80 years ago, nylon is a synthetic fibre used in clothing, flooring, car parts, and food packaging, with millions of tonnes produced each year. Nylon molecules are long chains, called polymers, made from two different smaller molecules called monomers.

SYNTHETIC POLYMERS
Many synthetic polymers have been developed with properties to suit various purposes. While some are designed to be hard and rigid, like PVC (polyvinyl chloride), others may be lightweight and waterproof, like PET (polyethylene terephthalate). Synthetic polymers are cheap to produce and can be more resilient than natural products.

Teflon pan coating

PVC is used for piping.

PET bottle

▶ NYLON ROPE TRICK
In this demonstration, a rope appears as if by magic from a beaker containing two liquids, which have been carefully layered one on top of the other. The liquids each contain a different monomer – molecules that join together to form long polymer molecules. At the point where they meet, a long strand of nylon polymer is created and can be pulled from the beaker as a long, continuous rope.

Carbon atoms form the backbone.

NYLON POLYMER
The nylon polymer is made of alternating monomer units from the two liquids. As the monomers join, two chlorine atoms are lost from each monomer in the top liquid and two hydrogen atoms are lost from each monomer in the bottom liquid. These atoms join together to make the byproduct hydrogen chloride.

The rope is pulled out slowly and wound around a rod.

Hydrogen chloride molecule

③ NYLON ROPE
As the nylon layer is pulled from the beaker, more monomers meet at the interface, creating more nylon. The process continues, creating a long nylon "rope", which can be several metres long.

Polymerization continues until all the monomers have been used up.

POLYMER PROBLEMS
Synthetic polymers are popular for their durability, but as a consequence they fail to break down in the way that natural materials do. Waste plastics can be carried into rivers and drains, which lead into the sea. These waste plastics at sea pose a serious threat to fish, mammals, and birds that eat them thinking they are food.

HOW HI-TECH MATERIALS WORK

Synthetic materials were first developed to improve on the properties of natural materials. Today, materials continue to be engineered that previously could only be dreamt of, from insulating aerogels to carbon fibre composites.

COMPOSITES

Composites combine materials with different properties to create a material with the benefits of both. Some brake discs (shown here in close-up), which help cars to slow down, are made from a composite of carbon fibre (thin carbon strands) encased in ceramic to both withstand heat and resist cracking.

AMAZING MATERIALS

Materials scientists are developing a mind-blowing array of materials with an ever-increasing range of properties. A combination of lucky discoveries and an increased understanding of how particles interact is leading to a new world of material possibilities.

GRAPHENE
Made of a single layer of carbon atoms, graphene is one of the strongest known materials.

METAL FOAM
Interspersing metal with air pockets can make it lightweight, while retaining its strength.

SELF-HEALING PLASTIC
Mimicking the way wounds heal, self-healing plastic releases a liquid to repair itself when damaged.

SPIDER SILK
Scientists are developing synthetic spider silk, which is stronger than steel, but more lightweight and elastic.

▼ AEROGEL

An aerogel is a material containing a network of nanoscopic (1,000 times smaller than microscopic) holes, or pores. These pores can form up to 90 per cent of the total volume, making aerogels some of the lightest and least dense solid materials known. The foam-like structure makes aerogels excellent insulators, like this silica aerogel that is protecting wax crayons from melting above a hot Bunsen flame.

The aerogel is held in place by a metal stand.

Also known as "frozen smoke", aerogels made from silica are transparent with a slightly blueish appearance.

Without the aerogel, the crayons would heat up and melt.

The solid part of this aerogel is made from silica, the compound that makes up most glass and sand.

Because they are made mostly of air, aerogels are very lightweight and are excellent insulators.

Air is a poor conductor of heat, so the air molecules trapped inside the aerogel provide insulation against the heat of the Bunsen flame.

MAKING AN AEROGEL

An aerogel is like a normal gel or jelly, but while gels have water in them, aerogels have air. To make an aerogel, the water content of a gel is replaced with air in a process called supercritical drying.

1 GEL
A gel is a colloid – a mixture in which one substance is dispersed in another (see page 35). In a gel, the solid part is dispersed in water. This gel is made from silica particles and water.

Solid silica particles

Water fills the spaces between particles.

2 AEROGEL
The aerogel is also a colloid, but this time the silica is dispersed in air instead of water. To create aerogel, gel is dried out to remove all water, leaving only air in the spaces between the silica particles.

Air now fills the spaces.

AEROGEL ON MARS

The incredibly low density of aerogels and their impressive insulation properties make them ideal for use in spacecraft. NASA's Mars exploration rovers needed to function at temperatures as low as -96°C (-140°F), so were insulated with aerogel.

SHARK SKIN

This scanning electron micrograph image shows
the skin of a spiny dogfish, a type of shark. Toothlike
scales, called denticles, on the skin's surface easily
cut through water as the dogfish swims. Experiments
have found that these denticles reduce drag,
allowing the predator to swim fast. Scientists are
developing synthetic materials inspired by this skin
that could help boats and swimmers to move faster
through water.

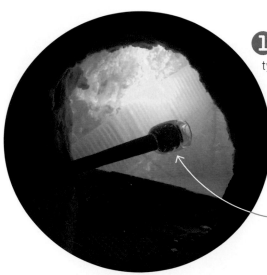

1 MELTING
The most commonly produced type of glass is soda-lime glass. When the ingredients are heated in a furnace to 500–900°C (930–1,650°F), they melt to form a thick, sticky liquid. A glass worker called a glassblower uses a long, metal pipe to pick up a small amount of molten glass to work with.

A blob of soft, molten glass is removed from the furnace on the end of a blowpipe.

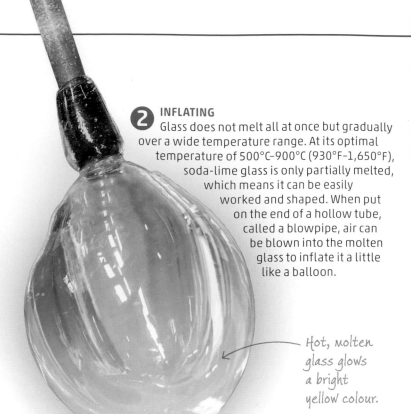

2 INFLATING
Glass does not melt all at once but gradually over a wide temperature range. At its optimal temperature of 500°C–900°C (930°F–1,650°F), soda-lime glass is only partially melted, which means it can be easily worked and shaped. When put on the end of a hollow tube, called a blowpipe, air can be blown into the molten glass to inflate it a little like a balloon.

Hot, molten glass glows a bright yellow colour.

HOW **GLASS** WORKS

Since at least 3,500 BCE, glass has been moulded into decorative and practical objects. A strong, transparent, waterproof, and malleable material, glass is used in windows, tableware, and technology, such as fibre optics. Glass workers make use of its sticky, stretchy consistency when hot to mould it to shape and can even inflate it like a balloon.

▲ GLASS WORKING
Glass is made of a substance called silica, or silicon dioxide, which is better known as sand. Because pure silica has a very high melting point, around 1,700°C (3,100°F), other chemicals are often added to make it easier to work with and improve its properties. Soda-lime glass, shown above, contains sodium oxide (soda) and calcium oxide (lime) to reduce its melting point so it can be melted, moulded, and inflated more easily.

LIGHTNING GLASS
When lightning strikes sand, a thin, glassy tunnel can form where the strike hits, as the extreme heat from the lightning turns the sand to glass. The hollow structures formed, like the one above, are called fulgurites. Natural glass can also be formed when meteors strike rock or when lava from volcanoes cools to form shiny glass called obsidian.

BULLETPROOF GLASS
The properties of glass can be altered using different ingredients or methods of construction. To make bulletproof glass, a soft plastic sheet, which absorbs some of the impact of a bullet, is layered over a thick sheet of hard glass.

Iron blowpipes have been used to blow glass for about 2,000 years.

3 **TAKING SHAPE**
A glassblower slowly blows more air through the blowpipe to inflate the glass to a larger size so it can be made into an object such as a vase. Colour can be added when the glass is molten by rolling it in powdered chemicals or coloured glass chips. By carefully and repeatedly heating and cooling the glass, and using a variety of tools and moulds, it can be blown and shaped into an amazing array of beautiful and useful objects. As it cools, the glass hardens and becomes transparent.

When the glass cools, it hardens and becomes transparent.

Air blown through the tube into the glass gradually inflates the glass from the inside.

Oxygen

Silicon

Sodium

Calcium

SODA-LIME GLASS
Sodium and calcium have been added to silica to make this glass. The sodium and calcium particles fit randomly within the irregular structure of the silica to lower the melting point and increase the strength of the glass, allowing it to be repeatedly softened and shaped.

▶ TURNING COPPER TO "GOLD"

In this experiment, a coin appears to turn from copper to silver, then gold. The copper coin is first plated with the metal zinc to make it appear silver. Heating this silvery coin then creates an alloy called brass, which gives the coin a gold-coloured coating.

❶ PREPARING THE COIN

Copper coins tarnish over time as they react with the air. To expose the pure, untarnished copper needed for this experiment, a coin must be scrubbed clean with wire wool.

Wire Wool

Coin cleaned with wire wool to expose the pure copper surface.

The solution has been heated to help the zinc to dissolve, but some solid zinc remains at the bottom of the beaker.

❷ PLATING

A solution of sodium hydroxide is heated to boiling point, then zinc powder is added. Some zinc reacts with the solution to make sodium zincate solution, while some remains solid at the bottom of the beaker. The copper coin is then dropped into the beaker and after several minutes of touching the solid zinc at the bottom, a layer of zinc appears on the surface of the coin.

ZINC COATING

When the zinc reacts with the solution, some of its atoms lose negatively charged particles, called electrons, and become positively charged zinc ions. When the zinc ions meet the surface of the copper coin, they gain electrons again and form a layer of zinc metal on top of the copper.

Layer of zinc atoms

Copper atoms

The Bunsen burner is turned off before the zinc powder is added because zinc powder is highly flammable.

The copper coin is plated with silvery zinc.

HOW ALLOYS WORK

An alloy is a combination of two or more different metals, or a combination of a metal and another element. Alloys are designed to improve on the properties of pure metals. The alloy brass, made in this demonstration, is stronger than pure copper and is created by mixing copper with zinc.

❸ ZINC-PLATED COPPER

When the coin is removed from the solution, it has changed colour from copper to silver. The copper coin looks silver because zinc from the solution has formed a layer over the coin.

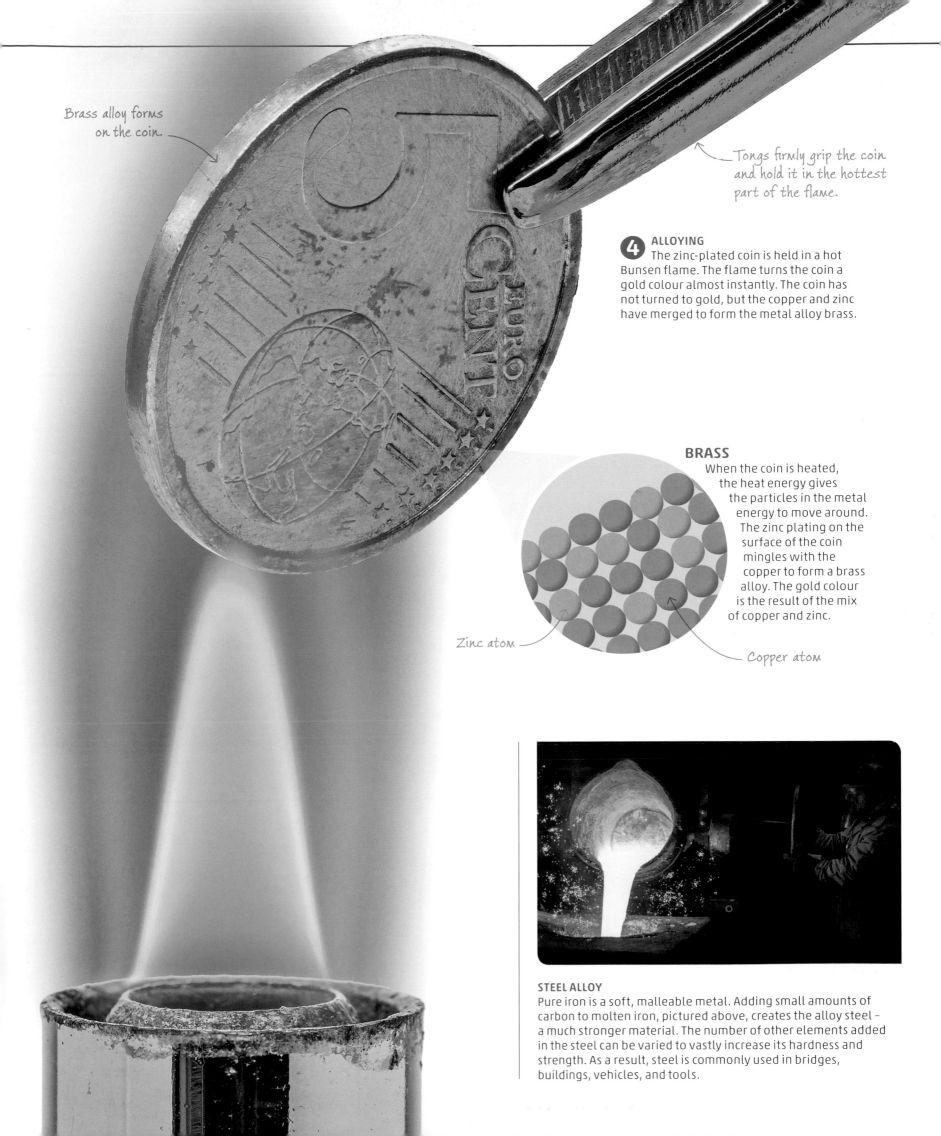

Brass alloy forms on the coin.

Tongs firmly grip the coin and hold it in the hottest part of the flame.

4 ALLOYING
The zinc-plated coin is held in a hot Bunsen flame. The flame turns the coin a gold colour almost instantly. The coin has not turned to gold, but the copper and zinc have merged to form the metal alloy brass.

BRASS
When the coin is heated, the heat energy gives the particles in the metal energy to move around. The zinc plating on the surface of the coin mingles with the copper to form a brass alloy. The gold colour is the result of the mix of copper and zinc.

Zinc atom

Copper atom

STEEL ALLOY
Pure iron is a soft, malleable metal. Adding small amounts of carbon to molten iron, pictured above, creates the alloy steel – a much stronger material. The number of other elements added in the steel can be varied to vastly increase its hardness and strength. As a result, steel is commonly used in bridges, buildings, vehicles, and tools.

HOW RECYCLING WORKS

Some rubbish put in landfill may take thousands of years to break down, or degrade. Aluminium cans take 500 years to degrade and glass bottles may take one million! Recycling recovers these materials and turns them into new products, often using less energy than the amount needed to make replacements from raw materials.

WHAT CAN BE RECYCLED?

Many materials can be recycled – from glass to food waste. Some waste, like bottles or boxes, can be reused at home. Other waste, such as cans and paper, is sent to recycling facilities to be remade into similar products.

 FOOD WASTE   **GLASS**   **PLASTIC**

 PAPER   **TEXTILES**   **METALS**

E-WASTE

Waste computers and phones are a growing problem – technology moves on so fast that products are rapidly outdated and thrown away. Some electronics companies now aim to recycle every component of their products to address the multitude of e-waste.

Most drinks cans are made from aluminium, the most abundant metal element in Earth's crust.

5 ROLLING SHEETS
The aluminium ingots are sent to a mill where they are passed though sets of rollers until they are shaped into sheets that are thin enough to be made into new cans – a process rather like rolling out pastry.

Aluminium is rolled into long, thin sheets.

6 NEW CANS
The thin aluminium sheets are fed into a press where they are shaped into new aluminium cans. These are then sent to be filled with new drinks. The whole process can take about six weeks.

An ingot can be as long as 15 m (50 ft).

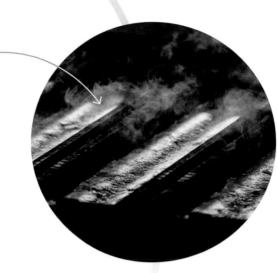

4 CASTING INGOTS
The liquid aluminium is poured into moulds and cooled with water jets. The metal hardens to form a large block, called an ingot. These ingots can be huge – each one can make 1.5 million cans.

RECYCLING ALUMINIUM

A staggering 180 billion aluminium cans are produced worldwide every year, 70 per cent of which are recycled. Recycling cans into new ones is more energy efficient than making them from scratch – it uses just 5 per cent of the energy that would be needed to use raw materials – and they can be recycled over and over again.

1 COLLECTING CANS
Once used, aluminium cans may be recycled. When they reach the recycling plant, cans are sorted from other materials, before a giant magnet is used to separate steel from aluminium.

3 MELTING
The shredded and cleaned aluminium is loaded into a searing hot furnace, which is heated to 750°C (1,382°F). The aluminium melts so it can be shaped at the next stage.

Inside the furnace the aluminium turns from solid to liquid.

2 BALING
Next, aluminium cans are compressed into square bales so they take up less space and can be easily moved. A 360 kg (800 lb) bale will contain about 19,000 cans. These bales are then shredded and blown with hot air to remove the decoration from the metal.

HOW IT WORKS

Vaccines teach the immune system to recognize disease-causing cells. Nanovaccines do this precisely because they are small enough to reach where they are needed. The yellow nanovaccine, shown on the right, tells immune cells how to recognize cancer cells so they can be killed.

Nanovaccine

1 **TAKE SAMPLES**
Doctors take a sample of a patient's immune cells, called dendritic cells, and mix them with the nanovaccine. This prepares the immune cells to fight cancer.

Dendritic cell

Treated dendritic cell

2 **VACCINATION**
The treated dendritic cells are returned to the patient's blood stream so they can be sent around the whole of the patient's body.

Blood vessel

Treated cell meets T cell.

3 **DISTRIBUTION**
As they are pumped around the body, the treated cells meet other immune cells, called T cells. The treated cells interact with the T cells, and trigger them to search for cancer cells.

T cell

Cancer cell

4 **SEEK AND DESTROY**
These T cells travel around the body in search of cancer cells. When a T cell meets a cancer cell, it releases a toxic cocktail that immediately kills and destroys the cancer cell.

Cancer cell is destroyed.

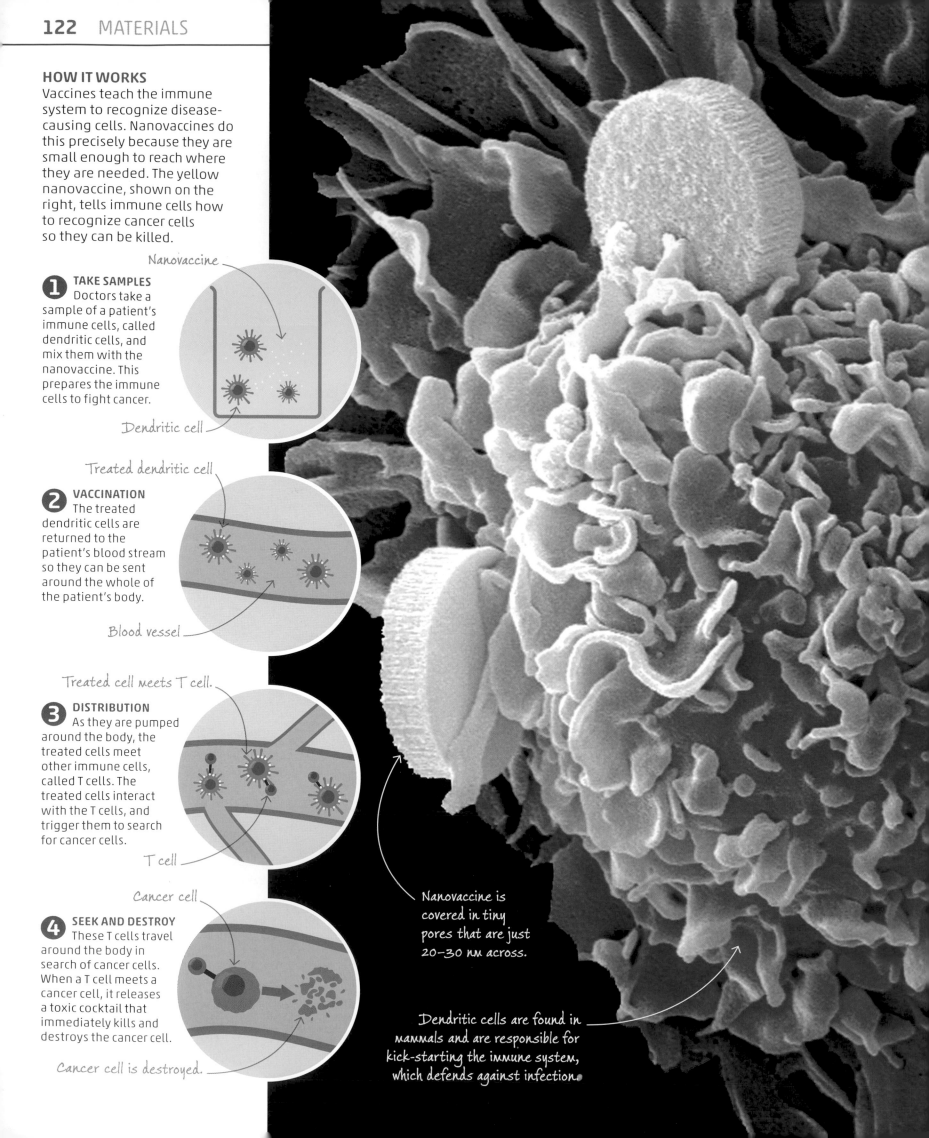

Nanovaccine is covered in tiny pores that are just 20–30 nm across.

Dendritic cells are found in mammals and are responsible for kick-starting the immune system, which defends against infection.

WHAT ARE NANOPARTICLES?

Nanomaterials contain particles that are so tiny they cannot be seen with a normal microscope. "Nano" means "one billionth", so nanoparticles are between 1 and 100 billionths of a metre in size. Their tiny size means that nanoparticles have many uses, from computing to medicine, and can have varying, often unexpected properties.

◄ NANOVACCINE

This coloured scanning electron micrograph (SEM) image shows an immune cell (blue), called a dendritic cell, from a cancer patient with nanovaccines (yellow discs) fixed to its surface. These silicon nanovaccines are covered with minuscule pores and loaded with molecules that will signal the patient's immune system to attack cancer cells when the dendritic cell is returned to the body.

HOW WIDE IS A NANOPARTICLE?

Nanoparticles are between 1 and 100 nm wide. A 1-nm-tall nanoparticle is one million times smaller than a 1-mm (0.04-in) pinhead. This difference in size is equivalent to the difference between a pinhead and a 1-km- (0.6-mile-) tall mountain, which is one million times taller than the 1-mm (0.04-in) pinhead.

1-nm-tall nanoparticle

X 1 MILLION

1-mm (0.04-in) pinhead

1-km- (0.6-mile-) tall mountain

X 1 MILLION

NANOPARTICLES

This coloured SEM image shows cotton fibres covered in nanoparticles (blue) to give the cotton stainproof and waterproof properties. The tiny nanoparticles prevent water and dirt particles from reaching the material. Textiles have been treated with a variety of nanoparticles to give them useful properties, such as antibacterial silver, which can be added to clothing to ward off bacteria and odours, and is used in some bandages.

Energy is what makes everything happen, from the blazing **heat** of a fire to the **light** reflected in a mirror or the **movement** of your muscles. Energy is everywhere. Most energy on Earth comes from the Sun, carried through space by **electromagnetic waves**. It can be **transferred** from one place to another, spread, and disperse – but it is **never created or destroyed**.

ENERGY

HOW ENERGY WORKS

Energy is what makes things happen, from moving muscles to heating a house or making a light bulb glow. Energy can be stored or transferred from one thing to another, but it can never be created or destroyed. When we say that energy is lost, we mean that it is not useful.

CONSERVATION OF ENERGY
The law of conservation of energy says that energy cannot be created and it cannot be destroyed – it is conserved. This means that the total amount of energy remains the same, no matter how many times it is transferred.

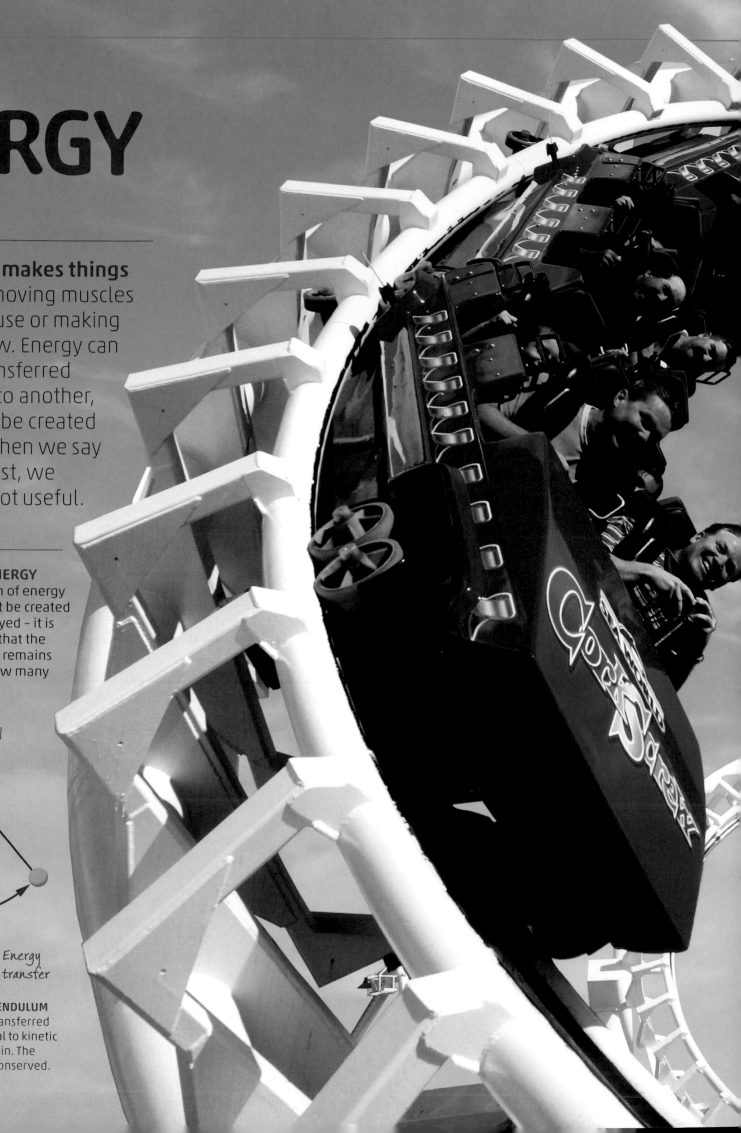

Maximum gravitational potential energy

Maximum kinetic energy

Energy transfer

ENERGY CONSERVED IN A PENDULUM
In a pendulum, energy is transferred from gravitational potential to kinetic energy stores and back again. The total amount of energy is conserved.

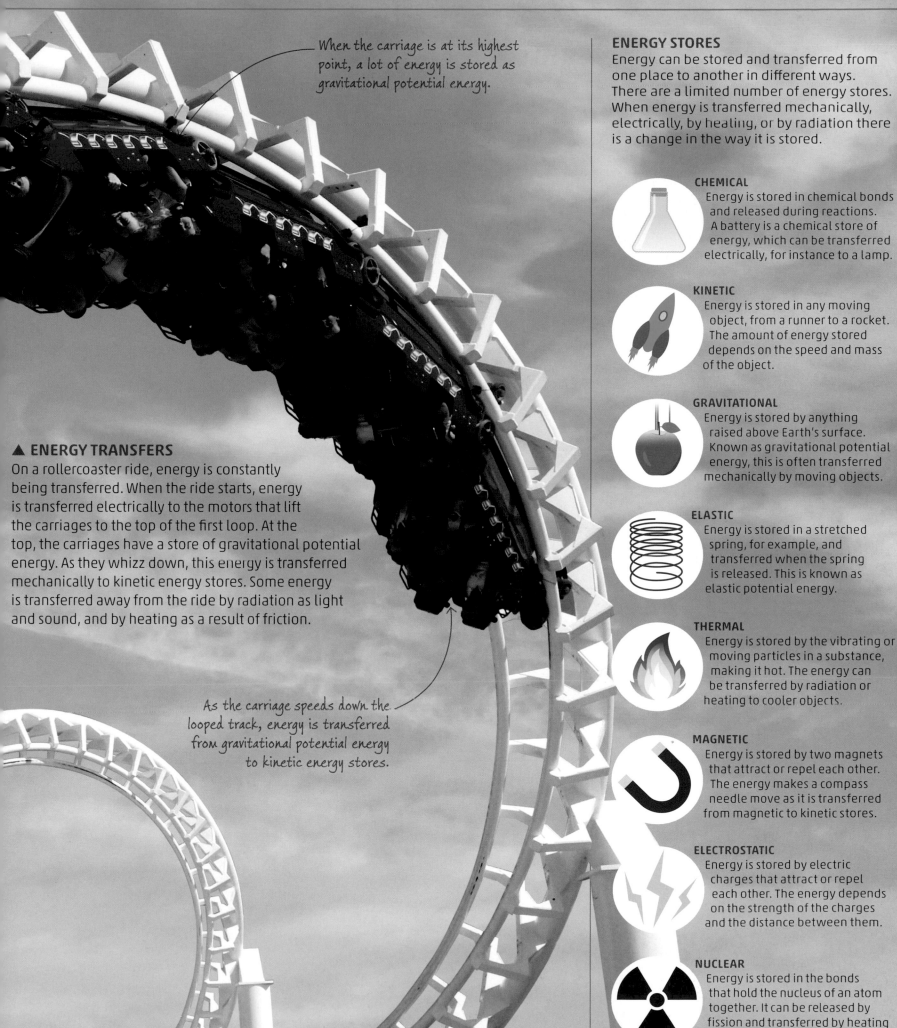

When the carriage is at its highest point, a lot of energy is stored as gravitational potential energy.

ENERGY STORES

Energy can be stored and transferred from one place to another in different ways. There are a limited number of energy stores. When energy is transferred mechanically, electrically, by healing, or by radiation there is a change in the way it is stored.

CHEMICAL
Energy is stored in chemical bonds and released during reactions. A battery is a chemical store of energy, which can be transferred electrically, for instance to a lamp.

KINETIC
Energy is stored in any moving object, from a runner to a rocket. The amount of energy stored depends on the speed and mass of the object.

GRAVITATIONAL
Energy is stored by anything raised above Earth's surface. Known as gravitational potential energy, this is often transferred mechanically by moving objects.

ELASTIC
Energy is stored in a stretched spring, for example, and transferred when the spring is released. This is known as elastic potential energy.

THERMAL
Energy is stored by the vibrating or moving particles in a substance, making it hot. The energy can be transferred by radiation or heating to cooler objects.

MAGNETIC
Energy is stored by two magnets that attract or repel each other. The energy makes a compass needle move as it is transferred from magnetic to kinetic stores.

ELECTROSTATIC
Energy is stored by electric charges that attract or repel each other. The energy depends on the strength of the charges and the distance between them.

NUCLEAR
Energy is stored in the bonds that hold the nucleus of an atom together. It can be released by fission and transferred by heating to hot water.

▲ ENERGY TRANSFERS

On a rollercoaster ride, energy is constantly being transferred. When the ride starts, energy is transferred electrically to the motors that lift the carriages to the top of the first loop. At the top, the carriages have a store of gravitational potential energy. As they whizz down, this energy is transferred mechanically to kinetic energy stores. Some energy is transferred away from the ride by radiation as light and sound, and by heating as a result of friction.

As the carriage speeds down the looped track, energy is transferred from gravitational potential energy to kinetic energy stores.

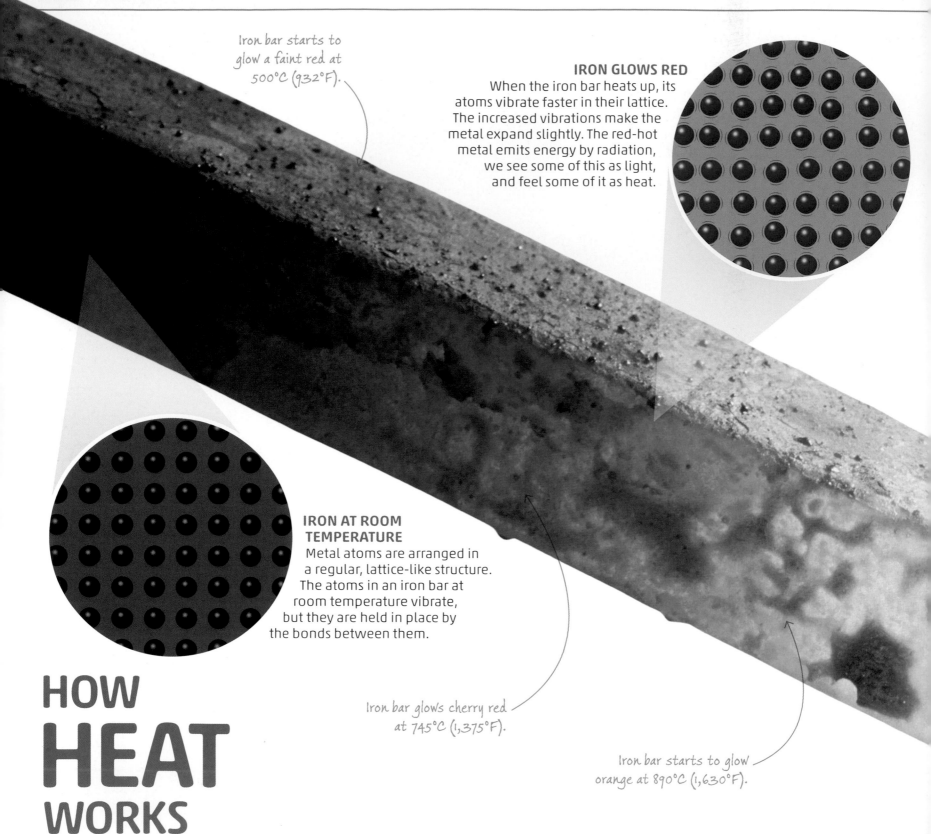

Iron bar starts to glow a faint red at 500°C (932°F).

IRON GLOWS RED
When the iron bar heats up, its atoms vibrate faster in their lattice. The increased vibrations make the metal expand slightly. The red-hot metal emits energy by radiation, we see some of this as light, and feel some of it as heat.

IRON AT ROOM TEMPERATURE
Metal atoms are arranged in a regular, lattice-like structure. The atoms in an iron bar at room temperature vibrate, but they are held in place by the bonds between them.

Iron bar glows cherry red at 745°C (1,375°F).

Iron bar starts to glow orange at 890°C (1,630°F).

HOW
HEAT
WORKS

Hot objects are stores of energy. When energy is stored this way, it is known as thermal energy. The thermal energy of an object is due to the motion of its particles. In a hot substance, particles move faster than in a cool substance. Hotter objects also transfer energy to cooler objects by heating. If an object is hot enough, it may also transfer energy by light.

▲ **HOT METAL BAR**
At normal temperatures, the atoms in an iron bar are constantly vibrating in all directions. The vibrating atoms have kinetic energy. When the bar is heated, the energy in it increases and its atoms vibrate more energetically. This is what makes it hot, and what causes it to glow.

TEMPERATURE AND HEAT

The temperature of a substance is the average kinetic energy of its particles – the faster they vibrate, the higher the temperature. Heat, on the other hand, is all the thermal energy stored in a hot object. This depends on the object's temperature, but also on its mass. So, for example, an iceberg stores more thermal energy than a hot cup of tea, because the iceberg, though colder, has a much greater mass.

WHITE-HOT SPARKS

The sparks of a sparkler are tiny fragments of iron so hot that they glow white. The sparks have a high temperature but a low mass, so they store little thermal energy. Although the temperature of the iron bar is lower, it has a much greater mass, so it stores more thermal energy.

White-hot sparks may reach temperatures of over 1,205°C (2,200°F).

IRON GLOWS YELLOW

As the iron bar gets hotter, its colour changes to yellow and then white. The atoms vibrate very energetically, moving fractionally apart within the lattice structure. This makes the metal expand even more.

Iron bar starts to glow yellow at 1,000°C (1,830°F).

THERMAL EQUILIBRIUM

Thermal energy is always transferred from hot to cool objects. If a hot iron bar is plunged into cold water, energy is transferred from bar to water until both are the same temperature.

❶ RED-HOT IRON, COLD WATER
The iron bar glows red hot, while the water in the bucket is cold.

❷ HOT IRON, HOT WATER
As energy is transferred from iron to water, the bar cools and the water heats up.

Energy makes water boil.

❸ FINDING EQUILIBRIUM
The bar and water will reach the same temperature, achieving thermal equilibrium.

CONDUCTION

Conduction transfers heat energy in solids. The particles that make up a solid are packed close together. When a solid is heated, its particles vibrate faster, colliding with other particles and making them vibrate faster too, so transferring energy from hotter to cooler areas.

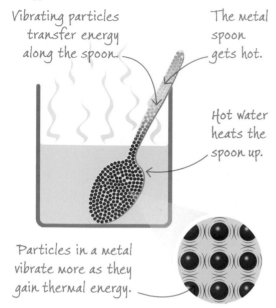

Vibrating particles transfer energy along the spoon.

The metal spoon gets hot.

Hot water heats the spoon up.

Particles in a metal vibrate more as they gain thermal energy.

RADIATION

Radiation is the transfer of energy by electromagnetic waves. All objects emit and absorb energy as infrared radiation. Unlike convection and conduction, which transfer energy through the motion of particles, radiation can transfer energy through space.

Energy is transferred by infrared waves.

Waves radiate in all directions.

HOW HEAT TRANSFER WORKS

Heat is constantly moving from place to place.
Energy is always transferred from hotter objects to cooler objects or surroundings. It can be transferred by heating in three different ways – convection, conduction, or radiation – depending on what it is moving through.

2 HEAT RISES
The dissolved crystals make a purple solution. When the water is heated, the molecules of the solution move apart, lowering its density. The less dense water rises, leaving a purple trail.

A concentrated trail of purple potassium permanganate solution rises with convection.

1 CRYSTALS ADDED
Purple potassium permanganate crystals are added carefully to the bottom of a beaker of cold water, and begin to dissolve.

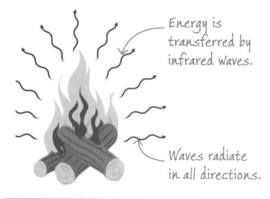

The crystals are added through a straw so they reach the bottom before dissolving.

Energy is transferred from the hot gases to the water in the beaker.

► CONVECTION

Convection transfers energy through gases and liquids. Convection can be shown in a beaker of water by adding a dye before heating it. As the water is heated, its particles gain energy, allowing them to move faster and farther apart. Hot water is less dense than cold water and rises. Cooler water moves in, creating a convection current.

Hot water rises and cold water sinks, setting up **CONVECTION CURRENTS.**

3 **CONVECTION CURRENT FORMS**
As the purple solution in the heated water reaches the top of the beaker, it cools down and becomes denser, causing it to sink. The circulation of hotter and cooler water forms a convection current.

As the purple solution cools, it spreads and begins to sink.

The purple solution continues to gain heat energy and rise by convection.

Heat is transferred through the glass beaker by conduction.

HOW WAVES WORK

Waves are all around us. The waves that we can see rippling across water, the waves that carry sound to our ears, and the waves that carry light to our eyes are just a few examples. All waves are vibrations that transfer energy as they travel. Some waves need a substance to travel through and others can travel through space, but there are features and behaviours that they share.

Floating rubber duck at peak of wave

▼ BOBBING IN ONE PLACE
It might look as if waves move water from one place to another, but this isn't the case. Waves in water don't move water forwards and sound waves don't move air forwards – their vibrations just transfer energy from place to place. A floating rubber duck bobs up and down, but the duck and the water don't travel with the wave.

TYPES OF WAVE
There are two main types of waves. Transverse waves, such as light, are made up of vibrations that move at right angles to the direction of travel. Longitudinal waves, such as sound, consist of vibrations that move parallel to the direction of travel. Some waves, such as ocean waves, can have features of both transverse and longitudinal waves.

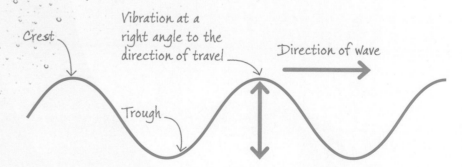

Crest

Vibration at a right angle to the direction of travel

Direction of wave

Trough

TRANSVERSE WAVE
In transverse waves, the vibrations go up and down at right angles to the direction of travel. Examples of transverse waves include all electromagnetic waves, such as light waves, microwaves, and radio waves.

MEASURING WAVES

All waves can be described by wavelength, frequency, and amplitude. Wavelength is the distance between two identical points of the wave, while frequency is the number of waves passing a set point in a given amount of time. Amplitude is the height of a crest or trough, measured from a central line.

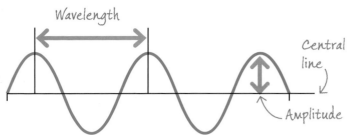

Wavelength

Central line

Amplitude

LONG WAVELENGTH, LOW FREQUENCY
For waves travelling at the same speed, waves with a longer wavelength have a lower frequency (fewer waves in a given amount of time).

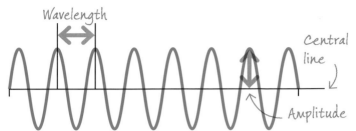

Wavelength

Central line

Amplitude

SHORT WAVELENGTH, HIGH FREQUENCY
For waves travelling at the same speed, waves with a shorter wavelength have a higher frequency (more waves in a given amount of time).

TRANSFER OF ENERGY

Waves involve the transfer of energy but not matter. As a water wave passes, it makes a duck bob up and down, but does not carry it in its direction of travel.

1 WAVE APPROACHES DUCK
The water wave disturbs the water surface, creating moving patterns of peaks and troughs.

2 DUCK RIDES THE WAVE
The wave causes the duck to bob in a fixed position on the surface of the water.

3 WAVE PASSES DUCK
The wave continues to travel, carrying energy but leaving the duck in place.

In this water tank conditions are carefully controlled. In the real world other forces, such as wind, currents, or tides, may cause a floating object to move.

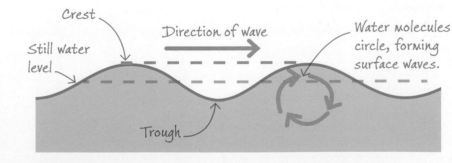

Surface of water forms alternating pattern of peaks and troughs.

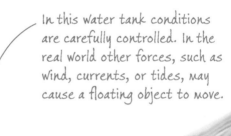

A stretched spring shows the motion of a longitudinal wave.

Vibration back and forth, parallel to the direction of travel

Direction of wave

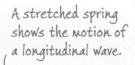

LONGITUDINAL WAVE
Longitudinal waves vibrate parallel to the direction of travel. Particles move back and forth through a medium, in a similar way to a stretched spring being pushed and pulled. Sound waves are longitudinal.

Crest

Direction of wave

Water molecules circle, forming surface waves.

Still water level

Trough

OCEAN WAVE
Ocean waves form when wind pushes against the surface of the water. Water particles move in circles, which makes the surface of the water rise and fall to form crests and troughs.

1 VIBRATIONS IN AIR
When a tuning fork is struck against a surface, its tines vibrate. They move so rapidly it can be difficult to see. The vibrations disturb particles in the air and travel through the air as invisible sound waves.

Tuning fork vibrates.

Sound waves travel through the air.

Glass contains water.

HOW SOUND WORKS

Sound is a vibration. When an object vibrates, it causes particles to move back and forth. The vibrations travel through a substance (solid, liquid, or gas), away from the source. These travelling vibrations are sound waves, and they transfer energy. They cannot travel in a vacuum – so there is no sound in space.

▶ SOUND VIBRATIONS
A sound wave causes particles to vibrate. The particles transfer sound but do not travel with the wave. Sound waves are invisible, but they are created by vibrating objects. You can show this using just a tuning fork and glass of water.

High pressure

Low pressure

PRESSURE WAVES
A sound vibration is made of changing regions of high and low pressure. The vibration pushes the particles of a substance forwards and backwards, parallel to the direction of energy transfer. When the tuning fork is placed in the glass its vibrations make sound waves travel through the water.

2 VIBRATIONS IN WATER
As the tuning fork is lowered into a glass of water, its vibrations disturb the surface of the water, making it splash. Once the tines are submerged they continue to vibrate and produce waves that travel through the water.

Tuning fork vibrates at a specific frequency, creating vibrations in the air that correspond to a particular pitch.

The vibrations of the tuning fork disturb the water, causing splashes.

Fork continues vibrating in the water.

PROPERTIES OF A SOUND WAVE
Sound vibrations can produce a range of different sounds: high and low, loud and quiet, and with different tones. The way we experience sounds depends on the properties of their waves.

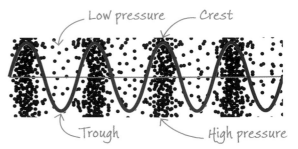

Low pressure   Crest

Trough   High pressure

REPRESENTING SOUND
The regions of high and low pressure in a sound vibration can be represented as waves. Crests show high pressure and troughs low pressure.

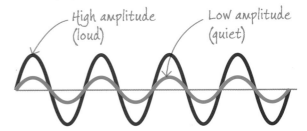

High amplitude (loud)   Low amplitude (quiet)

AMPLITUDE AND LOUDNESS
High-amplitude vibrations produce waves with more extreme regions of high and low pressure, which make loud sounds.

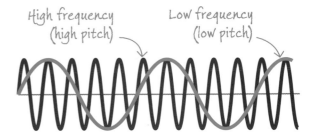

High frequency (high pitch)   Low frequency (low pitch)

FREQUENCY AND PITCH
A wave's frequency affects a sound's pitch. Low frequencies produce low-pitched sounds, while high frequencies produce high-pitched sounds.

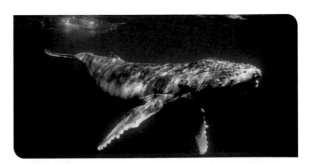

SPEED OF SOUND
Sound travels at different speeds in different substances, travelling fastest where particles are packed closest together, in solids. Sound waves travel faster in water than in air. Some marine animals, such as humpback whales, use sound to communicate underwater.

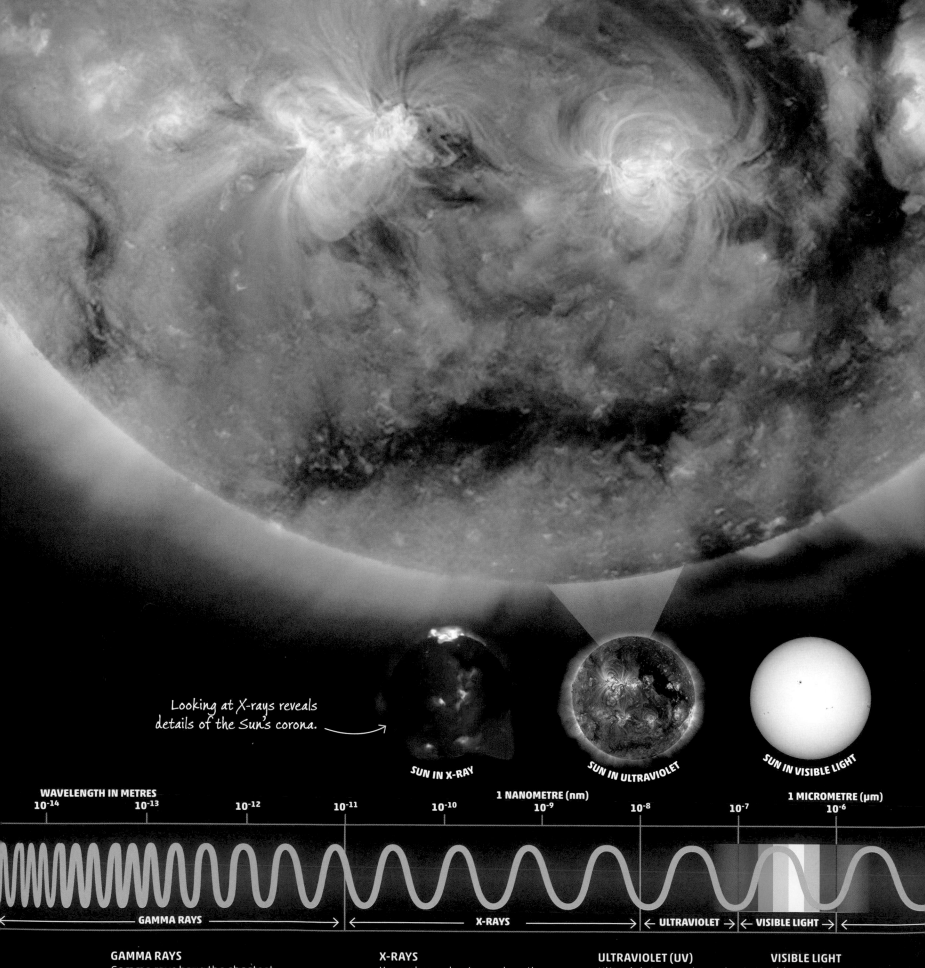

Looking at X-rays reveals details of the Sun's corona.

SUN IN X-RAY

SUN IN ULTRAVIOLET

SUN IN VISIBLE LIGHT

(see page 140)

WAVELENGTH IN METRES

10^{-14} 10^{-13} 10^{-12} 10^{-11} 10^{-10} **1 NANOMETRE (nm)** 10^{-9} 10^{-8} 10^{-7} **1 MICROMETRE (µm)** 10^{-6}

← GAMMA RAYS →   ← X-RAYS →   ← ULTRAVIOLET →   ← VISIBLE LIGHT →

GAMMA RAYS

Gamma rays have the shortest wavelengths and highest energies. This makes them useful for destroying cancer cells and sterilizing medical equipment, but exposure can be dangerous to humans.

X-RAYS

X-rays have short wavelengths and high energies. They are used to make images of inside the body because they pass through soft tissue but are absorbed by bone.

ULTRAVIOLET (UV)

Ultraviolet waves have shorter wavelengths than the violet wavelength of visible light. UV waves from the Sun can reach the surface of the Earth and cause sunburn and skin cancer.

VISIBLE LIGHT

This set of wavelengths is the part of the spectrum the human eye can see. The colour we see depends on the wavelength (see page 140).

HOW THE EM SPECTRUM WORKS

Visible light carries energy from the Sun to Earth. It is one part of a spectrum of waves that transfer energy around the Universe.
Known as the electromagnetic spectrum, this includes radio waves, microwaves, infrared, visible light, ultraviolet, X-rays, and gamma radiation. Each range of wavelengths has unique properties, but all travel through space at the speed of light. While the human eye can only detect visible light, special telescopes can also observe other parts of the spectrum.

▼ ELECTROMAGNETIC WAVES
The Sun emits waves across the whole electromagnetic spectrum. Most of these are invisible to the human eye. However, scientists can study the Sun's activity using special telescopes to detect other parts of the spectrum than visible light. Each of these false-colour images shows the Sun at different wavelengths.

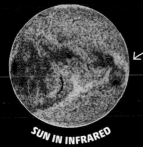

Infrared light is emitted from deeper within the Sun than visible light.

SUN IN INFRARED

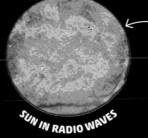

Radio waves are emitted from the Sun in huge bursts of gas from its outer layer.

SUN IN RADIO WAVES

| 10^{-4} | 10^{-3} | 10^{-2} | 10^{-1} | 1 METRE (m) 1 | 10^1 | 10^2 | 1 KILOMETRE (km) 10^3 | 10^4 |

INFRARED ─────→← ───────── MICROWAVES ───────── →← ───────── RADIO WAVES ─────────

INFRARED
Infrared waves have a longer wavelength and lower energy than the red part of the visible light spectrum. We feel infrared waves as heat.

MICROWAVES
Microwaves are used for sending communication signals, such as those for mobile phones and Wi-Fi. They are also used to heat food by making molecules vibrate in microwave ovens.

RADIO WAVES
Radio waves have the longest wavelengths in the electromagnetic spectrum. Vital in communications, they are used to broadcast radio and TV signals, for satellite navigation, and in wireless computer networks.

ALMA TELESCOPE

The Atacama Large Millimetre Array (ALMA) in Chile is an international observatory using telescope antennae that are sensitive to radio waves rather than visible light. The most powerful of its kind, this giant telescope has 66 antennae that detect faint radio signals from far-off stars and clouds of gas. The data collected is combined to create detailed images of the most distant galaxies in the Universe.

White light is composed of all the colours of the visible spectrum.

The prism bends light at different angles, depending on each colour's wavelength.

Red light has the longest wavelength and is refracted least.

Violet light has the shortest wavelength and is refracted most.

▶ **SPLITTING LIGHT**

White light can be split into different wavelengths and colours using a prism. When a light ray enters the prism, each wavelength of light travels at a slightly different speed and is bent by a different amount, revealing the spectrum of visible light.

HOW **LIGHT** WORKS

Light is the only part of the electromagnetic spectrum that the human eye can see. Visible light comes in a range of wavelengths often referred to as the visible spectrum. The eye can see colours from red (longest wavelength) to violet (shortest wavelength). When all the wavelengths are combined, light appears white.

RAINBOWS

The Sun is a powerful source of white light. Under certain conditions, water droplets in the sky scatter sunlight to reveal the full spectrum of visible light: a rainbow. In a double rainbow, the second spectrum is reversed.

REFLECTIVE COLOURS

The colour of an object depends on which wavelengths of light it absorbs and which it reflects. A yellow ball, for instance, absorbs all wavelengths of light that fall on it except the wavelength corresponding to that shade of yellow.

White ball reflects all wavelengths of the visible light spectrum.

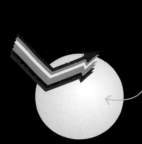

WHITE OBJECT
When all the colours of the spectrum are fully reflected from an object, the object appears pure white.

Yellow ball absorbs all wavelengths apart from yellow.

YELLOW OBJECT
When yellow light is reflected from an object, and all other colours are absorbed, the object appears yellow.

Black ball absorbs all wavelengths of the visible light spectrum.

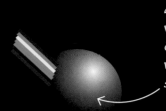

BLACK OBJECT
When all the colours of the spectrum are absorbed by an object, the object appears pure black.

Colours merge into each other.

VISIBLE LIGHT REGION OF THE ELECTROMAGNETIC SPECTRUM

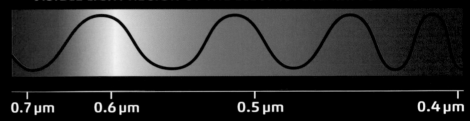

0.7 µm   0.6 µm   0.5 µm   0.4 µm

Orange blends into red and yellow.

VISIBLE WAVELENGTHS

All electromagnetic waves have different wavelengths. Visible light waves range in length from around 0.7 micrometres (µm; one millionth of a metre) to 0.4 µm – the size of a bacterium. Longer (infrared) or shorter (ultraviolet) waves are invisible.

The human eye can perceive more shades of green than of any other colour.

Indigo blends into violet. Although we talk about seven colours, they form a continuous spectrum.

Blue has a short wavelength.

Scorpion in **DAYLIGHT**

A special UV torch shines high-energy invisible ultraviolet light on the scorpion's cuticle.

EMISSION OF VISIBLE LIGHT
When UV light shines on the scorpion, it excites atoms that emit visible light in the blue region of the spectrum. The scorpion glows blue-green.

The scorpion's cuticle emits lower-energy visible blue light.

Scorpion's cuticle under **ULTRAVIOLET LIGHT**

REFLECTION OF VISIBLE LIGHT
In daylight, we see the scorpion as brown because it reflects a range of wavelengths from the visible light spectrum that includes yellows and reds.

HOW
FLUORESCENCE
WORKS

Light is made up of electromagnetic waves. Most objects can only be seen because they reflect light, but some objects produce their own light. Light can be generated when materials are hot enough to glow. It can also be emitted when electrons gain and lose energy within atoms. This is how a scorpion, such as this Asian forest scorpion, fluoresces.

HOW SCORPIONS GLOW
Light is emitted when the atoms in an object absorb energy and release it again as electromagnetic radiation in the visible light spectrum. This is known as luminescence. In scorpions, the energy that makes them fluoresce comes from ultraviolet light. In other types of luminescence, the energy may come from chemical reactions or an electric current.

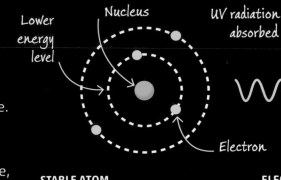

Lower energy level

Nucleus

UV radiation absorbed

Electron

Energized electron jumps to a higher level.

Electron falls back a level.

Light is emitted.

STABLE ATOM
Inside an atom, tiny charged particles called electrons fill up energy levels, which are often described as orbits or shells, around the nucleus.

ELECTRONS JUMP UP
When energy, such as that from ultraviolet radiation, is absorbed, electrons become excited, "jumping" to higher energy levels.

ELECTRONS FALL BACK
Electrons do not remain excited for long. They fall back to lower energy levels, releasing their excess energy as light.

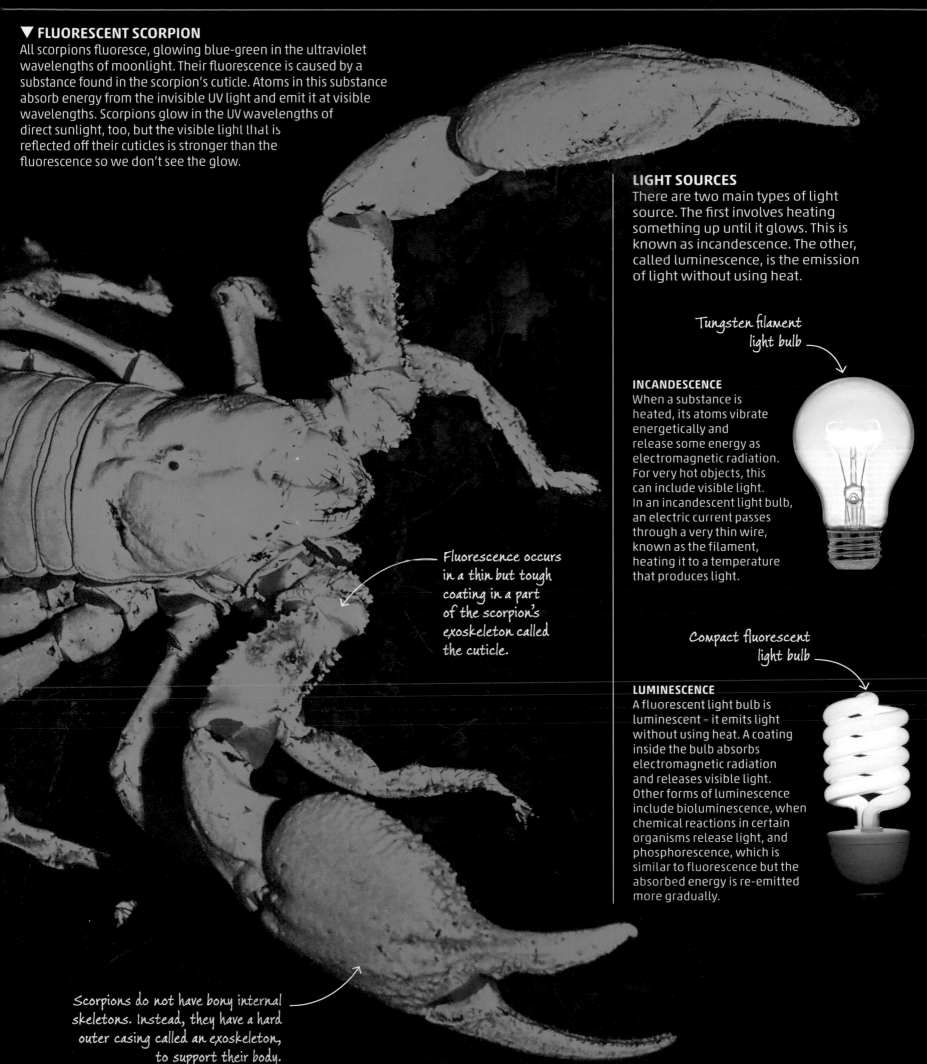

▼ FLUORESCENT SCORPION
All scorpions fluoresce, glowing blue-green in the ultraviolet wavelengths of moonlight. Their fluorescence is caused by a substance found in the scorpion's cuticle. Atoms in this substance absorb energy from the invisible UV light and emit it at visible wavelengths. Scorpions glow in the UV wavelengths of direct sunlight, too, but the visible light that is reflected off their cuticles is stronger than the fluorescence so we don't see the glow.

Fluorescence occurs in a thin but tough coating in a part of the scorpion's exoskeleton called the cuticle.

Scorpions do not have bony internal skeletons. Instead, they have a hard outer casing called an exoskeleton, to support their body.

LIGHT SOURCES
There are two main types of light source. The first involves heating something up until it glows. This is known as incandescence. The other, called luminescence, is the emission of light without using heat.

Tungsten filament light bulb

INCANDESCENCE
When a substance is heated, its atoms vibrate energetically and release some energy as electromagnetic radiation. For very hot objects, this can include visible light. In an incandescent light bulb, an electric current passes through a very thin wire, known as the filament, heating it to a temperature that produces light.

Compact fluorescent light bulb

LUMINESCENCE
A fluorescent light bulb is luminescent – it emits light without using heat. A coating inside the bulb absorbs electromagnetic radiation and releases visible light. Other forms of luminescence include bioluminescence, when chemical reactions in certain organisms release light, and phosphorescence, which is similar to fluorescence but the absorbed energy is re-emitted more gradually.

MIXING PIGMENTS

When combining pigments, such as paints or inks, colours mix in a different way. This is because pigments reflect the colour of light that we see and absorb other wavelengths (see page 141). When colours are mixed, more wavelengths of light are absorbed. In printing, the primary colours of cyan, magenta, and yellow are used to make all other colours.

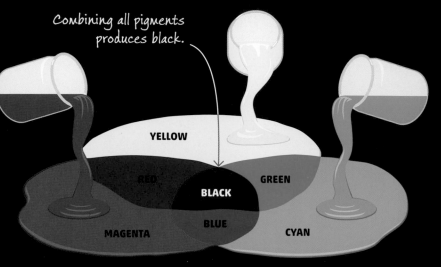

Combining all pigments produces black.

YELLOW

RED

GREEN

BLACK

MAGENTA

BLUE

CYAN

DIGITAL COLOUR

Digital displays combine red, green, and blue pixels of light to produce full-colour images; each pixel is made up of smaller red, green, and blue sub-pixels, which combine to make other colours.

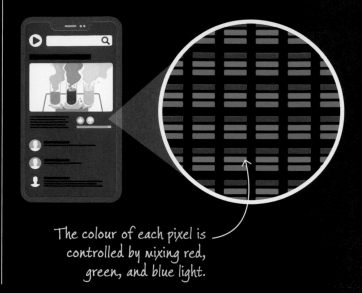

The colour of each pixel is controlled by mixing red, green, and blue light.

HOW COLOURS MIX

Colours seen by the human eye are produced by different wavelengths of visible light. The primary colours of light perceived are red, green, and blue. These can be combined to create any colour. If all the wavelengths are mixed, the eye sees white.

▶ MIXING LIGHT

A red, a green, and a blue light shine on a white ball in front of a screen. Where all the colours mix, the ball looks white. When our eyes detect all three primary colours of light (red, green, and blue), our brain interprets this as white. When our eyes detect only two of the three primary colours, we see cyan, magenta, or yellow.

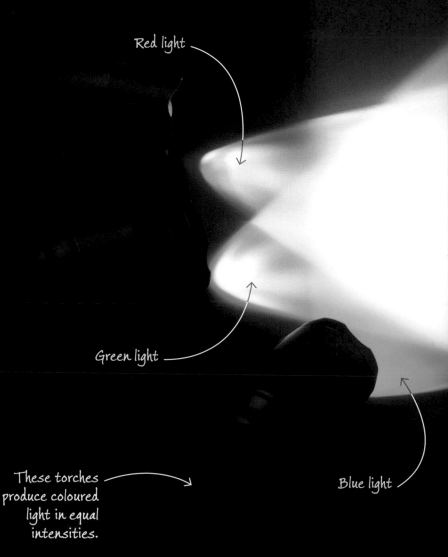

Red light

Green light

Blue light

These torches produce coloured light in equal intensities.

Blue light is blocked here. Red and green light mix to produce yellow.

Blue and green light are blocked here, so the eye sees red.

Green light is blocked here. Red and blue light mix to produce magenta.

Red, green, and blue light are blocked here. The absence of light is black.

Red and green light are blocked here, so the eye sees blue.

Red light is blocked here. Green and blue light mix to produce cyan.

Mixing equal parts of red, green, and blue light produces white light.

Parallel mirrors produce multiple images of robot's front and back.

HOW
REFLECTION
WORKS

Reflection happens when light meets a surface and bounces off it. Rays of light normally travel in straight lines, although they can be made to change direction. Almost all objects reflect light. Smooth surfaces such as mirrors reflect light at a predictable angle to produce a clear image, while rough surfaces reflect it in many directions.

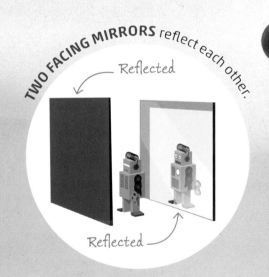

TWO FACING MIRRORS reflect each other.

Reflected

Reflected

PARALLEL MIRRORS
When an object is placed between parallel mirrors, a pattern of repetition can be seen: the images alternate from front to back view and from near to far apart.

Mirror produces clear reflected image of robot's front face.

◄ REPEATING REFLECTIONS
Positioning a pair of mirrors face-to-face can produce a series of smaller and smaller images reflected back and forth between the mirrors. Light rays reflect from both the front and back of the object.

The robot faces the mirror.

THE LAW OF REFLECTION
For very smooth surfaces such as mirrors, light rays follow the law of reflection. This states that the reflected light ray leaves the surface at the same angle that the incoming ray (known as the "incident" ray) meets the surface.

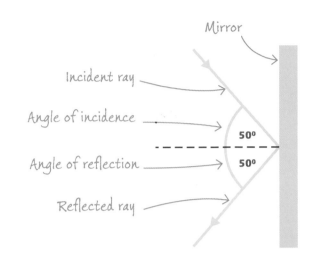

Mirror

Incident ray

Angle of incidence — 50⁰

Angle of reflection — 50⁰

Reflected ray

VIRTUAL REFLECTION
Placing an object in front of a mirror seems to conjure an identical object behind the mirror. This is a virtual image. In a flat mirror, the image appears as far behind the mirror as the object is in front.

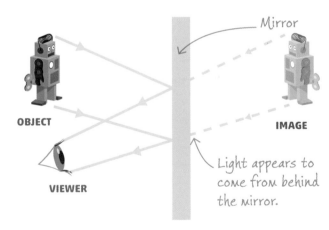

Mirror

OBJECT

IMAGE

VIEWER

Light appears to come from behind the mirror.

MIRROR IMAGE
A flat mirror creates reflections that appear reversed left to right. In reality, mirrors reverse images from front to back, through the surface of the mirror. Both the real and the reflected robot have their front closest to the mirror.

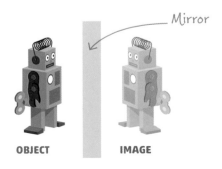

Mirror

OBJECT   IMAGE

▶ BENDING LIGHT

Inside this cardboard box is a powerful torch. When the torch is switched on, light emerges through slits in the sides of the box as straight beams of light. When these beams pass through glass blocks and lenses they seem to bend – the light changes direction as it passes from air to glass and back again.

Light bends again as it leaves the glass block and re-enters the air.

Light changes direction as it enters the block.

Light beam emerges parallel to the original beam.

Some light is reflected from the surface.

REAL AND APPARENT DEPTH

Light rays refract when they pass from water to air. This means that when you look from an angle at an object in water, it is not in fact where you see it. This is because your brain assumes that light travels in a straight line from the object. So a fish swimming in the water is deeper than it appears to be.

Light rays refract as they pass from water to air.

Image of the fish appears at a shallower depth than the real fish.

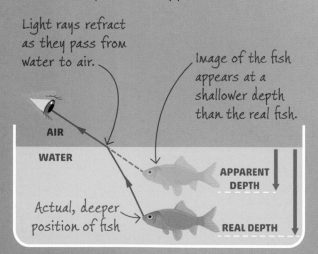

AIR

WATER

APPARENT DEPTH

Actual, deeper position of fish

REAL DEPTH

REFRACTION IN A GLASS BLOCK

As light passes from air to glass, it slows down and bends away from the surface. When it re-enters the air, it speeds up and bends back towards the surface. This is known as refraction. The amount it bends depends on how much the light speeds up or slows down as it passes through more or less dense substances. Light is refracted by the same angle as it enters and leaves the block.

HOW LENSES WORK

Light changes speed when it passes from one substance to another. This causes it to change direction, or refract. Refraction can be seen when light crosses the boundary between air and glass, or air and water. Lenses such as those found in glasses, telescopes, and other optical devices use refraction to make objects appear larger, closer, smaller, or simply clearer.

Light shines through slits in the light box from a hidden light source.

Concave lens curves inwards.

Lens causes light to diverge.

CONVEX LENS
A convex lens is shaped with a bulge in the middle. Light beams entering a convex lens are bent inwards and come together (converge) at a point on the other side called the focal point. The more curved the lens, the more the light converges.

Convex lens curves outwards.

Lens causes light to converge.

CONCAVE LENS
A concave lens is curved inwards with thicker edges. Light beams entering a concave lens are bent outwards and spread out (diverge), so that they appear to come from a focal point behind the lens. The more curved the lens, the more the light diverges.

Focal point

MAGNIFYING IMAGES
Depending on the type of lens and the position of an object in relation to it, images seen through a lens can appear smaller or larger. A convex lens can magnify a close-up object. Light from the object passes through the lens and is bent inwards, making it appear to have come from a much larger object behind the lens. This is known as a virtual image.

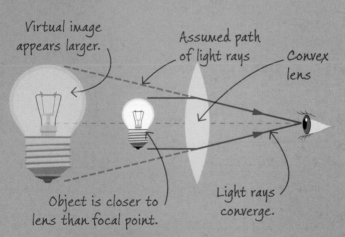

Virtual image appears larger.

Assumed path of light rays

Convex lens

Object is closer to lens than focal point.

Light rays converge.

SHRINKING IMAGES
A concave lens makes an object appear smaller. Light from the object spreads out as it passes through the lens, making it appear to have come from a much smaller object behind the lens. The brain sees this as a virtual image, because it assumes light travels in a straight line.

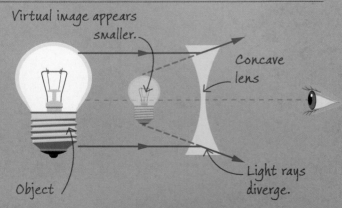

Virtual image appears smaller.

Concave lens

Object

Light rays diverge.

The laser emits a powerful beam of green light. This is not visible in air. A drop of milk added to the water scatters the light, making it easier to see.

▶ SHINING LIGHT

In this demonstration, a laser beam shines through a plastic bottle filled with water and along a stream flowing out of a hole in the bottle's side. The beam of light follows the curving path of the stream of water. This is a result of total internal reflection. The beam zig-zags inside the water stream, bouncing back and forth off its internal surface. This is because the light is reflected back into the water when it hits the boundary between water and air at or beyond a certain angle.

FIBRE-OPTIC COMMUNICATION

Total internal reflection allows information encoded in a beam of light to be carried down a thin strand of glass or plastic known as an optical fibre. These fibres can be used instead of electrical cables to transmit telephone and television signals, as well as data over the Internet. Signals travel at the speed of light. Each strand can carry thousands of signals at the same time. Fibre-optic cables can carry more data, faster than electrical cables.

OPTICAL FIBRES

The optical fibres used to send data between devices such as computers are made of glass that has been stretched into strands many times thinner than human hair. Like the light that travels through a stream of water, light can be sent through these glass optical fibres. The glass fibres make use of total internal reflection to send light zig-zagging to and fro along the strands as it is reflected off the inside. Light can travel long distances in this way.

HOW FIBRE OPTICS WORK

Total internal reflection causes the light beam to follow the curved path of the water.

The critical angle between water and air is 49°. This is the angle beyond which light reflects internally.

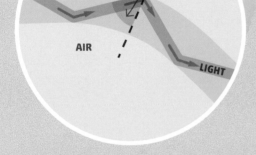

WATER

AIR

LIGHT

A laser beam bounces back and forth against the internal surface of a stream of water. This causes the beam of light to follow the path of the water. The same behaviour, known as total internal reflection, can be seen in transparent substances such as glass, and is the principle by which fibre-optic communications work. Data signals, encoded as light, travel at great speed across vast networks of optical fibres – strands of glass many times thinner than a human hair.

The light beam scatters when the stream of water pools at its end.

TOTAL INTERNAL REFLECTION

Light travels at different speeds in different substances. When light passes from one transparent substance to another, it bends, or refracts. How much it refracts depends on how much it changes speed and the angle at which it hits the boundary between substances. Beyond a certain angle, light travelling from water to air is reflected inside the water instead of being refracted. This angle is known as the critical angle.

FIBRE CABLES

Hundreds of optical fibres can be bundled together to form cables. Electrical signals from a computer are converted into light signals and sent down these cables to their destination. They are converted back into electrical signals at the other end. Individual fibres within each cable are able to transmit multiple signals at once, because light beams can follow different paths. Each cable is capable of sending huge quantities of information at a time.

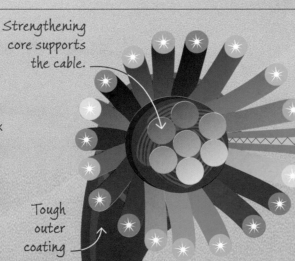

Strengthening core supports the cable.

Protective cladding keeps light inside the fibre.

Optical fibre

Tough outer coating

Light travels down the fibre by bouncing to and fro off its walls.

Plastic coating

HOW MAGNETISM WORKS

Magnetism is an invisible force that can push or pull objects. Magnetic force acts strongly on certain materials, such as iron, nickel, or cobalt, which are called magnetic materials. These have small regions called domains, which are like tiny magnets. When a piece of iron is magnetized, all the domains line up to produce a magnetic field.

Iron filings align with the magnetic field, because iron is a magnetic material.

The iron filings on top of the magnet stand up, because the magnetic field acts in three dimensions.

The iron filings are closest together near the magnet's poles, because this is where the magnet's field is strongest.

SOUTH POLE

▶ MAGNETIC FORCE FIELD

Every magnet is surrounded by a magnetic field. When iron filings are scattered over a magnet, they are pulled into line with the field. All magnets have a north and a south pole. The force field curves out from one pole and back to the other.

This bar magnet is made of steel, an iron alloy. Magnets can also be made from cobalt, nickel, or neodymium.

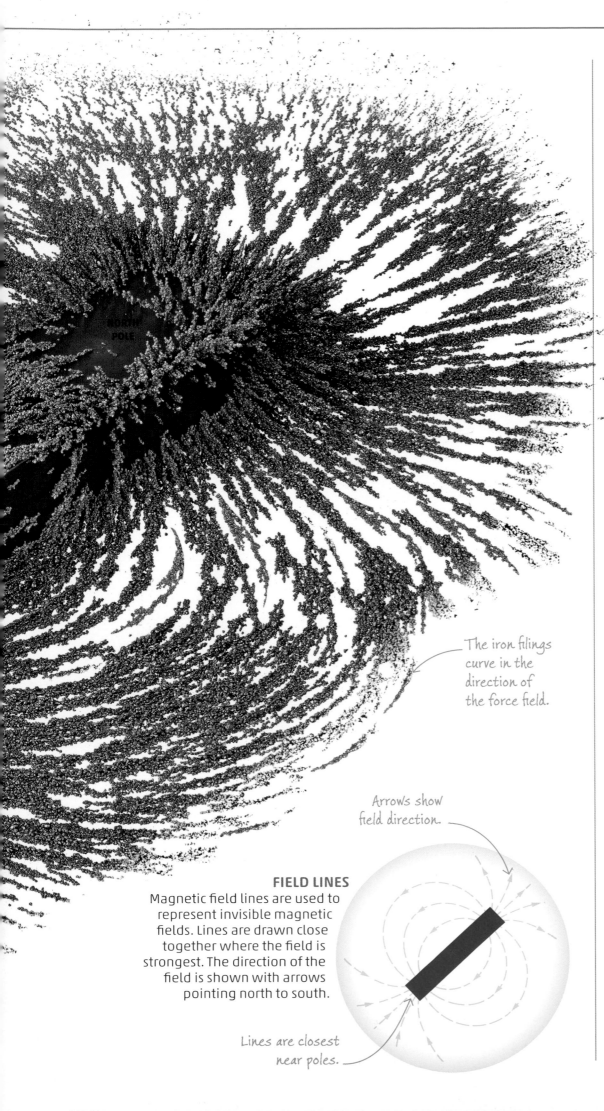

The iron filings curve in the direction of the force field.

ATTRACTION AND REPULSION
Magnets interact with the fields of other magnets, causing them to attract or repel each other. This effect can be seen using two bar magnets and a heap of iron filings.

OPPOSITE POLES ATTRACT
North and south poles are attracted to each other. When the opposite poles of two bar magnets are close, a magnetic force pulls them together. Iron filings reveal the attraction.

LIKE POLES REPEL
Like poles (north and north, or south and south) repel each other. When like poles of two bar magnets are close, a magnetic force pushes them apart. Iron filings show the repulsion.

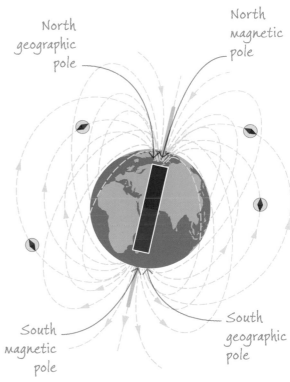

North geographic pole

North magnetic pole

South magnetic pole

South geographic pole

EARTH'S MAGNETIC FIELD
The Earth is a giant magnet, with a field, known as the magnetosphere, that extends tens of thousands of kilometres into space. The north magnetic pole acts like the south pole of a bar magnet, because it attracts the north poles of compasses. Earth's field reverses about once every million years. The magnetic poles are a few degrees away from the geographic poles.

Arrows show field direction.

FIELD LINES
Magnetic field lines are used to represent invisible magnetic fields. Lines are drawn close together where the field is strongest. The direction of the field is shown with arrows pointing north to south.

Lines are closest near poles.

AURORA BOREALIS

This spectacular light show dancing across the sky over Qaleraliq glacier, Greenland is known as the aurora borealis, or the northern lights. The lights appear hundreds of times per year, when electrically charged solar winds stream past the Earth and disturb the Earth's magnetic field. Charged particles rain into the atmosphere above the magnetic poles. The charged particles produce a coloured glow. When this occurs around the South Pole it is called aurora australis.

HOW STATIC ELECTRICITY WORKS

Static electricity is charge that builds up in one place. Objects are not usually charged, because positive charges in the nuclei of their atoms are balanced by negatively charged electrons. However, if electrons are transferred between objects, for example by rubbing one against another, the objects end up with opposite charges of static electricity.

CHARGE GENERATOR

A Van de Graaff generator is a device that builds up a positive charge on a metal dome by transferring negatively charged electrons away from it. A person touching the dome and insulated from the ground will also lose electrons and become positively charged. If the boy lets go and touches a metal object, the charge on him will run to earth through the object. He may feel a small shock where the charge passes from him to earth.

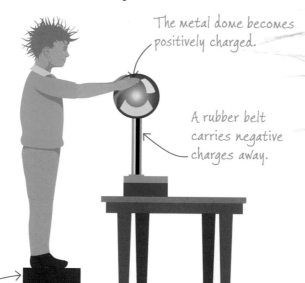

The metal dome becomes positively charged.

A rubber belt carries negative charges away.

An insulating stool prevents the charge from flowing to earth.

STATIC CHARGE

Static electricity can build up when certain materials rub against each other, causing electrons to be transferred from one to the other. This creates a positive charge in one and a negative charge in the other. Charged objects attract or repel each other.

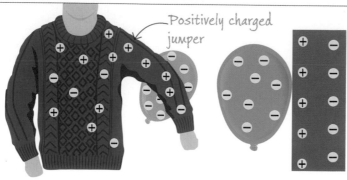

Positively charged jumper

Transferring electrons
Rubbing a balloon on a woolly jumper transfers electrons from the jumper to the balloon, so it becomes negatively charged.

Electrostatic attraction
The charged balloon repels electrons in a wall, making the wall's surface positively charged, so the balloon sticks.

Electrostatic repulsion
If you rub two balloons on a woolly jumper, they will both become negatively charged and repel each other.

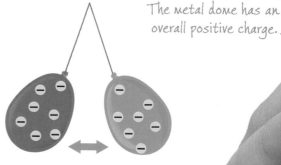

The metal dome has an overall positive charge.

◀ **HAIR-RAISING EFFECTS**
When a person touches the dome of the Van de Graaff generator, negative charges travel from them to the dome, leaving them with a positive charge. As a result, the positively charged hairs on this boy's head repel each other, making his hair stand on end.

ELECTRICAL REPULSION
Electrically charged objects interact with other charged objects: opposite charges attract while like charges repel each other. The hairs become positively charged, so they repel each other.

When a person makes contact with the dome, they lose electrons and become positively charged.

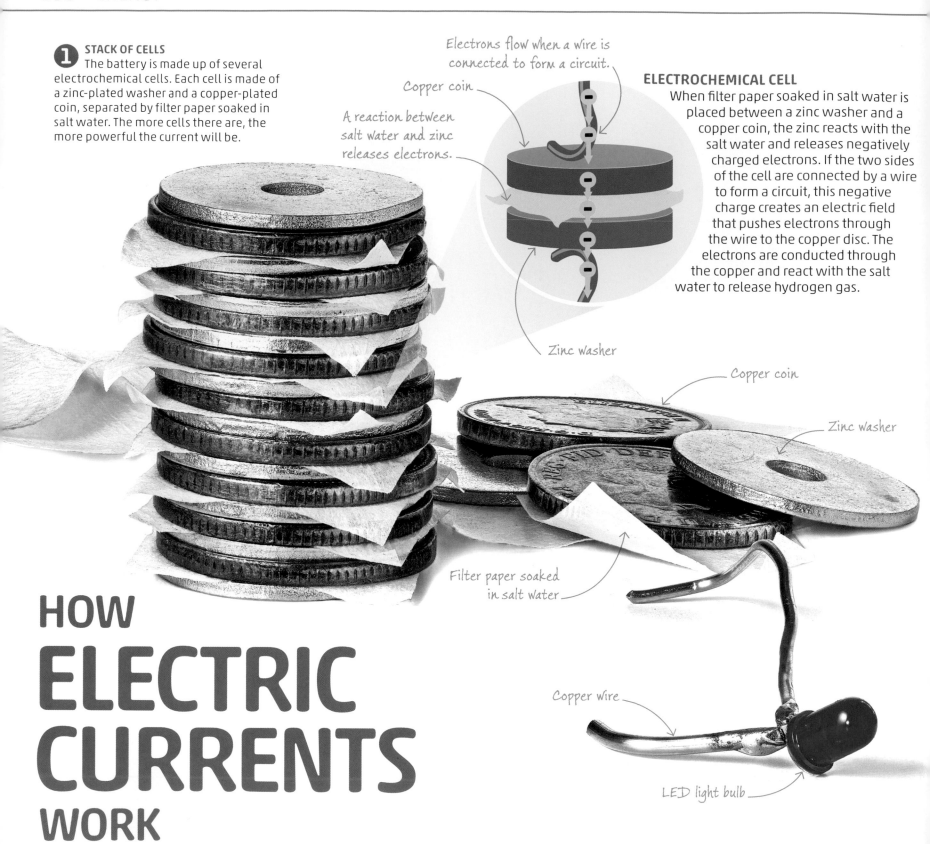

1 STACK OF CELLS
The battery is made up of several electrochemical cells. Each cell is made of a zinc-plated washer and a copper-plated coin, separated by filter paper soaked in salt water. The more cells there are, the more powerful the current will be.

Electrons flow when a wire is connected to form a circuit.

Copper coin

A reaction between salt water and zinc releases electrons.

Zinc washer

ELECTROCHEMICAL CELL
When filter paper soaked in salt water is placed between a zinc washer and a copper coin, the zinc reacts with the salt water and releases negatively charged electrons. If the two sides of the cell are connected by a wire to form a circuit, this negative charge creates an electric field that pushes electrons through the wire to the copper disc. The electrons are conducted through the copper and react with the salt water to release hydrogen gas.

Copper coin

Zinc washer

Filter paper soaked in salt water

Copper wire

LED light bulb

HOW ELECTRIC CURRENTS WORK

An electric current is a flow of negatively charged particles called electrons. Some materials, such as metals, contain electrons that can move easily. These materials are known as electrical conductors. All the electrical devices we use rely on flowing electric current. Electricity can also flow through liquids by electrolysis.

▶ SIMPLE BATTERY
A battery is a device that releases energy from chemical stores. The energy is carried around a circuit by an electric current to power devices. In this simple battery, electrochemical "cells" are stacked to produce a stronger electric field in the wire – known as the voltage of the battery. A higher voltage can produce a higher current, used here to power an LED light bulb.

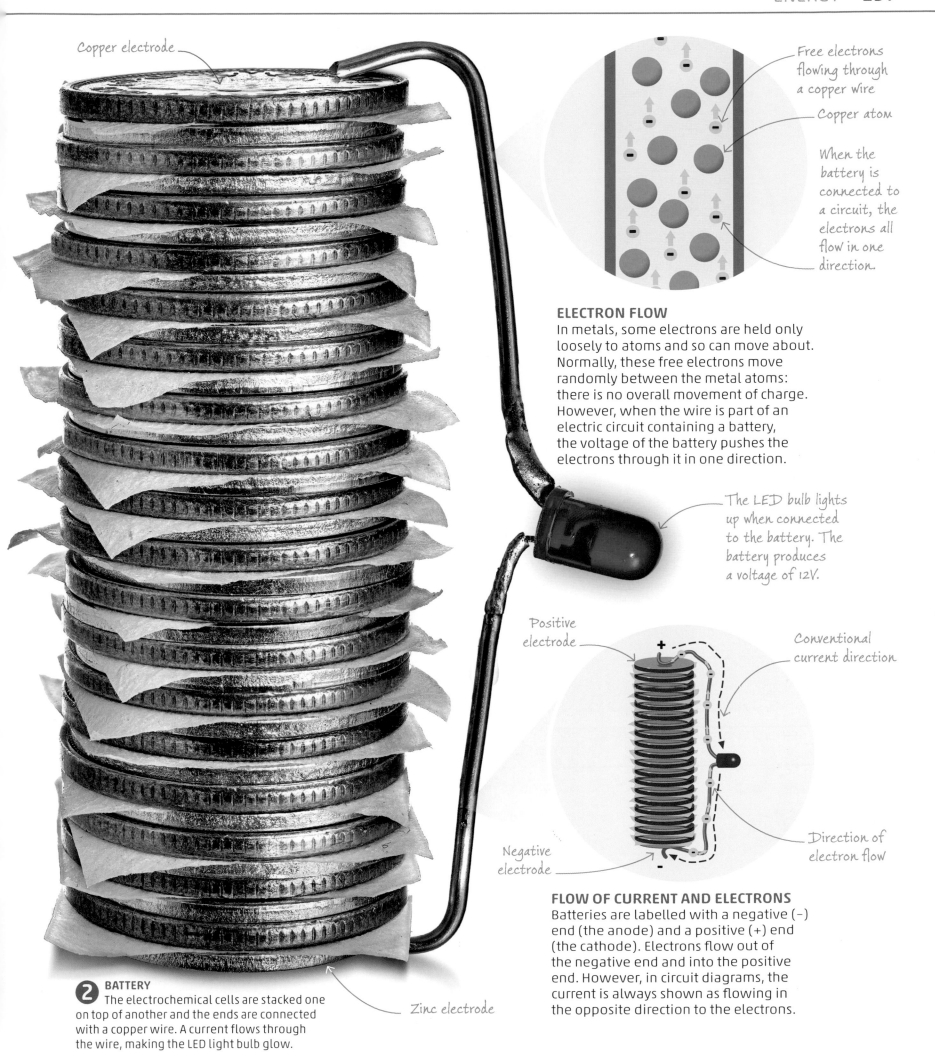

Copper electrode

Free electrons flowing through a copper wire

Copper atom

When the battery is connected to a circuit, the electrons all flow in one direction.

ELECTRON FLOW
In metals, some electrons are held only loosely to atoms and so can move about. Normally, these free electrons move randomly between the metal atoms: there is no overall movement of charge. However, when the wire is part of an electric circuit containing a battery, the voltage of the battery pushes the electrons through it in one direction.

The LED bulb lights up when connected to the battery. The battery produces a voltage of 12V.

Positive electrode

Conventional current direction

Direction of electron flow

Negative electrode

2 **BATTERY**
The electrochemical cells are stacked one on top of another and the ends are connected with a copper wire. A current flows through the wire, making the LED light bulb glow.

Zinc electrode

FLOW OF CURRENT AND ELECTRONS
Batteries are labelled with a negative (–) end (the anode) and a positive (+) end (the cathode). Electrons flow out of the negative end and into the positive end. However, in circuit diagrams, the current is always shown as flowing in the opposite direction to the electrons.

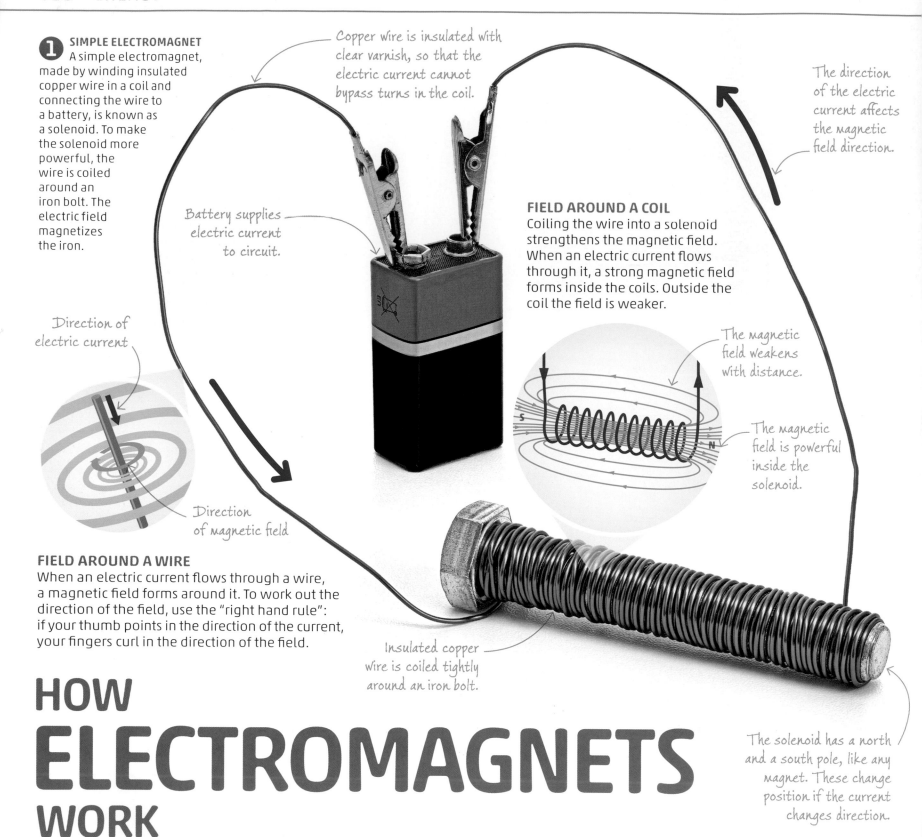

1 SIMPLE ELECTROMAGNET
A simple electromagnet, made by winding insulated copper wire in a coil and connecting the wire to a battery, is known as a solenoid. To make the solenoid more powerful, the wire is coiled around an iron bolt. The electric field magnetizes the iron.

Copper wire is insulated with clear varnish, so that the electric current cannot bypass turns in the coil.

The direction of the electric current affects the magnetic field direction.

Battery supplies electric current to circuit.

FIELD AROUND A COIL
Coiling the wire into a solenoid strengthens the magnetic field. When an electric current flows through it, a strong magnetic field forms inside the coils. Outside the coil the field is weaker.

Direction of electric current

The magnetic field weakens with distance.

The magnetic field is powerful inside the solenoid.

Direction of magnetic field

FIELD AROUND A WIRE
When an electric current flows through a wire, a magnetic field forms around it. To work out the direction of the field, use the "right hand rule": if your thumb points in the direction of the current, your fingers curl in the direction of the field.

Insulated copper wire is coiled tightly around an iron bolt.

HOW ELECTROMAGNETS WORK

The solenoid has a north and a south pole, like any magnet. These change position if the current changes direction.

Electricity and magnetism are closely related. The moving charges in an electric current can create a magnetic field, while a magnetic field can make electric current flow. Electromagnets are powerful magnets in which electricity is used to control the magnetism. The magnetic force can be switched on and off, have its direction reversed, or be made more or less powerful. Electromagnets drive electric generators and motors.

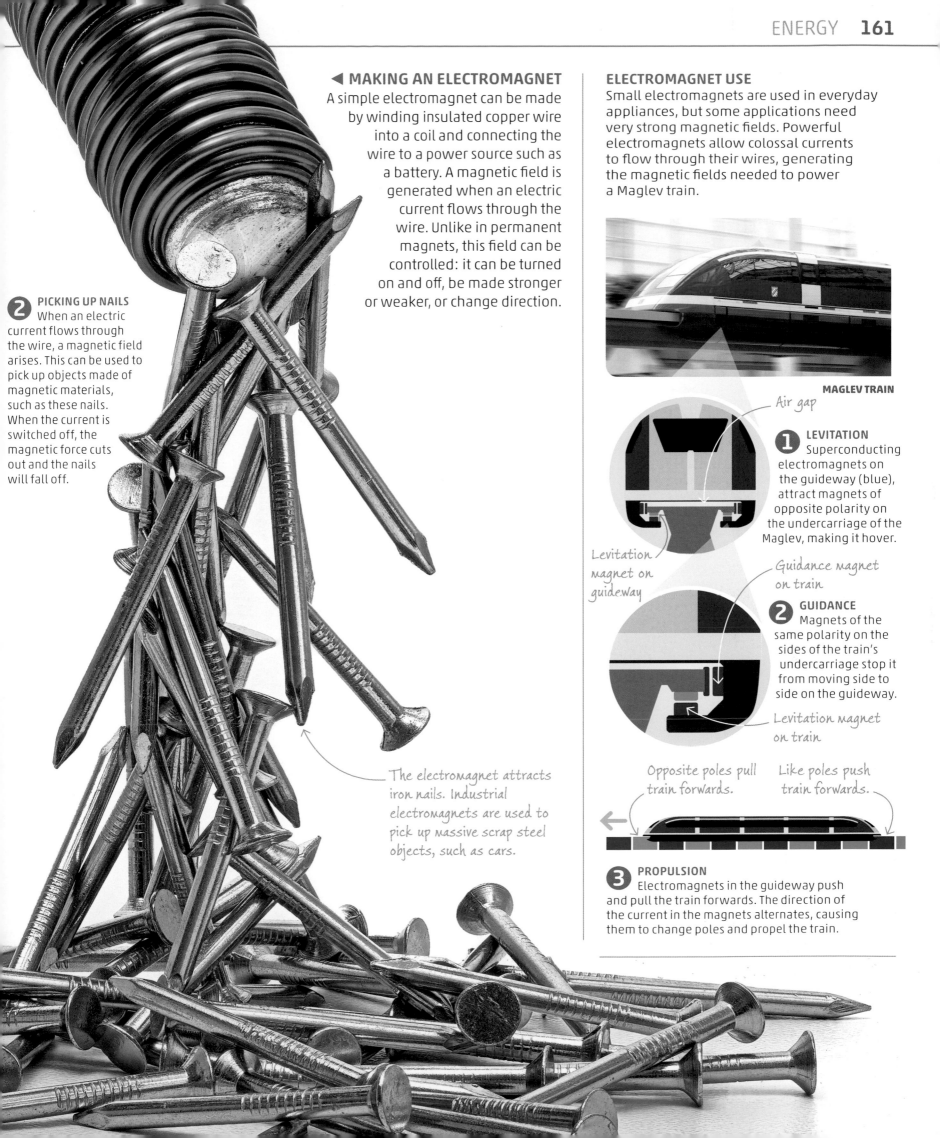

◀ MAKING AN ELECTROMAGNET

A simple electromagnet can be made by winding insulated copper wire into a coil and connecting the wire to a power source such as a battery. A magnetic field is generated when an electric current flows through the wire. Unlike in permanent magnets, this field can be controlled: it can be turned on and off, be made stronger or weaker, or change direction.

2 PICKING UP NAILS
When an electric current flows through the wire, a magnetic field arises. This can be used to pick up objects made of magnetic materials, such as these nails. When the current is switched off, the magnetic force cuts out and the nails will fall off.

The electromagnet attracts iron nails. Industrial electromagnets are used to pick up massive scrap steel objects, such as cars.

ELECTROMAGNET USE

Small electromagnets are used in everyday appliances, but some applications need very strong magnetic fields. Powerful electromagnets allow colossal currents to flow through their wires, generating the magnetic fields needed to power a Maglev train.

MAGLEV TRAIN

Air gap

1 LEVITATION
Superconducting electromagnets on the guideway (blue), attract magnets of opposite polarity on the undercarriage of the Maglev, making it hover.

Levitation magnet on guideway

Guidance magnet on train

2 GUIDANCE
Magnets of the same polarity on the sides of the train's undercarriage stop it from moving side to side on the guideway.

Levitation magnet on train

Opposite poles pull train forwards.

Like poles push train forwards.

3 PROPULSION
Electromagnets in the guideway push and pull the train forwards. The direction of the current in the magnets alternates, causing them to change poles and propel the train.

HOW NUCLEAR ENERGY WORKS

Nuclear power works by releasing immense energy from tiny atoms. This energy comes from strong forces that hold the nucleus of an atom together. Splitting the atom's nucleus (fission) or fusing two nuclei (fusion) releases the energy. Both processes require large amounts of energy but release much more.

▶ NUCLEAR FISSION REACTOR CORE

Nuclear reactors harness the energy from the fission of uranium fuel to produce electricity. Fission takes place in the reactor core. A steel pressure vessel contains the core. In it are fuel rods and control rods. These are surrounded by water, which transfers heat released by fission to the generator.

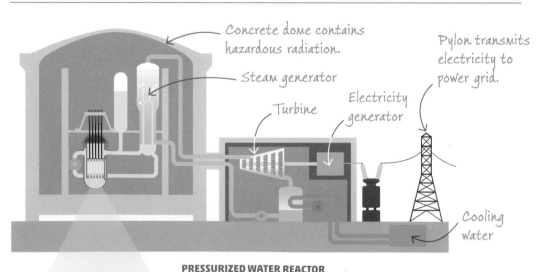

Concrete dome contains hazardous radiation.

Steam generator

Turbine

Electricity generator

Pylon transmits electricity to power grid.

Cooling water

PRESSURIZED WATER REACTOR

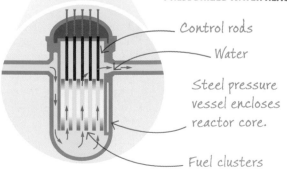

Control rods

Water

Steel pressure vessel encloses reactor core.

Fuel clusters

REACTOR CORE

NUCLEAR POWER STATION

Energy from fission reactions in the reactor core heats water under pressure to very high temperatures. The energy is transferred from the reactor to a steam generator, where it boils more water to steam. This spins a turbine, driving a generator to make electricity.

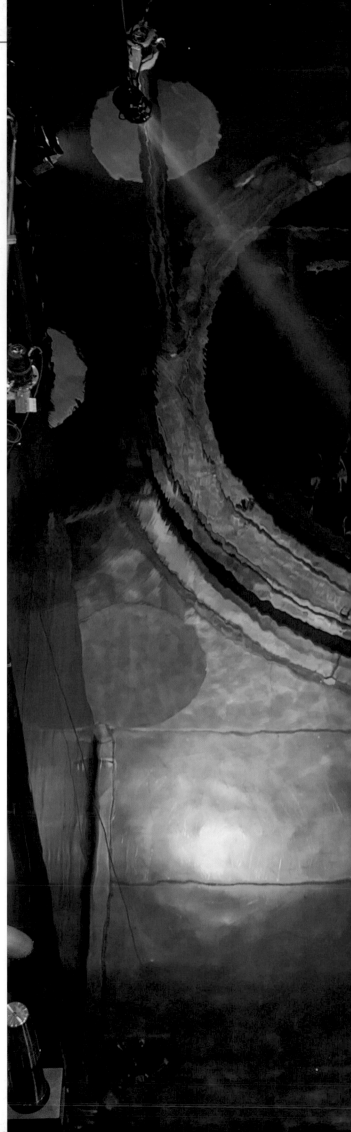

NUCLEAR FISSION

Fission takes place in unstable forms of certain elements, such as uranium, that can be split. A particle called a neutron from the nucleus of an atom hits the nucleus of a uranium atom. This splits the uranium nucleus, releasing energy and more neutrons. If these neutrons travel slowly, they hit more nuclei and cause new fission reactions, in what is known as a chain reaction.

Neutron hits nucleus.

Nucleus splits, releasing energy.

Uranium nucleus

More neutrons are released, starting a chain reaction.

CONTROLLING FISSION

A nuclear reactor generates energy, which heats water, from a fuel such as uranium. This starts a chain reaction. Conditions inside a reactor are controlled to start, stop, and keep reactions going in a safe way.

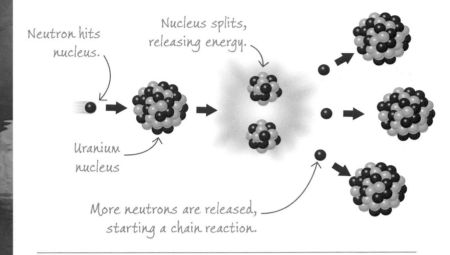

Control rod

FUEL CLUSTERS AND CONTROL RODS

The reactor core contains clusters of fuel rods (see below) and control rods. Naturally occurring neutrons start a chain reaction in the fuel, and fission produces fast neutrons. Water flowing through the core slows the neutrons down to keep the reaction going. The control rods, made of a substance that absorbs neutrons, can be lowered into the fuel to control the reaction by preventing further reactions.

Cluster of fuel rods

Uranium pellet

FUEL RODS

Pellets of uranium fuel are stacked into long metal tubes known as fuel rods. Clusters of these fuel rods are then inserted into the reactor core. A nuclear power station uses tiny amounts of fuel, but the spent fuel is radioactive and dangerous to human health. Unlike power stations that burn fossil fuels, however, nuclear power does not produce high levels of greenhouse gases.

Fuel rod

When a jet plane takes off, a rollercoaster loops the loop, or a car screeches to a halt, **forces** are at work. A force is a **push or a pull**. It can act at close range or from far away and it can be **weak or strong**. Forces are at work throughout the Universe, holding **tiny atoms** and **massive stars** together and keeping the planets in **orbit** around the Sun.

FORCES

HOW FORCES WORK

A force is a push or pull that can make an object start or stop moving, speed up or slow down, change direction, or change shape. Some forces act when objects come into contact with each other, others can act at a distance. When several forces act on an object at once, we call their combined effects "resultant force". If the forces in one direction are balanced by the forces in the opposite direction, they cancel each other out and the resultant force is zero.

▶ **CHANGING MOTION AND SHAPE**
Many forces act on a ball during a tennis game to make it speed up and slow down. When a tennis ball hits a surface such as a wall, it exerts a force on the wall and the wall exerts a reaction force (see page 171) back on the ball, causing it to change direction and shape.

A racket has applied a force to the tennis ball, making it move in the direction of the wall.

As the ball travels, the force of air resistance, or drag, slows it down.

CONTACT FORCES
A force can be thought of as a push or a pull in a particular direction. Many of the forces we are aware of are contact forces, which act between two objects that are physically touching each other. These include friction and air resistance, as well as the physical force applied by a person or another object. These forces do "work" on an object when energy is transferred. For example, in a tennis game, work is done when the racket applies a force to the ball.

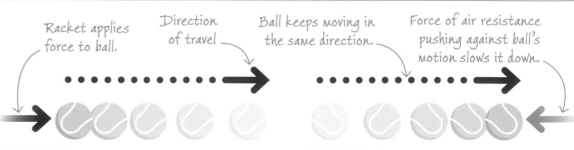

Racket applies force to ball.

Direction of travel

Ball keeps moving in the same direction.

Force of air resistance pushing against ball's motion slows it down.

SPEEDING UP
A force acting in the direction of an object's motion causes it to speed up, or accelerate. How much it accelerates depends on force and mass. It takes a larger force to accelerate a more massive object.

SLOWING DOWN
A force applied in the opposite direction to an object's motion causes it to slow down, or decelerate. The force of friction or drag often causes moving objects to slow down, as here.

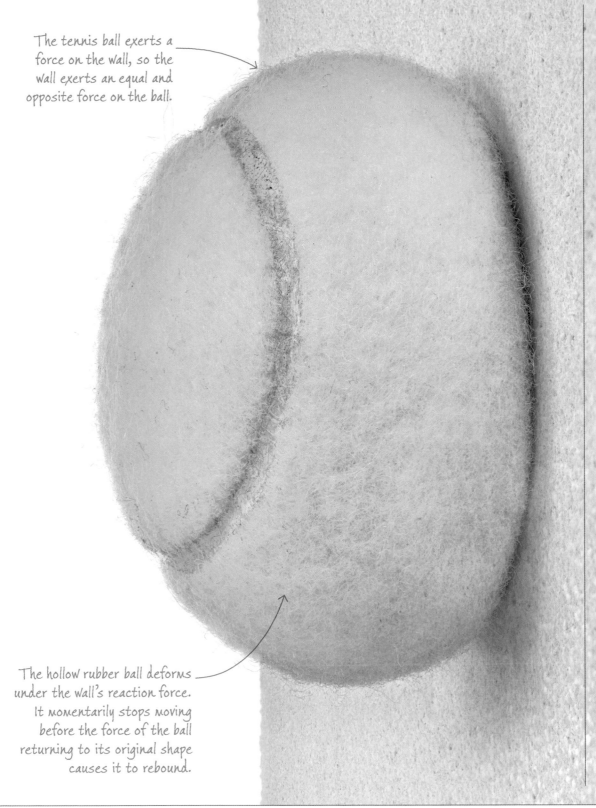

The tennis ball exerts a force on the wall, so the wall exerts an equal and opposite force on the ball.

The hollow rubber ball deforms under the wall's reaction force. It momentarily stops moving before the force of the ball returning to its original shape causes it to rebound.

NON-CONTACT FORCES

Non-contact forces are forces that act between objects that are not physically touching each other. Examples include magnetism, static electricity, and gravity. Unlike other forces, gravity can only pull and not push.

MAGNETIC FORCE

A magnetic force field surrounds magnets. This pushes and pulls other magnets and objects made of magnetic materials, such as iron, within the field.

ELECTROSTATIC FORCE

An electric force field surrounds electrically charged objects. This can push or pull other objects within the field that have an electrostatic charge.

GRAVITATIONAL FORCE

Gravity is a force of attraction between all objects, but we only notice it if at least one of the objects is massive – such as Earth. Earth's gravity makes objects fall to the ground.

MEASURING FORCES

The standard unit for measuring force is the newton (N). Weight is a force, so it is measured in newtons. An object's weight is the force of gravity on its mass. The force required to accelerate a mass of 1 kg (2.2 lb) at a rate of 1 m/s² (3.28 ft/s²) is 1 N.

A force meter is used to measure some forces.

An apple with a mass of 100 g (3.5 oz) weighs 1 N.

The greater the force applied, the more the ball changes shape.

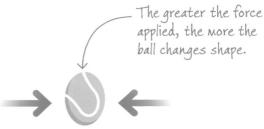

CHANGING SHAPE
Applying forces to objects can squash, stretch, bend, or twist them. Some objects return to their original shape after being deformed in this way, while others stay deformed or break.

Ball keeps moving in the same direction.

If a racket hits the ball, the force of the racket pushing against the ball's motion changes its direction.

New direction of travel

CHANGING DIRECTION
When a force applied to an object is in a different direction to the object's motion, the object will change direction. Forces are usually described by both their size and their direction.

HOW DOMES WORK

A dome's arched shape has amazing strength.
The curved structure spreads forces downwards
and outwards evenly through its walls. These unique
properties mean that even very thin-walled domes
can support extremely heavy weights.

► **EGGSHELL DOMES**
Eggshells appear fragile, but they are surprisingly
strong. Four half-eggshells placed dome-up on the
ground have enough strength to support a stack of
bricks between them. The force exerted by the bricks
is distributed evenly throughout the four eggshells.

Force is measured
in newtons (N). A
3.2-kg (7-lb) brick
exerts a downward
force of 32 N.

The weight
of the bricks
exerts a force
on the eggshells.

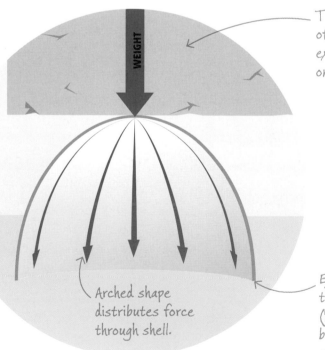

WEIGHT

Arched shape
distributes force
through shell.

Eggshell is less
than 0.5 MM
(1/32 in) thick,
but can support
a heavy weight.

STRENGTH OF A DOME
Vertical forces, such as the weight of
the bricks, are transferred outwards
and downwards through the dome to the
ground. This distribution of force means
that no point is put under too much stress.

Each eggshell
supports a quarter
of the total weight.

3 X 32 N = 96 N

Weight of bricks exerts downward force.

RESULTANT
FORCE = 0 N

BALANCED FORCES

When two or more forces act on an object, the resultant force can be found by adding up the individual forces. The weight of the bricks pushes down with a force of 96 N. An equal and opposite reaction force pushes up on the bricks – 24 N per egg. When all the forces are added up, the resultant force is 0 N.

Four eggshells push up on bricks with equal reaction force.

2 X 24 N = 48 N   2 X 24 N = 48 N

STRONG STRUCTURES

For thousands of years, architects have made use of arches and domes for their structural strength. In astonishing feats of engineering, bridges, and buildings support their own weight as well as heavy loads.

RAILWAY VIADUCT

Arched bridges, such as the Landwasser Viaduct in Switzerland, are built with arches because they can support weight above open spaces.

Weight transfers down the arch at either side to the ground.

CATHEDRAL DOME

The huge dome of Florence Cathedral, in Italy, was completed in 1436. Stone arches and interior rings of stone and wood support the structure's own weight.

1 INCREASING PRESSURE
The bottle rocket is half-filled with water and corked, then placed upside down on the ground, resting on its fins. Pumping air into the bottle through a valve increases the air pressure inside it.

At first, pressure is equal inside and outside the bottle, but internal pressure builds as air is pumped in.

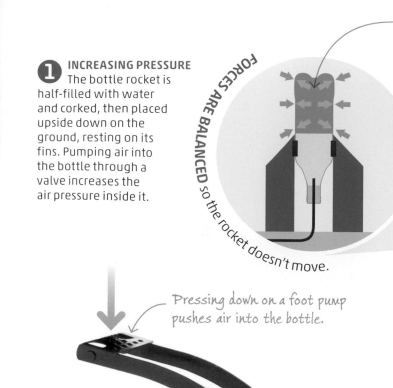

FORCES ARE BALANCED so the rocket doesn't move.

Pressing down on a foot pump pushes air into the bottle.

▶ BOTTLE ROCKET LAUNCH
A plastic bottle can be launched like a rocket by using air pressure to force water out of its neck, creating thrust. A foot pump is used to push air into the upturned bottle until the rocket shoots into the air – showing how forces cause changes in motion.

A plastic bottle is half-filled with water.

Cardboard fins are attached with sticky tape.

Air is pumped through a tube.

Fins support the bottle on the ground.

Cork

A valve pushed through the cork allows air to enter but not exit the bottle.

Fins stabilize the rocket's flight.

HOW FORCES AND MOTION WORK

How an object moves depends on the forces acting on it. When the forces on an object are balanced, it stays still or continues moving in the same way. If the forces on it are unbalanced, its motion changes: it may speed up, slow down, or change direction. Launching a rocket shows these changes in action.

2 PRESSURE CREATES THRUST
Eventually enough air pressure builds up inside the bottle to force the cork out of the bottle. Water is pushed out, applying an upward force of thrust on the bottle and launching it into the air.

NEWTON'S LAWS OF MOTION

English scientist Isaac Newton's three laws of motion describe the relationship between an object and the forces acting on it. The laws, first set out in 1686, remain accurate today, except if applied to very small or fast objects.

FIRST LAW
An object does not change its motion unless a force acts upon it. If the forces on the rocket are balanced, it remains still or continues moving at a constant speed in a straight line.

Forces are balanced, so rocket remains still.

Reaction force of ground (see Third Law) pushes up.

Weight pushes down.

ROCKET AT REST

SECOND LAW
When a force acts on an object it makes the object accelerate. The acceleration depends on the size of the force and the object's mass. The more mass an object has, the more force it takes to accelerate it.

The rocket accelerates upwards.

Thrust pushes rocket up.

Resultant (overall) force pushes the rocket up.

Weight pushes down.

ROCKET ACCELERATES

THIRD LAW
Every action has an equal and opposite reaction. As water rushes out of the bottle, the bottle is pushed upwards with equal force.

The bottle is pushed upwards with equal force; this is the reaction.

Water is forced rapidly downwards out of the rocket; this is the action.

ROCKET LIFTS OFF

Water rushes downwards when pressure forces the cork out.

HOW MOMENTUM WORKS

A moving object keeps moving because it has momentum. The object will carry on moving until a force stops it. That force might be friction or a collision. Momentum can be transferred between objects, but the total momentum is always conserved.

Fragments and fluids fly in different directions, but the overall momentum is the same as the original momentum of the paintball.

1 PAINTBALL MOMENTUM
A paintball is fired towards an egg. The heavier an object is and the faster it moves, the greater its momentum. The paintball is light, but travels fast, so it has considerable momentum.

The paintball has momentum.

Egg balanced on bottle

The paintball is slowed down by the collision but continues travelling in the same direction.

▶ PAINTBALL AND EGG COLLISION

When a paintball collides with an egg, it transfers some of its momentum to the egg. The total momentum remains the same before and after the impact, with most of the mass flying in the same direction as the paintball was originally moving. The more mass an object has and the faster it moves, the more momentum it has – and the harder it is to stop, so the more damage it causes in a collision.

Pieces of egg gain momentum and are knocked away, mostly in the direction of motion.

2 PAINTBALL COLLISION
The paintball crashes into the egg. Some of its momentum is transferred to the egg, cracking the eggshell and sending bits of shell and egg fluid flying off in the same direction.

Direction of momentum

The eggshell is smashed by the force of collision.

COLLISIONS

If a car hits a wall, the forces on it depend on its original momentum and how long it takes to come to a stop – how fast its momentum changes. To reduce these forces, modern cars have crumple zones. These are designed to collapse in a controlled way on impact, to slow the change in momentum. This reduces the risk of injury to the driver and passengers in a crash.

A seat belt stops the dummy's momentum. It stretches to slow the change in momentum of the dummy, reducing the forces on it.

An air bag slows the change of momentum of the dummy's head and reduces the forces on it.

Crash-test dummy

The crumple zone slows the change in momentum of the car, and of the dummy if it is wearing a seat belt.

③ TOTAL MOMENTUM
The paintball bursts on impact and its casing, the eggshell, and a mixture of fluids fly in several directions. The total momentum of all the solids and fluids is equal to the original momentum of the paintball.

The paintball continues in the original direction of its motion.

The forces of air resistance and gravity will slow and eventually stop the motion of the flying paintball and egg fragments.

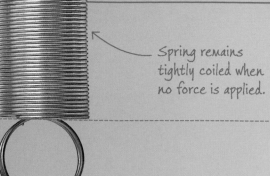

Spring remains tightly coiled when no force is applied.

No extension in spring

Spring extends under force.

▶ ELASTIC DEFORMATION

Elastic objects change their shape when forces are applied, then return to their original shape once the forces are removed. However, elastic objects are elastic only up to a point. For example, overstretching a spring will cause it to be plastically deformed – it will stay stretched even after the force is removed. How much a spring extends depends on how much force is applied. Twice the force equals twice the extension.

The hanger and discs weigh 100 g (3.5 oz) each.

0.5 KG (1.1 LB)

Five 100-g (3.5-oz) weights are added to the spring, exerting a downward force on it that makes it extend.

HOW SPRINGS WORK

Applying forces can stretch, compress, bend, twist, or break an object, changing its shape. This change of shape is called deformation. If an object returns to its original size and shape after the forces are removed, this is known as elastic deformation. If the object's shape is changed permanently, this is called plastic deformation.

Spring extends
twice as much if
the weight doubles.

Adding five more 100-g
(3.5-oz) weights pulls
down with more force
and causes significant
deformation in
the spring.

1 KG (2.2 LB)

PLASTIC DEFORMATION

A permanent change to an object's shape is
known as plastic deformation. For example,
a crushed can has reached the "point of no
return" and will no longer resume its original
shape and size. Applying force
has caused permanent
(plastic) change.

BEYOND DEFORMATION

When objects pass the points of
elastic and plastic deformation,
they will break. However, when
force is applied to an object made
from a brittle material such as
glass or porcelain, it reaches
breaking point with almost no
elastic or plastic deformation first.

COMPRESSING, STRETCHING, AND BENDING

Changing the shape of an object requires more
than one force. For example, compressing an
object needs two forces pushing from two sides,
such as a force pushing down while another
force pushes up.

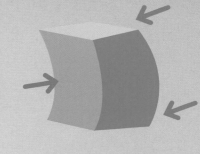

COMPRESSING
An object is compressed
when forces push inwards
from different points,
causing it to be squashed.
Depending on how the
forces are applied, its size,
shape, or both can change.

STRETCHING
An object is under tension
when forces pull in opposite
directions, causing it to
stretch. Materials, such as
gold, that can be stretched
very thin without breaking
are called ductile materials.

BENDING
Bending an object involves
both compressing and
stretching it. When several
forces act in different places
and different directions,
the object will bend, and
may even snap.

SHATTERED ROSE

When a rose is dipped in liquid nitrogen, which has a temperature lower than –196ºC (–320ºF), the water in its cells freezes and expands, breaking down cell walls and membranes in the process. The ice-packed flower becomes rigid and brittle. When thrown to the ground, the rose shatters into pieces, whereas a rose at room temperature would crumple and deform.

PULLING APART

As the cars move away from each other, the interleaved pages of the books are squashed together more tightly. This forces the imperfections on the surface of the pages closer together too, helping them to grip each other and prevent the books from separating. The harder the cars pull, the harder the books become to pull apart.

Two cars accelerate away from each other.

When the cars move, the pages squeeze together.

▶ CLINGING ON

The friction between the pages of two interleaved books can be so great that even powerful vehicles cannot overcome it. Here, two cars have been attached to the spines of two books with their pages interleaved. No matter how hard the cars pull, the books cannot be pulled apart – the books are more likely to rip first.

When pulled from both sides, the books do not separate because the force of friction between the pages is very strong.

Pages of two books have been interleaved.

GRIPPING SURFACES

Even surfaces that look smooth, like the pages of this book, are covered in tiny bumps and pits. When two surfaces are in contact, these bumps catch on each other so the surfaces resist motion. Rough surfaces produce more friction than smooth surfaces.

Bumps and pits increase friction.

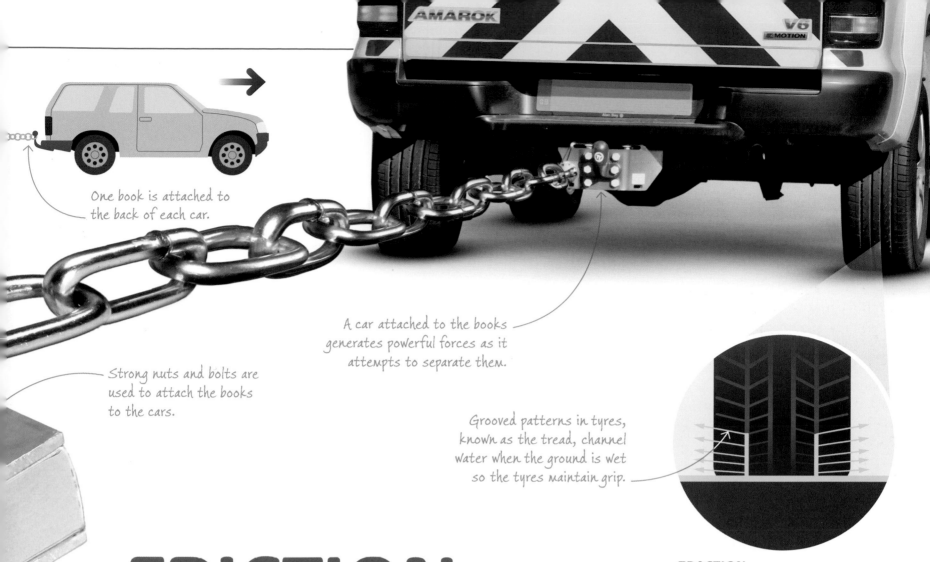

One book is attached to the back of each car.

Strong nuts and bolts are used to attach the books to the cars.

A car attached to the books generates powerful forces as it attempts to separate them.

Grooved patterns in tyres, known as the tread, channel water when the ground is wet so the tyres maintain grip.

HOW **FRICTION** WORKS

When two objects or substances rub or slide against each other, they are resisted by a force called friction.
Friction always acts against the direction of movement, and the amount of friction between objects depends on the roughness of their surfaces and how hard they are pressed together. Sometimes friction is useful, such as when brakes are applied to the wheel of a bicycle, but at other times it is inconvenient, such as when pushing a heavy object across the ground.

TRACTION
Friction allows a car tyre to grip the ground so that, when the wheel is turned by a motor, the vehicle is propelled forward. This grip is known as traction. Tyres are designed with deep grooves that channel water so the tyre can maintain its grip even in wet conditions. However, the friction between the ground and the tyre can create heat and will eventually cause the tyre tread to wear down.

OVERCOMING FRICTION
Ice skaters minimize friction by wearing skates with thin, smooth blades that allow them to travel on ice with very little friction or loss of speed. Ice is slippery because a very thin layer at its surface melts, providing lubrication that reduces friction between the skating blade and ice.

DRAG
Friction does not only act between solids – it also affects objects that move through fluids. This air and water resistance is known as drag. Boats can minimize drag in water using a structure called a hydrofoil, which raises the boat's hull out of the water so that drag only affects the sleek foils.

HOW **GRAVITY** WORKS

Gravity is the force that holds planets, stars, and galaxies together. Gravity also acts between us and the Earth, keeping our feet firmly on the ground or pulling us downwards if we jump from a height. We experience gravity as weight, the gravitational pull on our mass. In reality, gravity is a force of attraction between all objects – gravity pulls us towards the Earth, but we also pull the Earth imperceptibly towards us.

A skydiver in free fall in the head down position may reach a terminal velocity of up to 290 km/h (180 mph).

LAW OF GRAVITATION
Every object with mass exerts a gravitational force on every other object with mass in the Universe. Objects with more mass and objects that are close together experience stronger gravitational attraction.

FORCE OF
GRAVITY = 1

MASS = 1

NORMAL MASS AND DISTANCE
Gravitational force depends on mass and distance.

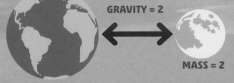

FORCE OF
GRAVITY = 2

MASS = 2

MASS DOUBLES
If the mass doubles, the gravitational force doubles.

FORCE OF
GRAVITY = 4

MASS = 1
DISTANCE = ½

DISTANCE HALVES
If the distance halves, the force is four times as strong.

▼ DEFYING GRAVITY

When skydivers leap from a plane, the Earth's gravity pulls them towards the ground. For a few exhilarating moments, they enter free fall. There is little air resistance and gravity is the main force acting on them. As they gather speed, air resistance increases until they reach a steady speed, known as terminal velocity.

Each skydiver has a parachute. Depending on the height of the jump, they will open their parachutes after around 35–40 seconds.

GRAVITY AND ACCELERATION

Gravity makes falling objects accelerate, speeding up as they fall. However, objects that fall for a long time will reach a maximum, or terminal, velocity. This happens when the downward pull of gravity is balanced by the upward push of air resistance. The gravitational force of the Earth pulls objects towards its centre. They also pull the Earth towards them, but this is less noticeable.

GRAVITY

AIR RESISTANCE

1 SPEED INCREASES
When a skydiver leaps out of a plane, the force of gravity between her and the Earth causes her to accelerate towards the ground. The acceleration of all falling objects due to gravity is 9.8 metres per second every second (32 ft/s²).

Skydiver speeds up when gravity is greater than air resistance.

2 TERMINAL VELOCITY
As the skydiver speeds up, the force of air resistance pushing up on her body also increases. After about 12 seconds, gravity and air resistance are close to equal. When the forces are balanced, acceleration stops. The skydiver continues to fall at terminal velocity – about 195 km/h (122 mph).

Skydiver falls at a steady speed when forces are balanced.

Skydiver slows down when air resistance increases.

3 SPEED DECREASES
Opening a parachute creates a rapid increase in the upward force of air resistance, causing the skydiver to decelerate (slow down) as she approaches the ground. She will reach a new, slower, terminal velocity.

The blade of an axe is blunt at one end, tapering to a thin edge at the other end.

HOW SIMPLE MACHINES WORK

A simple machine is a tool that can be used to change the size or direction of a force. Most simple machines work by increasing a force to make a hard job easier. This is known as mechanical advantage. There are six kinds of simple machine. Many of the machines that we use are complex machines, which combine more than one simple machine.

Downward force is applied to the blunt end of the axe.

WEDGES
A wedge is thick at one end and thin at the other. When a force is applied downwards to the thick end of the wedge, the thin end increases the force and directs it sideways, cutting or splitting an object apart. This is how an axe works to split a log.

The downward force is converted into sideways forces by the tapered edge of the axe, splitting the log.

Pushing an object up the ramp requires less force than lifting it to the same height.

RAMPS
A ramp is a surface with one end higher than the other. It takes less force to move an object up a ramp than to lift it the same height vertically. The mechanical advantage depends on the distance travelled and the height.

DISTANCE

HEIGHT

LEVERS

A lever is a rigid bar that moves around a fixed point called a fulcrum. The force applied is called the effort and the force overcome is called the load. If the effort is applied to the lever further from the fulcrum than the load, it increases the force. Levers can work in different ways, depending where the effort is applied and where the force acts in relation to the fulcrum.

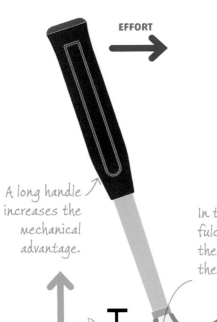

EFFORT

A long handle increases the mechanical advantage.

In this lever, the fulcrum is between the effort and the load.

LOAD

The head of the nail stops the nail slipping through the gap in the hammer's claw.

The effort applied to the hammer increases the force on the nail, making it easier to pull it out.

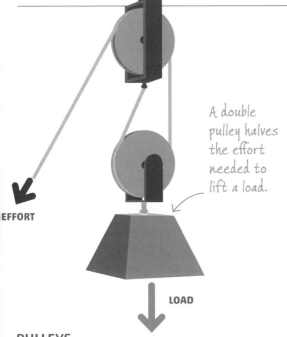

A double pulley halves the effort needed to lift a load.

EFFORT

LOAD

PULLEYS

A pulley is a rope or a cable that runs around a wheel. A single pulley changes the direction of a force (pulling down on a rope lifts a load up), while other types of pulley reduce the effort to lift a load.

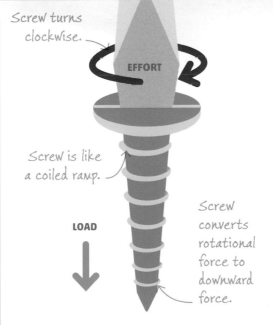

Screw turns clockwise.

EFFORT

Screw is like a coiled ramp.

LOAD

Screw converts rotational force to downward force.

SCREWS

A screw works like a ramp wrapped around a cylinder. Each turn of the screw pushes it a little further into the wood. Screws are also found in devices such as taps, the lids of jars and bottles, and corkscrews.

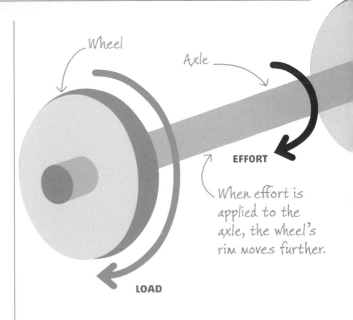

Wheel

Axle

EFFORT

When effort is applied to the axle, the wheel's rim moves further.

LOAD

WHEEL AND AXLE

A wheel turns around a small central rod called an axle. Together, they work as a circular lever. Wheels and axles can be used to either magnify forces or increase the distance moved.

HOW PRESSURE WORKS

Pressure is the result of a force pushing on a surface. The same force can produce high or low pressure depending on how much surface area it pushes on. High pressure can make objects change shape. Pressure can be applied to and by solids, liquids, and gases.

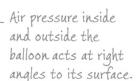

Internal pressure is greater than external pressure.

▶ BALLOON ON A BED OF NAILS

If you push a nail into an inflated balloon, the balloon bursts. This is because the tip of the nail is very small, so it applies high pressure to the balloon. However, if you construct a bed of nails and press the balloon down on it with a similar force, it stays intact. This is because the contact area between the sharp points of the nails and the balloon's surface is much greater, spreading out the force and reducing the pressure.

AIR PRESSURE

Air particles are constantly whizzing around and colliding with things. This creates air pressure. When a balloon is inflated, the air inside is compressed so more air particles bump against its inner surface than its outer surface – so the internal pressure is higher.

Air pressure inside and outside the balloon acts at right angles to its surface.

DESERT CREATURES

Animals and vehicles travelling in the desert are in danger of sinking into the soft sand. Some desert-dwelling animals have adapted in ways that allow them to get around this. For instance, camels have very broad feet, which bring a large surface area into contact with the ground at every step. This spreads out the camels' weight and prevents them from sinking in as they walk.

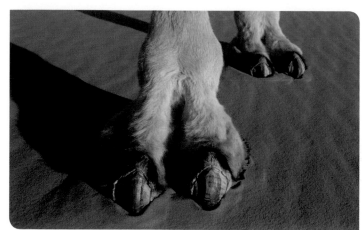

CAMEL'S FOOT IN THE SAHARAN SAND

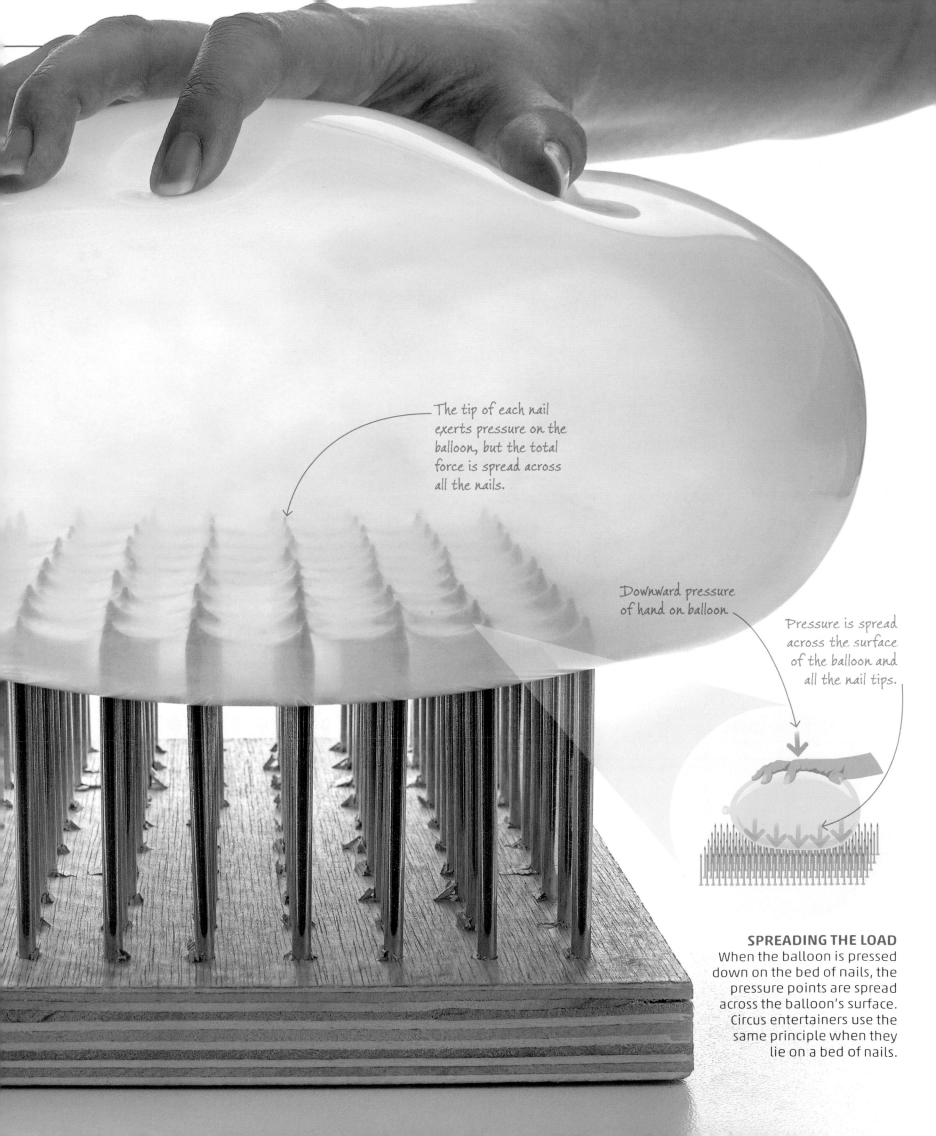

The tip of each nail exerts pressure on the balloon, but the total force is spread across all the nails.

Downward pressure of hand on balloon

Pressure is spread across the surface of the balloon and all the nail tips.

SPREADING THE LOAD
When the balloon is pressed down on the bed of nails, the pressure points are spread across the balloon's surface. Circus entertainers use the same principle when they lie on a bed of nails.

DENSITY, MASS, AND VOLUME

An object's density is its mass divided by its volume. Mass is the amount of matter in an object, while volume is the space it occupies. The three cubes below all have the same mass, but each has a different volume, so they have different densities.

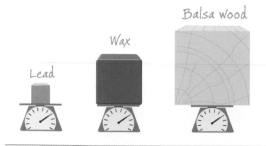

Balsa wood

Wax

Lead

RELATIVE DENSITY

The density of substances can be compared to that of water. This is known as relative density. A cube of liquid water with a volume of 1 cm³ has a mass of 1 g, so its density is 1 g/cm³. Substances with a relative density of more than 1 sink in water.

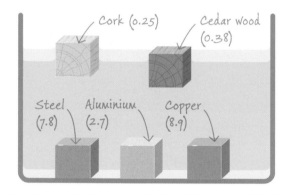

Cork (0.25)   Cedar wood (0.38)

Steel (7.8)   Aluminium (2.7)   Copper (8.9)

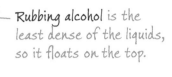

Rubbing alcohol is the least dense of the liquids, so it floats on the top.

Vegetable oil is less dense than water, and does not mix with it.

Water has been dyed purple in this density tower to make it visible.

Washing-up liquid is denser than oil and water. It would mix with both if shaken together.

Maple syrup has a lower density than corn syrup and floats on top of it.

Clear corn syrup is more dense than maple syrup, but less dense than honey.

Honey – even the runny kind – is very dense, so sinks to the bottom.

HOW DENSITY WORKS

Density is a measure of the mass (amount of matter) of a substance compared with its volume. Objects of the same size usually do not have the same mass, because they have different densities. Dense substances, such as lead, feel heavy for their size. Density depends on the size and mass of the atoms and molecules in a substance, and how tightly they are packed together.

▲ **DENSITY TOWER**

When liquids that do not easily mix are poured into a container, they form separate layers, arranged by density. As shown here, the densest liquid sinks to the bottom and the least dense floats on the top. A solid object dropped into the tower will float or sink depending on how dense it is relative to each liquid layer. A metal bolt sinks to the bottom.

When a dense solid object is dropped into the tower, the liquid layers are disturbed. However, if left to settle they will separate again into distinct layers.

Water is relatively dense because its molecules are tightly bonded together.

A steel bolt is denser than all the liquids in this tower, so it sinks to the bottom.

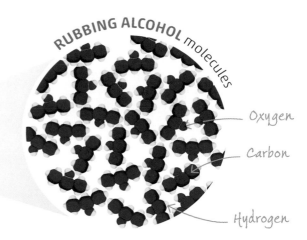

RUBBING ALCOHOL
A molecule of rubbing alcohol is made of carbon and hydrogen plus one oxygen atom. Because of their shape, the molecules do not pack close.

VEGETABLE OIL
A vegetable oil molecule is a chain of carbon and hydrogen plus two oxygen atoms. Oil is denser than alcohol because its molecules pack closer.

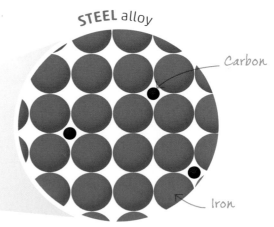

STEEL
A dense alloy (metal mixture), steel is made of iron atoms – which have a very high atomic mass – and carbon atoms, packed together in a lattice.

HOW FLOATING WORKS

Why do some objects float and others sink? It's all about density – if the object is denser than water it sinks but if it is less dense then it will float. Ships have lots of air space inside them, so a ship made of heavy steel floats because its average density is less than that of water. Similarly, an aluminium foil boat laden with copper coins floats, even though the coins on their own would sink.

▼ FLOATING IN WATER
A boat floats because of a force called upthrust. This upward force acts on any object in a fluid (liquid or gas). Upthrust is equal to the weight of the fluid displaced by the object, which depends on the object's volume. If the object is less dense than water, the upthrust is large enough to balance its weight and it will float.

The large, submerged hull of the boat holds air and so has a low average density.

1 SINKING COPPER COIN
A small coin made of copper-plated steel is dropped in water. The metal it is made of is denser than the water. This means that the weight of the water the coin displaces is less than the weight of the coin, and so the upthrust is less than the coin's weight and it sinks.

UPTHRUST

WEIGHT

2 BOAT FLOATS
An aluminium foil boat laden with coins floats. The boat is shaped to hold air, so that its average density is less than that of the water that it displaces. The upthrust on the boat is equal to its weight, and so the boat floats.

High-density metal coin sinks in water.

FLOATING IN AIR

A hot-air balloon uses heat to create upthrust and lift the balloon off the ground. The air in its "envelope" (the colourful fabric balloon) is heated by a propane burner until it has a lower density than the air around it. The balloon floats when the downward force of its weight is smaller than or equal to the upthrust exerted by the surrounding air.

The hot air inside the envelope is less dense than the cool air outside.

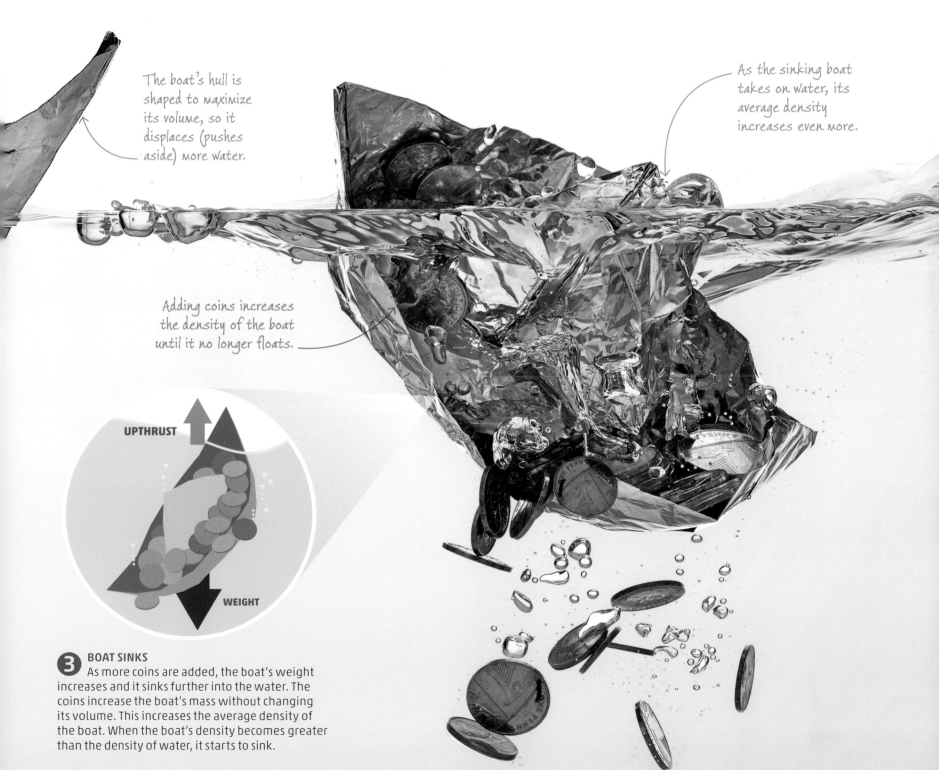

The boat's hull is shaped to maximize its volume, so it displaces (pushes aside) more water.

As the sinking boat takes on water, its average density increases even more.

Adding coins increases the density of the boat until it no longer floats.

UPTHRUST

WEIGHT

3 BOAT SINKS
As more coins are added, the boat's weight increases and it sinks further into the water. The coins increase the boat's mass without changing its volume. This increases the average density of the boat. When the boat's density becomes greater than the density of water, it starts to sink.

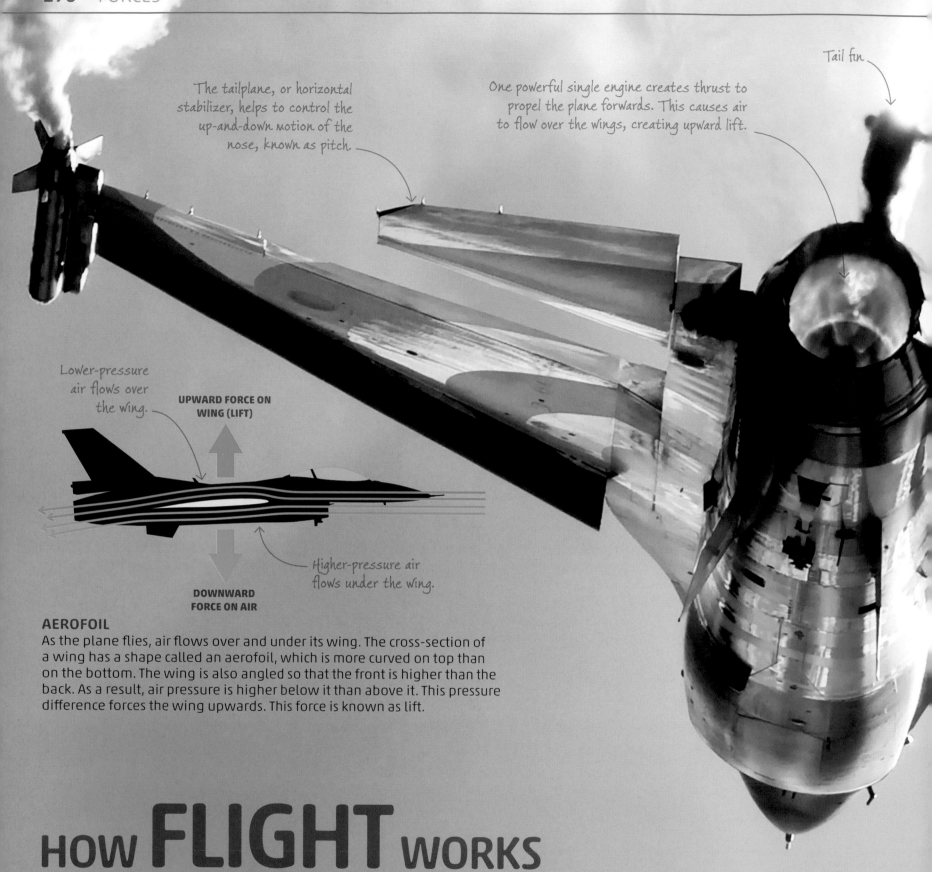

The tailplane, or horizontal stabilizer, helps to control the up-and-down motion of the nose, known as pitch.

One powerful single engine creates thrust to propel the plane forwards. This causes air to flow over the wings, creating upward lift.

Tail fin

Lower-pressure air flows over the wing.

UPWARD FORCE ON WING (LIFT)

Higher-pressure air flows under the wing.

DOWNWARD FORCE ON AIR

AEROFOIL

As the plane flies, air flows over and under its wing. The cross-section of a wing has a shape called an aerofoil, which is more curved on top than on the bottom. The wing is also angled so that the front is higher than the back. As a result, air pressure is higher below it than above it. This pressure difference forces the wing upwards. This force is known as lift.

HOW FLIGHT WORKS

Planes appear to defy gravity to take to the sky. Heavier than air, they have to overcome their weight to take off from the ground. To make this happen, powerful engines propel the plane forwards with a force called thrust. This pushes fast-flowing air over the plane's wings, generating an upward force known as lift.

▲ AERODYNAMIC DISPLAY

Specialized F-16 Falcon fighter planes are designed to be agile for military combat and are often used for airborne stunts in aerodynamic displays. Unlike most aircraft, they have engines that enable planes to fly upside down or on their side, known as flying knife-edge.

THE FORCES OF FLIGHT

Four forces act on a plane in flight. Engine thrust pushes the plane forwards, while drag slows it down. As the plane moves, the flow of air over the wings creates the upward force of lift. This is balanced by the downward pull of weight. When the forces are balanced, the plane flies horizontally at a steady speed. At take-off, thrust and lift must be greater than drag and weight.

In this display, canisters attached to the wings release smoke trails for effect. In normal flight, air flowing over the wings creates a vortex of low-pressure air at the tips. This can make water vapour condense, leaving contrails in the sky.

CONTROLLING MOVEMENT

Once a plane is in flight, its movement can be controlled by moving flaps that affect how air flows over different parts of the plane. The pilot steers by moving these horizontal and vertical flaps. Changing any one of the three types of motion affects the other two.

Tilting the elevators down creates more lift at the tail, pitching the tail up and the nose down.

Raising an aileron reduces lift, causing the wing to go down.

Lowering an aileron increases lift.

Turning the rudder to the left causes the plane's nose to turn to the left.

1 PITCH
Moving the parts on the tailplane known as elevators (the horizontal stabilizers on the plane's tail) alters the amount of lift acting on the tail. This pitches the nose and tail up or down.

2 ROLL
Moving the parts on the wings known as ailerons in opposite directions increases lift in one wing and decreases it in the other, causing the plane to roll left or right. This helps it to turn.

3 YAW
Moving the rudder on the tail fin (the vertical stabilizer) from one side to the other causes a sideways force called yaw on the plane's tail, which pushes its nose in the other direction.

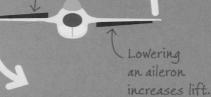

Life on Earth comes in many **different forms**, from tiny microscopic **microbes** to **complex organisms** such as humans and other large mammals. Everything living is made up of one or more tiny units called **cells** and carries out a range of processes to keep itself alive. **Plants** and **animals** have the most **specialized body systems**, which have **evolved** over millions of years.

LIFE

KINGDOMS OF LIFE

Organisms (living things) belong to one of seven main groups, called kingdoms. Some are multicellular: their bodies are made up of countless microscopic units called cells. Other creatures are single-celled: they consist of just one individual cell.

ANIMALS
This kingdom of complex, multicellular species includes all mammals, birds, reptiles, amphibians, fishes, and invertebrates.

PLANTS
Plants are multicellular. They absorb nutrients and water through their roots and receive energy from the Sun with their leaves.

FUNGI
Fungi can be single or multicelled. Many are rooted to the spot like plants. They feed by decomposing and absorbing dead material.

ALGAE
Like plants, algae make their food by using photosynthesis, but they have simpler bodies and may have just a single cell.

PROTOZOANS
These complex single-celled beings consume food, like animals – but they do so on a much smaller scale.

BACTERIA
Along with archaea, bacteria are the smallest and simplest organisms. They are single-celled and can live almost anywhere.

ARCHAEA
These tiny, single-celled organisms resemble bacteria, but many live in extreme habitats such as hot acidic pools.

WHAT IS LIFE?

Living things can be as different as pea plants and people, or bacteria and barnacles, but there are seven activities that all living things do. They consume or make food, release energy for their own use, excrete waste, sense their surroundings, move, grow, and eventually reproduce.

▶ **LIFE IN THE SLOW LANE**
In their Australian homeland, koalas eat the leaves of eucalyptus trees and little else. This food provides nutrients and the energy needed to drive life's processes – such as moving, growing, and making offspring. But eucalyptus leaves are poor-quality food, so koalas do everything slowly and spend up to 20 hours a day resting or sleeping.

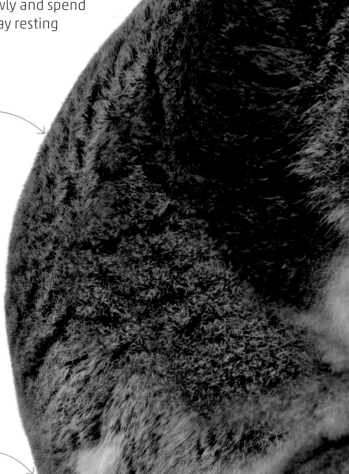

Animals must use senses such as hearing to perceive their environment.

Koalas belong to the group of animals known as marsupials.

Animals like the koala remove waste carbon dioxide through respiration and other waste products through their urine.

The koala's forward-facing eyes help it judge distances in trees.

Like all animals, koalas grow because their cells increase in size and multiply.

DEFINING LIFE
There are seven features essential to life that are shared by living things.

NUTRITION
Living things must obtain or make food to survive.

RESPIRATION
The cells in a living thing must release energy.

EXCRETION
A living thing's cells make waste that must be lost.

SENSITIVITY
Living things respond to environmental changes.

MOVEMENT
Living things must move to grow or get around.

GROWTH
Living things get bigger or change form.

REPRODUCTION
Living things produce more of their kind.

Animals can move quickly because they have contracting muscles, but koalas are slower than many other mammals.

After giving birth, a mother koala cares for her baby in her pouch for 6 months.

Koalas get almost all their food from just 20 species of eucalyptus trees.

HOW CELLS WORK

All plants and animals are made up of units that are so small they can only be seen through a microscope. These are cells – the building blocks of life. Each cell contains tiny working parts.

▼ EXAMINING ONION CELLS

Most cells are transparent, and in order to show up under a microscope must be stained with special dyes. The thin, pale layers of an onion are ideal for this process, as they do not contain much pigment. Once coloured, the multitude of cells packed into this plant can be seen much more clearly.

A single onion can contain billions of living cells.

Cells in the tough outer coat of an onion are dead.

The blue dye does not stick well to the jelly-like cytoplasm of a cell, so it stays mainly colourless.

This thin sheet of onion skin is just one-cell thick.

A dropping pipette helps to add just one drop of dye at a time.

X400 MAGNIFICATION

① SEPARATING THE CELLS
An onion is made up of lots of layers – each containing millions of cells. A very thin, transparent sheet in the inner surface of each layer is an ideal place to view these. By carefully using tweezers, this flimsy sheet can be detached and examined.

Tiny square of cells cut from the thin layer of onion

② STAINING
A small square is cut from the onion layer and placed on a glass microscope slide. The square is pulled flat to remove wrinkles, then a drop of blue dye – called methylene blue – is added on top.

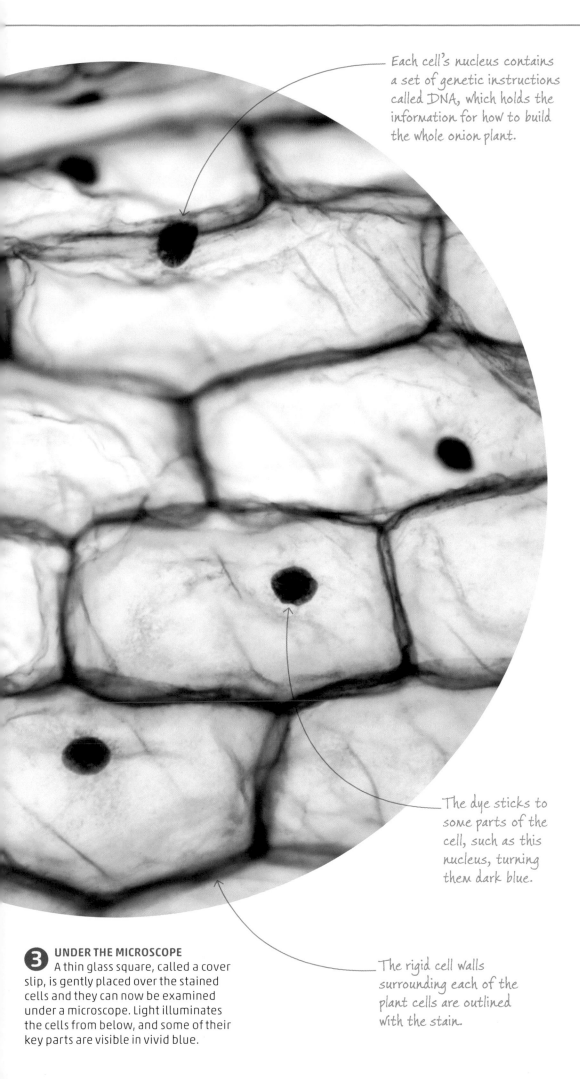

Each cell's nucleus contains a set of genetic instructions called DNA, which holds the information for how to build the whole onion plant.

The dye sticks to some parts of the cell, such as this nucleus, turning them dark blue.

3 **UNDER THE MICROSCOPE**
A thin glass square, called a cover slip, is gently placed over the stained cells and they can now be examined under a microscope. Light illuminates the cells from below, and some of their key parts are visible in vivid blue.

The rigid cell walls surrounding each of the plant cells are outlined with the stain.

ANIMAL CELLS
Both animal and plant cells contain a runny jelly called cytoplasm surrounded by an oily cell membrane that acts as a thin outer layer. Embedded in the cytoplasm is a nucleus (containing the cell's genetic information) and lots of mitochondria that power the cell.

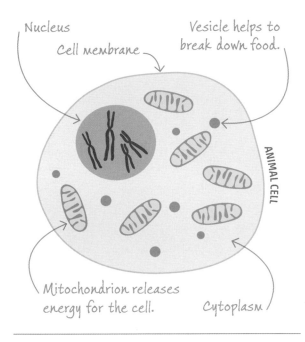

Nucleus

Cell membrane

Vesicle helps to break down food.

ANIMAL CELL

Mitochondrion releases energy for the cell.

Cytoplasm

PLANT CELLS
In addition to the parts of an animal cell, plant cells have a solid cell wall, making their edges easier to see under a microscope. They also contain a sap-filled vacuole, and many cells also have chloroplasts that make the plant's food.

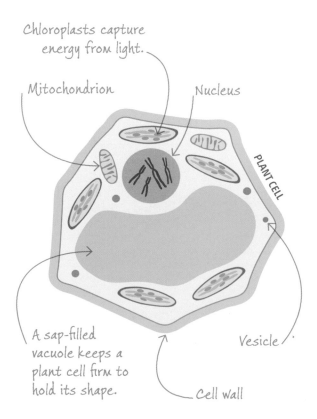

Chloroplasts capture energy from light.

Mitochondrion

Nucleus

PLANT CELL

A sap-filled vacuole keeps a plant cell firm to hold its shape.

Vesicle

Cell wall

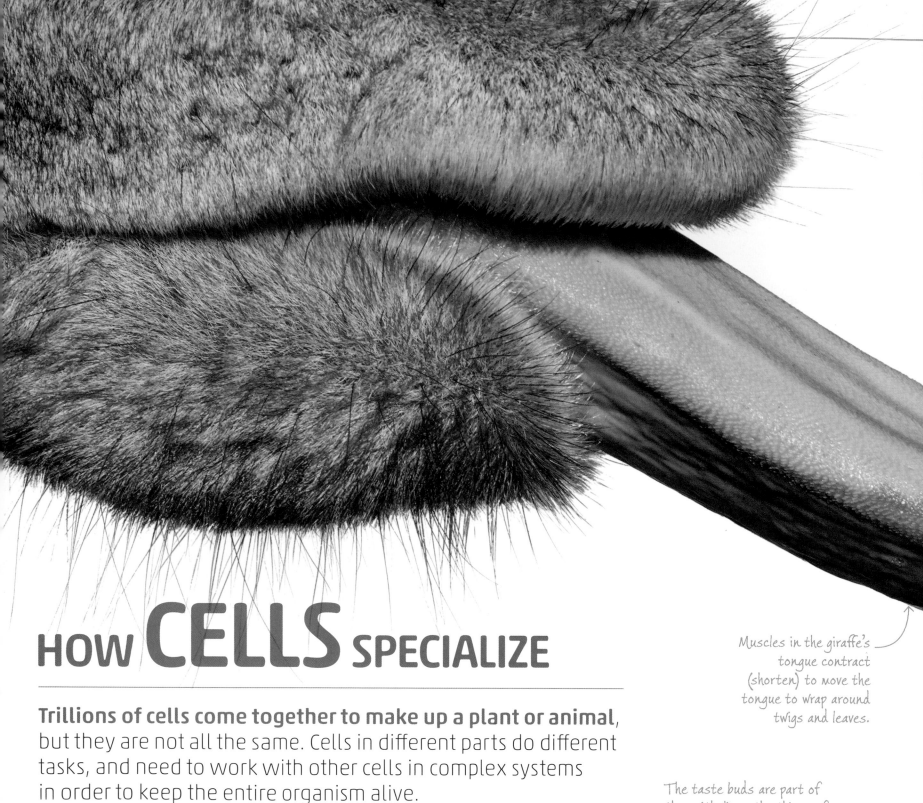

HOW **CELLS** SPECIALIZE

Trillions of cells come together to make up a plant or animal, but they are not all the same. Cells in different parts do different tasks, and need to work with other cells in complex systems in order to keep the entire organism alive.

▶ BUILDING A BODY

Each part of the body is precisely organized – all the way from microscopic cells up to large organ systems. The long tongue of a giraffe is made up of layers of tissues, which in turn are made up of many specialized cells. And the tongue itself is part of two of the giraffe's body systems – the muscle system that allows the giraffe to move its body, and the digestive system that processes its food.

Muscles in the giraffe's tongue contract (shorten) to move the tongue to wrap around twigs and leaves.

The taste buds are part of the epithelium, the thin surface layer of the tongue.

1 CELLS
Every part of the body is made of tiny cells, all adapted for different purposes. Across the surface of the tongue, some cells are specialized for tasting food, and these are grouped into bundles called taste buds.

These cells detect taste and together make up a taste bud.

Cell nucleus

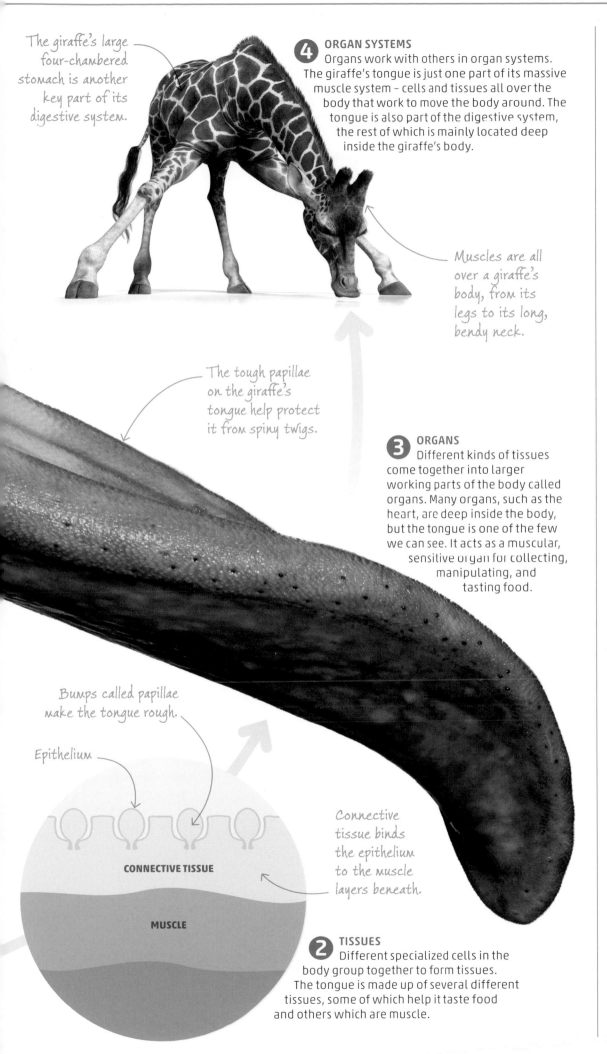

The giraffe's large four-chambered stomach is another key part of its digestive system.

4 ORGAN SYSTEMS
Organs work with others in organ systems. The giraffe's tongue is just one part of its massive muscle system – cells and tissues all over the body that work to move the body around. The tongue is also part of the digestive system, the rest of which is mainly located deep inside the giraffe's body.

Muscles are all over a giraffe's body, from its legs to its long, bendy neck.

The tough papillae on the giraffe's tongue help protect it from spiny twigs.

3 ORGANS
Different kinds of tissues come together into larger working parts of the body called organs. Many organs, such as the heart, are deep inside the body, but the tongue is one of the few we can see. It acts as a muscular, sensitive organ for collecting, manipulating, and tasting food.

Bumps called papillae make the tongue rough.

Epithelium

Connective tissue binds the epithelium to the muscle layers beneath.

CONNECTIVE TISSUE

MUSCLE

2 TISSUES
Different specialized cells in the body group together to form tissues. The tongue is made up of several different tissues, some of which help it taste food and others which are muscle.

TYPES OF CELLS
Specialized cells have different shapes and contain special features to help them perform their unique tasks. All the cells in a plant or animal contain genetic instructions in their DNA (see pages 244–245), but they use these in different ways, depending on what kind of cell they are.

RED BLOOD CELL
This oxygen-carrying animal cell is part of the blood. In mammals it is disc-shaped and has no nucleus.

FAT CELL
A large fat droplet acts as a store of food energy for the animal's body.

BONE CELL
This animal cell releases the minerals needed to make bone.

GUARD CELL
Two guard cells surround a plant's pores. These pores collect and release gases.

ROOT HAIR CELL
A long hair-like projection in plants helps gather water and minerals from the soil.

STEM CELLS
Animals and plants develop from tiny balls of cells called embryos. Before they have started to specialize – in a process known as differentiation – these cells are called embryonic stem cells (pictured below). Because these cells have the potential to turn into any kind of cell, they are often used in medical research.

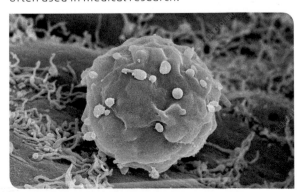

HOW **BACTERIA** WORK

Bacteria are the tiniest of single-celled living things. They live anywhere they can feed and respire, sometimes in huge numbers. There are about as many alive in your mouth as there are people living on the planet. Some can cause diseases, but bacteria are vital to life – helping to break down food and regulate the health of our bodies.

VARIETIES OF BACTERIA
There are millions of different kinds of bacteria. The vast majority help life to flourish by breaking down dead matter and helping to produce food, but some bacteria spread harmful diseases.

HELPFUL BACTERIA
Most bacteria are beneficial because they act as decomposers. They also recycle nutrients in the soil. A few live in nodules on roots and help certain kinds of plants take nitrogen from the air.

HARMFUL BACTERIA
Some bacteria cause disease by living inside our bodies as parasites. An example of these are the spherical bacteria called staphylococci. They are the kind of bacteria that can cause dangerous infections.

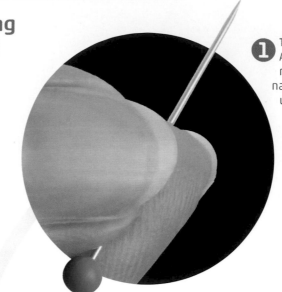

① TOO SMALL TO SEE
Although bacteria are much too tiny to see with the naked eye, they are all around us. They even live inside our bodies or on objects that look entirely lifeless. Thousands of bacteria can fit on the end of a pin.

Bacteria grow and divide faster where there is more food available.

X35 MAGNIFICATION

▶ LIFE ON A PIN
Bacteria float in the air – in tiny droplets of water or as dry spores – before setting up home, dividing, and spreading when they land somewhere suitable – even on the tip of a pin less than 1 mm across. These bacteria can survive by decomposing organic matter. By magnifying many times we can look into their world.

X175 MAGNIFICATION

② CLOSE UP
By using a very high-powered instrument called a scanning electron microscope, the bacteria become visible as tiny clusters on the tip of the pin. The pin has been coloured purple and the bacteria orange to make them stand out more clearly.

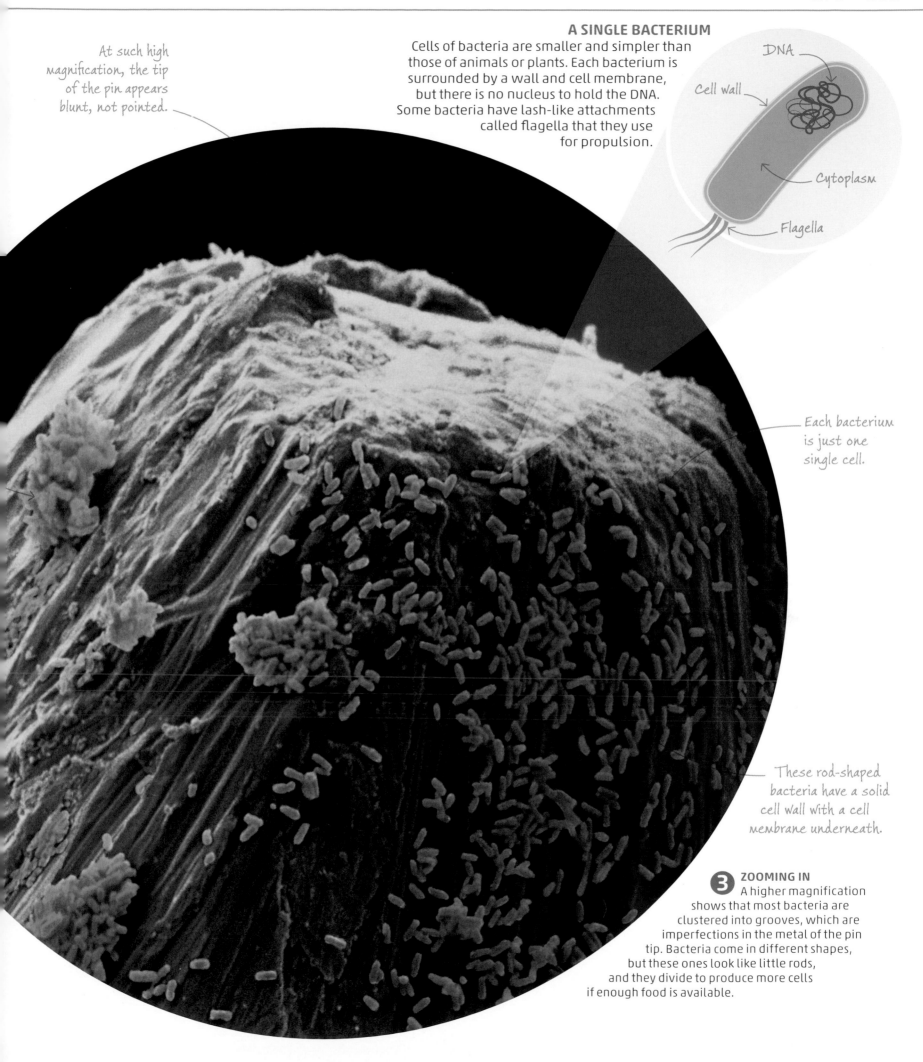

At such high magnification, the tip of the pin appears blunt, not pointed.

A SINGLE BACTERIUM
Cells of bacteria are smaller and simpler than those of animals or plants. Each bacterium is surrounded by a wall and cell membrane, but there is no nucleus to hold the DNA. Some bacteria have lash-like attachments called flagella that they use for propulsion.

DNA

Cell wall

Cytoplasm

Flagella

Each bacterium is just one single cell.

These rod-shaped bacteria have a solid cell wall with a cell membrane underneath.

3 ZOOMING IN
A higher magnification shows that most bacteria are clustered into grooves, which are imperfections in the metal of the pin tip. Bacteria come in different shapes, but these ones look like little rods, and they divide to produce more cells if enough food is available.

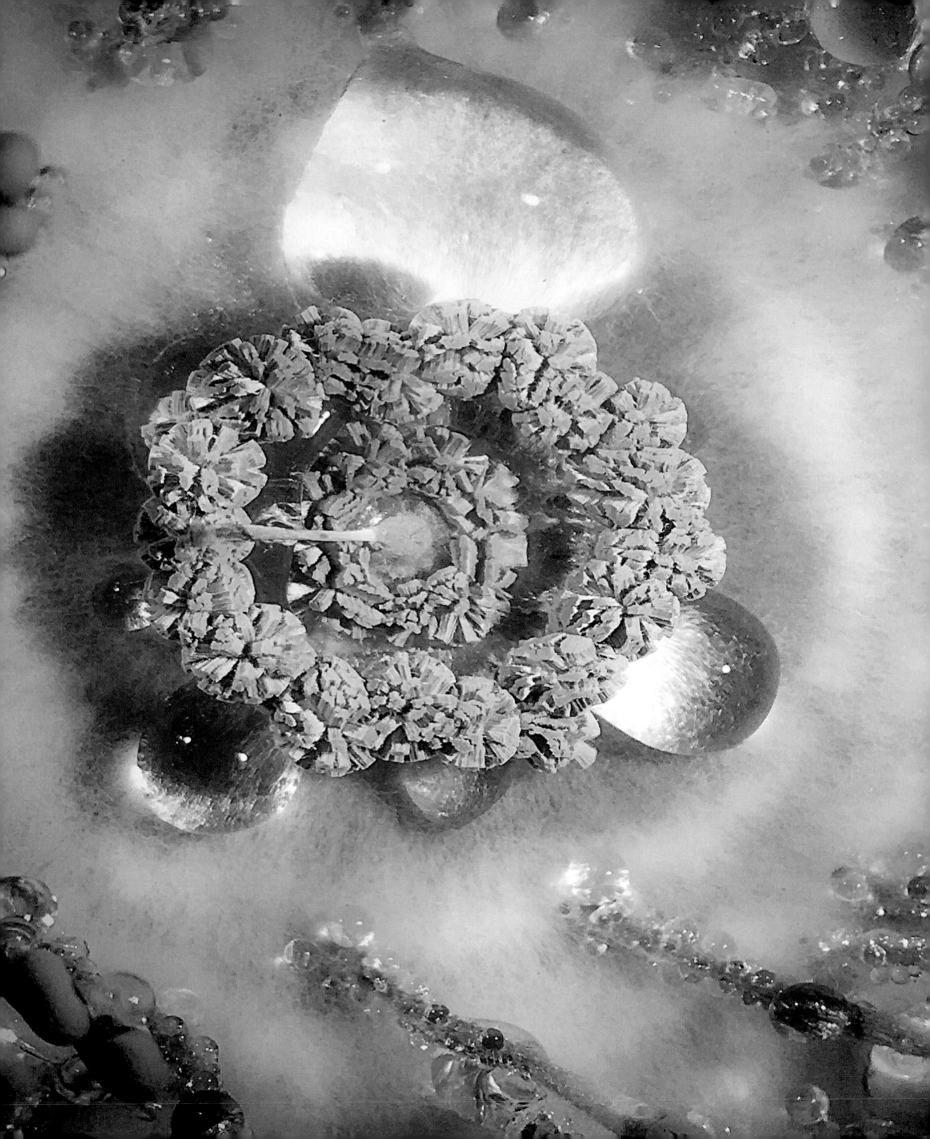

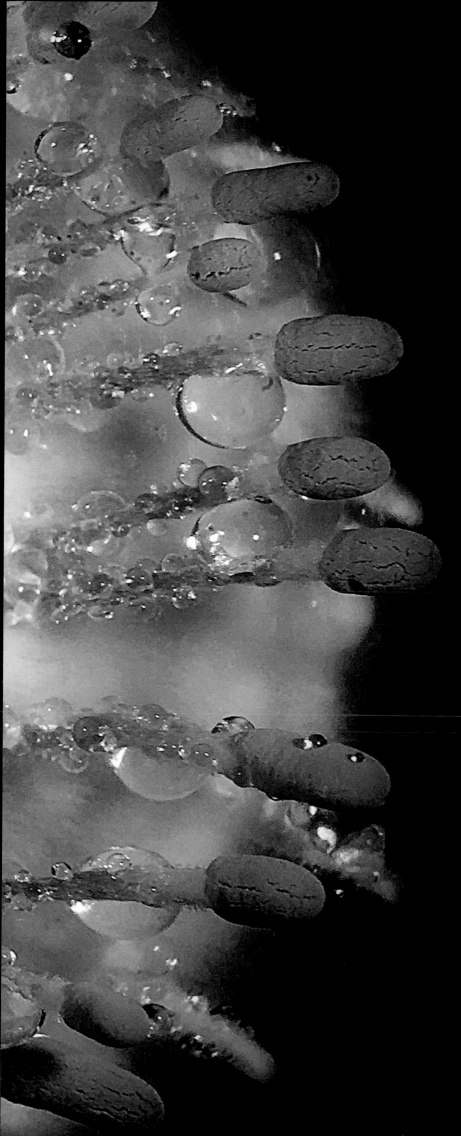

PENICILLIUM VULPINUM

Many life forms, such as bacteria and protozoans, are very small – sometimes only visible under a microscope. This tiny mould is part of the fungi kingdom, belonging to a large group of moulds called *Penicillium*. Its striking matchstick-like spore capsules (which contain green spores that new moulds develop from) grow on rabbit droppings. Other moulds in the *Penicillium* group can be used to produce life-saving medicines.

1 **REMOVING THE SHELL**
When eggs are soaked in vinegar for a few days, the acid in the vinegar reacts with the egg shell and dissolves it. This leaves the naked egg protected by only a thin membrane.

The eggs are in the vinegar for 48 hours.

2 **SOAKING THE EGGS**
The shell-less eggs are carefully placed into glass beakers. One egg is placed in a beaker of pure water, while the other is put in corn syrup – a highly concentrated liquid.

NAKED EGG IN WATER

NAKED EGG IN CORN SYRUP

HOW OSMOSIS WORKS

Plant and animal cells can absorb water like a bath sponge, as the water particles can pass through their thin protective membranes. But if the cells' surroundings are very salty or sugary, they lose water instead. This effect is due to osmosis – the way water moves around within organisms.

▲ TESTING NAKED EGGS
A raw egg that is carefully stripped of its shell still hangs together because its liquid insides are surrounded by a delicate membrane. This "naked" egg acts like a giant cell and can be used to demonstrate osmosis when placed in solutions of different concentrations.

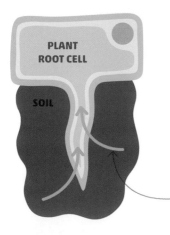

OSMOSIS IN PLANTS
Land-based plants take in water from the soil by osmosis. A steady intake of water pushes against their cell walls and keeps the plant firm. However, if the cells do not get enough water, they shrivel and the plant wilts.

PLANT ROOT CELL

SOIL

Water is absorbed by spindly root hair cells.

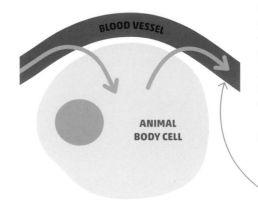

OSMOSIS IN ANIMALS
In humans and other animals, water is carried around the body by the blood. The insides of the body cells and the blood need to have the same concentration of water, so water constantly moves in and out of cells by osmosis to maintain this balance.

BLOOD VESSEL

ANIMAL BODY CELL

Water moves both in and out of animal cells by osmosis.

The water is a dilute solution – not many other particles are dissolved in it.

3 OSMOSIS TAKES PLACE
After 24 hours, the egg in pure water has swelled, whereas the egg in corn syrup has shrivelled. Both of these effects are due to osmosis – when water passes from a dilute solution to a more concentrated one. At the start of the experiment, the liquid inside the egg is more concentrated than the water, but less concentrated than the corn syrup. At the end, the eggs and the liquid they are sitting in are more equally concentrated.

Water flows from the more dilute solution in the beaker to the more concentrated liquid inside the egg.

NAKED EGG IN WATER

The corn syrup is a concentrated solution – it has lots of sugars dissolved in it.

Water flows out of the egg to even out the molecules of water and sugars in the syrup.

NAKED EGG IN CORN SYRUP

THE EGG SWELLS
The solution inside the naked egg contains some water, but also a high concentration of natural sugars and salts, so some of the water in the beaker moves into the egg to dilute it. The egg's membrane is semi-permeable, so only lets the water through and not the salts and sugars.

Water particle

Sugar particle

The semi-permeable membrane only lets water molecules across.

THE EGG SHRINKS
In this beaker, the corn syrup is more concentrated than the liquid inside the egg. Water moves by osmosis from the egg's more dilute solution to the more concentrated solution in the syrup. This makes the concentrations more equal – inside the egg becomes more concentrated, while the corn syrup becomes less concentrated.

HOW
PHOTOSYNTHESIS
WORKS

Plants make their own food, in a process called photosynthesis. Their cells contain a green pigment called chlorophyll that absorbs the energy in sunlight and uses it to make the sugars they need to stay alive. The two main ingredients that plants take from their surroundings to do this are water and carbon dioxide.

The experiment can be varied by placing the light source at different distances from the plant and comparing how fast oxygen is released.

As more gas collects in the tube, more water is displaced, and the water level in the tube drops.

2 RELEASING OXYGEN
As photosynthesis occurs, the oxygen produced emerges from the pondweed as tiny bubbles. These float up and gather at the top of the test tube.

After about five minutes, bubbles of oxygen from photosynthesis will start to rise up the tube.

The experiment starts with the test tube completely filled with water.

1 TAKING IN LIGHT
The pondweed is placed in a beaker of water, with an upturned glass funnel on top. A test tube full of water is positioned on top of the funnel's neck, and a strong light source is directed towards the plant. After a few minutes, photosynthesis will start to take place.

▶ PHOTOSYNTHESIS IN ACTION
When plants photosynthesize, they convert water and carbon dioxide into sugar, and release oxygen as a waste product. This demonstration shows photosynthesis in *Elodea*, a type of pondweed. Aquatic plants such as this use carbon dioxide that is dissolved in water, and when they release waste oxygen it is clearly visible as tiny bubbles in the water.

FACTORS AFFECTING PHOTOSYNTHESIS

A plant with bigger leaves and more chlorophyll can trap more energy, but the surroundings of a plant can speed up photosynthesis as well.

LIGHT
Brighter light means more energy can be absorbed by the plant.

TEMPERATURE
Warm conditions make the reactions involved in photosynthesis happen faster.

CO₂
More carbon dioxide in the air or water speeds up photosynthesis.

THE PHOTOSYNTHESIS REACTION

Photosynthesis takes place inside a chloroplast. The light energy from sunlight is trapped by the chlorophyll and used to power the chemical reactions in this process. These change water and carbon dioxide into oxygen and a vital sugar called glucose, which powers the plant.

The pigment chlorophyll forms an oily membrane around each disc.

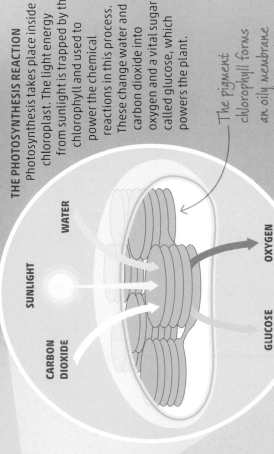

SUNLIGHT

WATER

CARBON DIOXIDE

OXYGEN

GLUCOSE

LEAF TIP

At magnification x40, the thin layer of cells that make up the leaves of pondweed are visible. Inside each cell photosynthesis takes place inside rounder green structures called chloroplasts. Chloroplasts are what give most plant leaves a green colour.

The rectangular cells of the plant's leaves are filled with green chloroplasts.

The pondweed releases oxygen from small holes in its leaves and stems.

The pondweed has lots of small oval leaves attached to soft, bendy stems.

PLANT CELL

Chloroplast

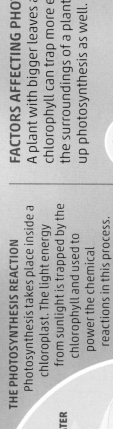

LEAF CELLS

Most plant cells are packed with chloroplasts – especially those in the upper section of a leaf. Chloroplasts are bean-shaped granules, each filled with tiny discs covered in a green pigment called chlorophyll.

HOW DIGESTION WORKS

All animals consume food to supply them with the nutrients they need to grow and the energy their body needs to perform vital functions. Solid food is broken down in a process called digestion to release these nutrients, so they can be transported to cells around the body.

▶ **GIANT HERBIVORE**
A hippopotamus gets all the nourishment it needs from eating vegetation – consuming around 40 kg (88 lb) of grass every day. Its digestive system must work hard to release the nutrients found in these tough leaves. The process begins by chewing using jaws bigger than any other land animal, before the meal is swallowed ready for the stomach juices to play their part.

Unlike most herbivores, hippopotamuses have long canine teeth, which are used for attacking competing males.

HUMAN DIGESTIVE SYSTEM
Humans are omnivores, which means they eat both plant matter and meat. Their digestive system has a one-chambered stomach. Like in the hippopotamus, food begins to be digested in the mouth and then passes through several other organs before it is fully broken down and its nutrients absorbed into the bloodstream.

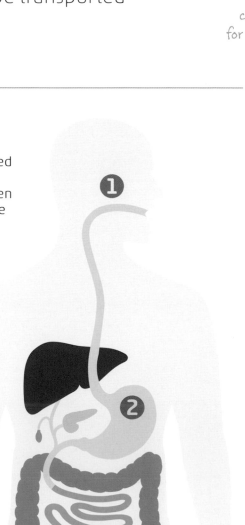

1 MOUTH
Grinding teeth mash up the food, and enzymes within saliva begin digesting it. Muscles push the mixture of food and saliva down the oesophagus and into the stomach.

2 STOMACH
Digestive juices from the stomach wall contain acid, which provides the right conditions for stomach enzymes to continue breaking down food.

3 INTESTINES
After being digested a bit more, most of the food's nutrients are absorbed into the blood from the small intestine. In the large intestine any indigestible food is prepared to be removed from the body.

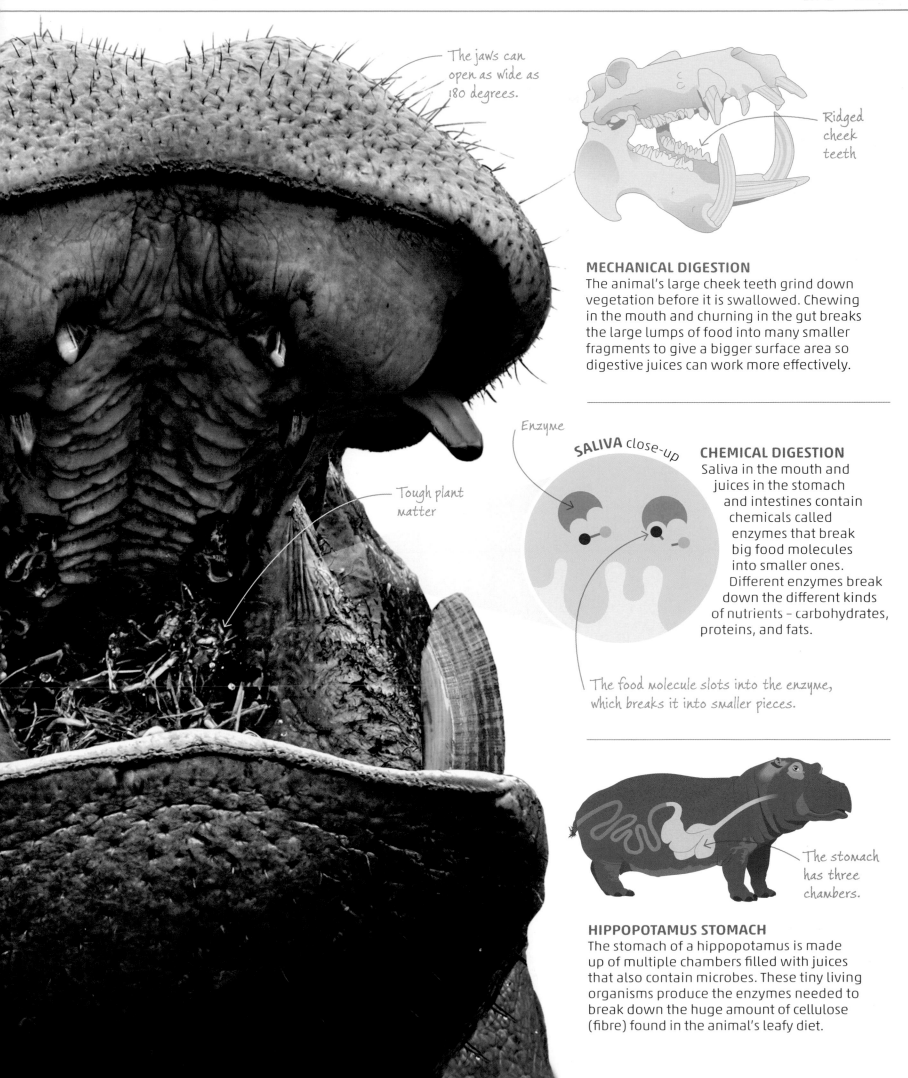

The jaws can open as wide as 180 degrees.

Ridged cheek teeth

MECHANICAL DIGESTION
The animal's large cheek teeth grind down vegetation before it is swallowed. Chewing in the mouth and churning in the gut breaks the large lumps of food into many smaller fragments to give a bigger surface area so digestive juices can work more effectively.

Enzyme

Tough plant matter

SALIVA close-up

CHEMICAL DIGESTION
Saliva in the mouth and juices in the stomach and intestines contain chemicals called enzymes that break big food molecules into smaller ones. Different enzymes break down the different kinds of nutrients – carbohydrates, proteins, and fats.

The food molecule slots into the enzyme, which breaks it into smaller pieces.

The stomach has three chambers.

HIPPOPOTAMUS STOMACH
The stomach of a hippopotamus is made up of multiple chambers filled with juices that also contain microbes. These tiny living organisms produce the enzymes needed to break down the huge amount of cellulose (fibre) found in the animal's leafy diet.

HOW BREATHING WORKS

Animals need to breathe to bring oxygen into their bodies. This is needed in cells to release energy to power the body. Many animals, such as humans, breathe by using muscles to pull air into their lungs.

▶ **MODELLING THE HUMAN LUNGS**
The human lungs are inflatable – just like balloons. In this demonstration, the rubber at the bottom of the bell jar simulates the action of a muscle called the diaphragm. As it is pulled downwards, the balloons, representing the lungs, inflate as they are filled with air. When it is released, they deflate.

The balloons draw in air from outside and inflate.

Air passes into the lungs through the windpipe.

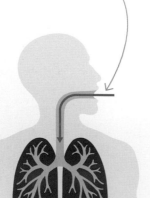

The bell jar represents the chest cavity.

When breathing in, the diaphragm contracts into a flat shape.

1 INHALING
The diaphragm is a sheet of muscle that sits below the lungs. When a person breathes in, it flattens, expanding the chest cavity and causing the pressure inside the lungs to decrease. Air flows from areas of high pressure to areas of low pressure, so air is then sucked into the lungs from outside the body.

Pulling down increases the space inside the jar.

Air enters and leaves through a hole in the top of the jar.

This plastic tubing represents the stiff-walled windpipe that carries air to the lungs.

The balloons completely deflate, but real lungs always contain some air to keep them open.

When the rubber sheet is released, the balloons deflate.

Stale air, containing carbon dioxide, is pushed back out of the body.

The diaphragm springs up to form a dome shape when it relaxes.

② EXHALING
To breathe out, the muscles relax and the diaphragm becomes dome-shaped. This decreases the space inside the chest cavity, pushing air from the lungs out of the body.

INSIDE THE LUNGS
The lungs are filled with microscopic sacs called alveoli, which are covered with blood vessels. In these, oxygen from the air passes from the lungs into the blood (shown here in red) and carbon dioxide from the blood (shown in blue) passes back into the lungs.

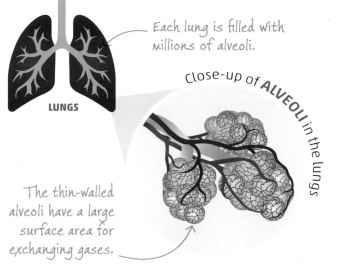

Each lung is filled with millions of alveoli.

LUNGS

Close-up of **ALVEOLI** in the lungs

The thin-walled alveoli have a large surface area for exchanging gases.

OTHER WAYS OF BREATHING
Not all animals have lungs, but they still need a way to take in oxygen and pass out carbon dioxide. Across the animal kingdom there are a diverse range of respiratory systems to carry out this gas exchange.

FISH
Fish gulp water into their mouth and pass it through feathery structures called gills. The gills contain lots of tiny blood vessels that absorb oxygen from the water.

Gills

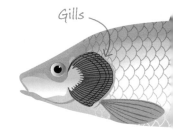

AMPHIBIANS
Frogs have small lungs, but absorb extra oxygen through their thin skin. This passes straight into the blood. Their aquatic tadpoles breathe with gills, like fish.

Oxygen also enters through the skin.

INSECTS
The bodies of insects are punctured by small holes called spiracles. These draw air through tiny tubes straight to cells, so oxygen reaches them directly without having to travel by blood.

Spiracles connect to tiny air-carrying tubes called tracheae.

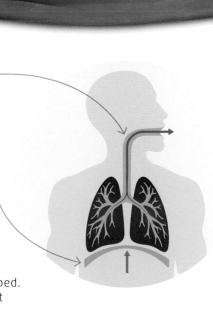

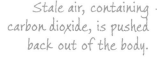

HOW RESPIRATION WORKS

Everything alive needs energy to keep itself functioning effectively.
Organisms obtain this energy through a chemical reaction called
respiration. This releases energy by breaking down a specific
kind of sugar called glucose, and is most efficient when the
sugar reacts with oxygen – called aerobic respiration.
Living things therefore need both food and
oxygen: food supplies the sugar, and
oxygen helps to unlock its energy.

BURNING SUGAR
When sugar in a bowl
is burned it produces
brown caramel, but
does not ignite
completely. Only
when surrounded
with plenty of
oxygen will the sugar
react explosively and
release all its energy.

A pipe directs the
powdered sugar and
oxygen into the flame.

When it flows out
of the tube, the sugar
disperses in a big cloud.

The flame ignites
the puff of sugar
and oxygen.

▶ ENERGY FROM SUGAR
This brilliant orange explosion shows the power of food. A cloud of
powdered sugar is blown into a flame. Because of the large surface
area as it disperses, the sugar is surrounded by lots of oxygen in the
air, and the flame causes the sugar and oxygen to react. The result
is an explosive release of the sugar's energy – representative of
the energy present in lots of the food the body takes in.

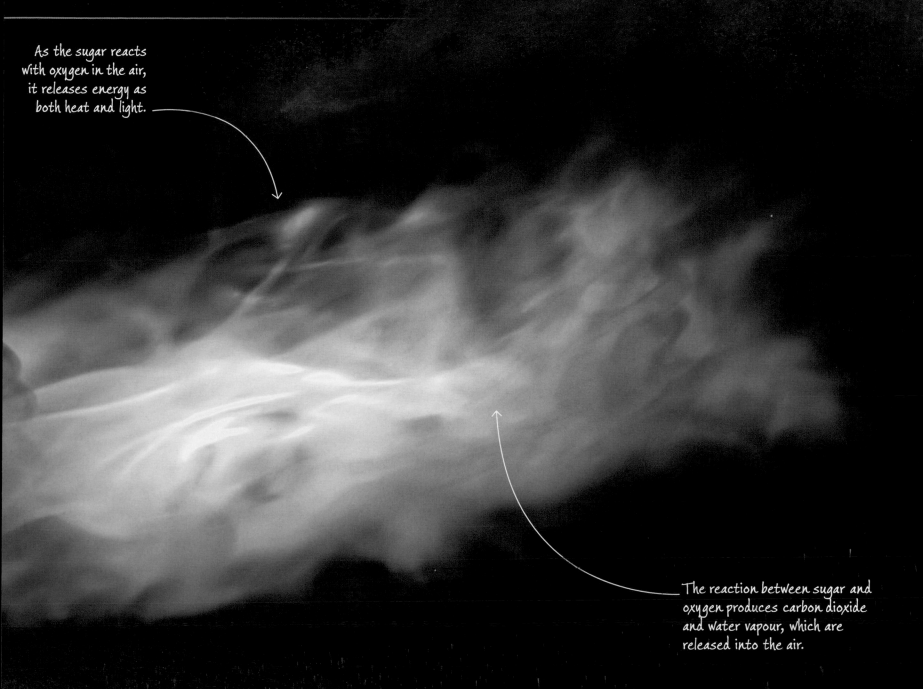

As the sugar reacts with oxygen in the air, it releases energy as both heat and light.

The reaction between sugar and oxygen produces carbon dioxide and water vapour, which are released into the air.

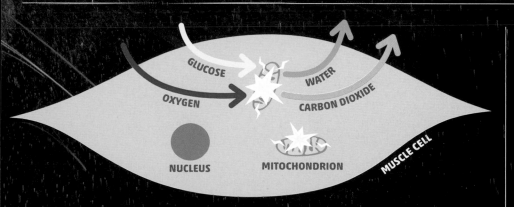

GLUCOSE

WATER

OXYGEN

CARBON DIOXIDE

NUCLEUS

MITOCHONDRION

MUSCLE CELL

RESPIRATION IN A CELL
Glucose is released from food when it is digested, and much of it is used in respiration. This reaction takes place inside every cell of the body, mostly within small oval structures called mitochondria. Here, glucose reacts with oxygen to release energy, as well as carbon dioxide and water. However, the process is carefully controlled, so that energy is released in small, useable amounts, and not in one huge burst like in the experiment above.

GETTING EXTRA ENERGY
When an animal runs, its muscles demand more energy, but the body can only work so fast to bring in oxygen. To get some extra energy, extra glucose is broken down without oxygen – a process called anaerobic respiration. This makes the waste product lactic acid, which causes muscle cramp.

HOW THE HEART WORKS

The heart is an organ that is practically all muscle, and in humans it beats about 70 times each minute. Unlike other muscles it works tirelessly, beating nonstop for our whole lives. At the centre of the circulatory system, it needs to be strong in order to pump blood all around the body.

BLOOD VESSELS

Blood must circulate around the body so that it can deliver food and oxygen to cells and carry away their waste carbon dioxide. Two main types of blood vessel – arteries and veins – carry out this job. Where they meet, they branch into fine, microscopic vessels called capillaries that run directly to the cells.

ARTERIES
Arteries carry the blood travelling away from the heart, and need thick walls to cope with the high pressure. They pass blood into capillaries.

VEINS
Blood returns from capillaries and back to the heart through veins. These are thin-walled and have valves to stop blood flowing back the wrong way.

► HARD-WORKING ORGAN
This scan shows the human heart. About the size of a clenched fist, it is made up of four chambers with muscular walls for pumping blood. The upper chambers, called atria, move blood into the ventricles below. Ventricles have thicker muscle to pump blood the much greater distance around the body.

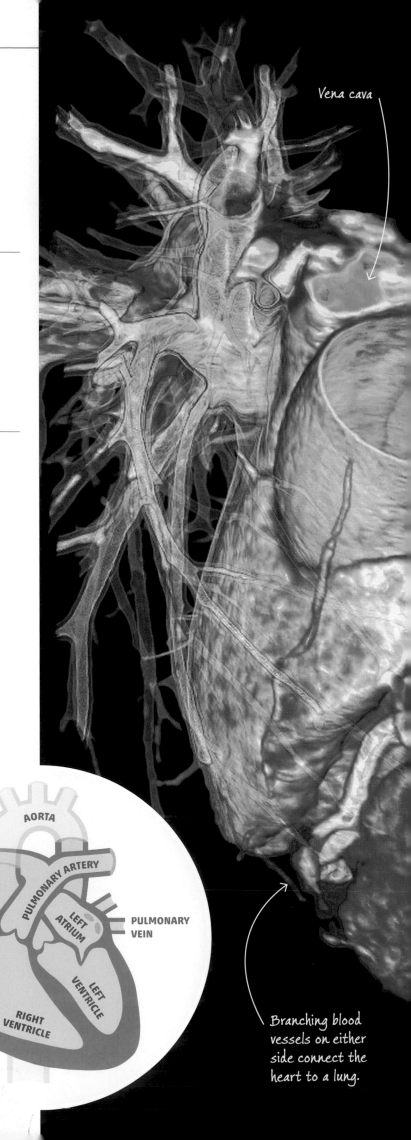

Vena cava

VENA CAVA

AORTA

PULMONARY ARTERY

LEFT ATRIUM

PULMONARY VEIN

RIGHT ATRIUM

LEFT VENTRICLE

RIGHT VENTRICLE

Branching blood vessels on either side connect the heart to a lung.

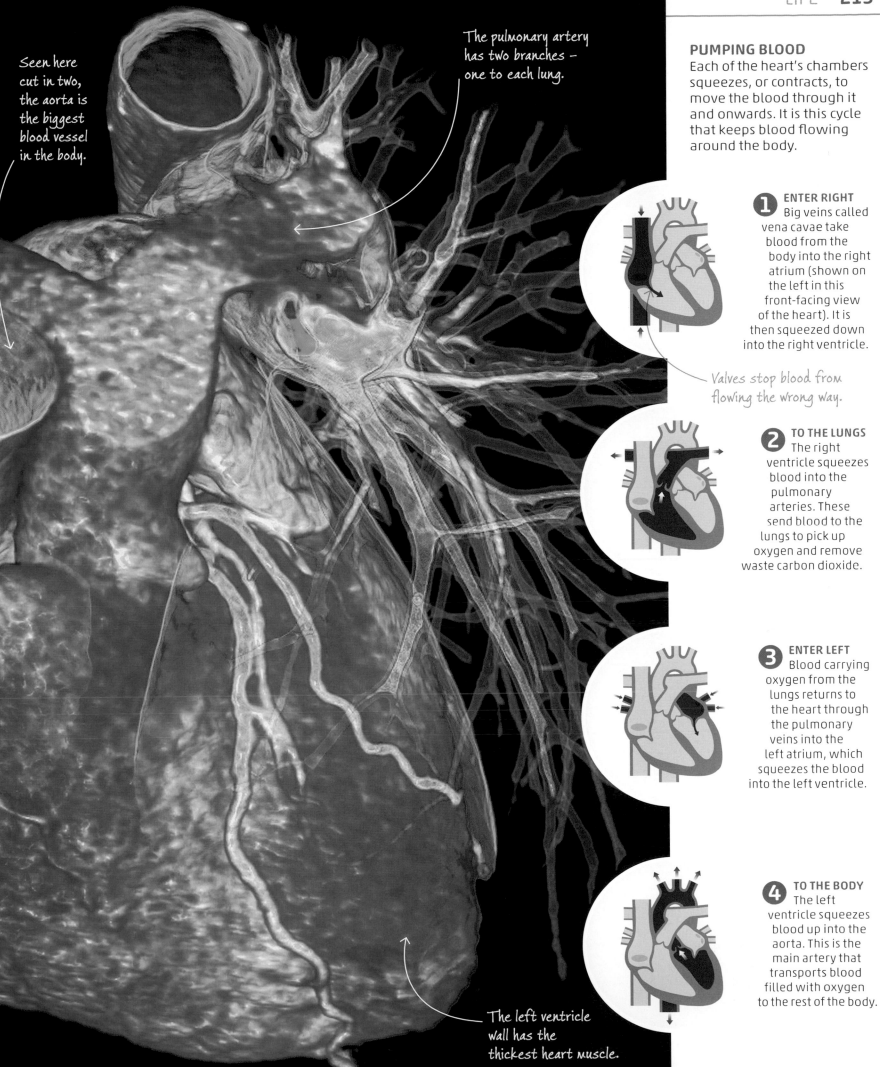

Seen here cut in two, the aorta is the biggest blood vessel in the body.

The pulmonary artery has two branches – one to each lung.

The left ventricle wall has the thickest heart muscle.

PUMPING BLOOD

Each of the heart's chambers squeezes, or contracts, to move the blood through it and onwards. It is this cycle that keeps blood flowing around the body.

1 ENTER RIGHT
Big veins called vena cavae take blood from the body into the right atrium (shown on the left in this front-facing view of the heart). It is then squeezed down into the right ventricle.

Valves stop blood from flowing the wrong way.

2 TO THE LUNGS
The right ventricle squeezes blood into the pulmonary arteries. These send blood to the lungs to pick up oxygen and remove waste carbon dioxide.

3 ENTER LEFT
Blood carrying oxygen from the lungs returns to the heart through the pulmonary veins into the left atrium, which squeezes the blood into the left ventricle.

4 TO THE BODY
The left ventricle squeezes blood up into the aorta. This is the main artery that transports blood filled with oxygen to the rest of the body.

HOW PLANTS
TRANSPORT
WATER

Plants need a steady flow of water to ensure their leaves stay firm and do not wilt. Those that grow in the ground pull both water and minerals from the soil with their roots and transport these up through the plant. When the water reaches the top, it evaporates from leaves and petals, pulling more water upwards. This process is called transpiration.

▶ COLOURING A ROSE
This experiment uses a food-colouring dye to show how water rises through a plant. The stem of a single flower is cut down the middle so that one half carries dyed water to turn half the flower blue, while the other side carries colourless water, which does not affect the flower's colour.

When water evaporates from the petals, the blue dye remains inside the flower, staining this side of the petals blue.

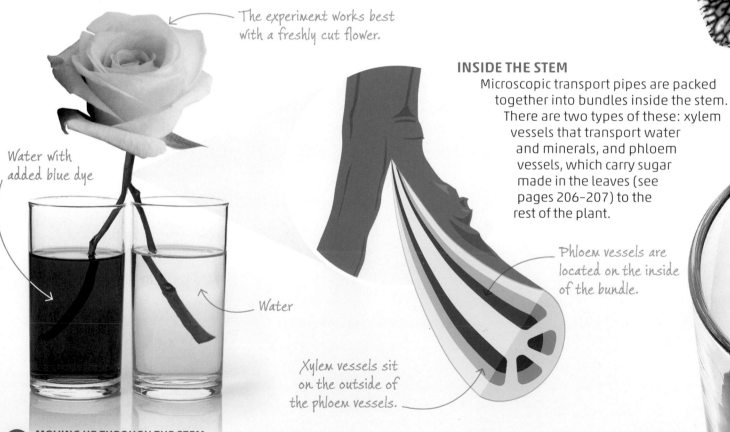

The experiment works best with a freshly cut flower.

Water with added blue dye

Water

INSIDE THE STEM
Microscopic transport pipes are packed together into bundles inside the stem. There are two types of these: xylem vessels that transport water and minerals, and phloem vessels, which carry sugar made in the leaves (see pages 206–207) to the rest of the plant.

Phloem vessels are located on the inside of the bundle.

Xylem vessels sit on the outside of the phloem vessels.

❶ MOVING UP THROUGH THE STEM
The rose's stem is divided in two and each half placed in a different glass of water - one with added dye and the other with clear water. Both liquids then travel up though one half of the stem in xylem vessels - microscopic pipes that stretch right up into the petals.

The blue-dyed water is carried up xylem vessels in one side of the split stem.

Traces of dye begin to reach the petals after just a few hours.

2 ENTERING THE PETALS
On one side of the plant, the mixture of water and dye travels up the xylem vessels as one. As it moves up into half the petals, the dye turns these a brilliant blue. The other side of the plant receives normal water and so its petals do not change colour.

The rose's petals provide a large surface area for water to evaporate from.

Each stoma in the surface layer of the petal is kept open by two supporting guard cells.

Water inside xylem vessels enters the petal.

ROSE PETAL cross-section in close-up

STOMATA
Water evaporates from the petal through holes called stomata. As more water from the xylem replaces this lost moisture, this pulls on the columns of water further down in the xylem vessels, helping this water stream rise through the stem.

HOW ANIMALS
REGULATE
TEMPERATURE

Humans and other animals need conditions just right for their bodies to work as well as they can. They must regulate the body in a balancing act called homeostasis. Temperature is one of the conditions that must be controlled. Some animals can keep their body temperature constantly warm, but for others it depends on their surroundings.

BALANCING THE BODY

Homeostasis involves the body sensing when a factor gets too high or too low, then triggering a response to bring it back to the right level. The amount of water in the body, temperature, and sugar levels are all controlled this way.

WATER
The body gains water when drinking and loses it through sweating and urination. The kidneys help to regulate water levels (see pages 220–221).

TEMPERATURE
Heat can be absorbed from or lost to the surroundings, and is generated during exercise. Warm-blooded animals generate heat inside their bodies.

SUGAR
Sugar levels in the blood rise after eating sugar-rich food and drop when sugar is burned in exercise. Hormones help to control sugar levels.

The leopard gecko is a small lizard with distinctive black and yellow markings.

The fingertips are darker, showing that they are cooler than the rest of the hand.

▶ REGULATING TEMPERATURE

Reptiles, such as this leopard gecko, are cold-blooded, meaning their temperature varies with their surroundings. Mammals, such as humans, are warm-blooded – they can generate heat internally to keep them warm. This thermal image, taken with a camera that detects infrared, was captured on a cold morning. The cold gecko appears purple and the warmer human hand is orange.

STAYING WARM
Animals need to keep their internal temperature constant so that their cells work properly. A gecko relies on its environment to either warm up or cool down, but humans have mechanisms in their bodies that help keep their temperature steady.

BASKING
A gecko must sit in the sun to absorb heat and warm up. It will then move to the shade if it feels itself getting too hot.

The reptile's feet are beginning to absorb some warmth from the hot hand.

The reptile's body absorbs the heat from the Sun.

Surface of the skin

HAIRS AND SWEAT
When cold, humans raise hairs on the skin to trap warm air close to the body. If they get too hot, they release sweat, which cools the body as it evaporates.

A tiny muscle contracts to pull each hair upright.

A sweat gland releases sweat.

The cold-blooded gecko is closer to the background temperature than the warm-blooded human.

BLOOD
Blood vessels in the skin give off heat. These constrict when the human body gets cold, allowing less blood near the surface of the skin. They open wider when it gets too warm.

This blood vessel can open wider to cool the body down.

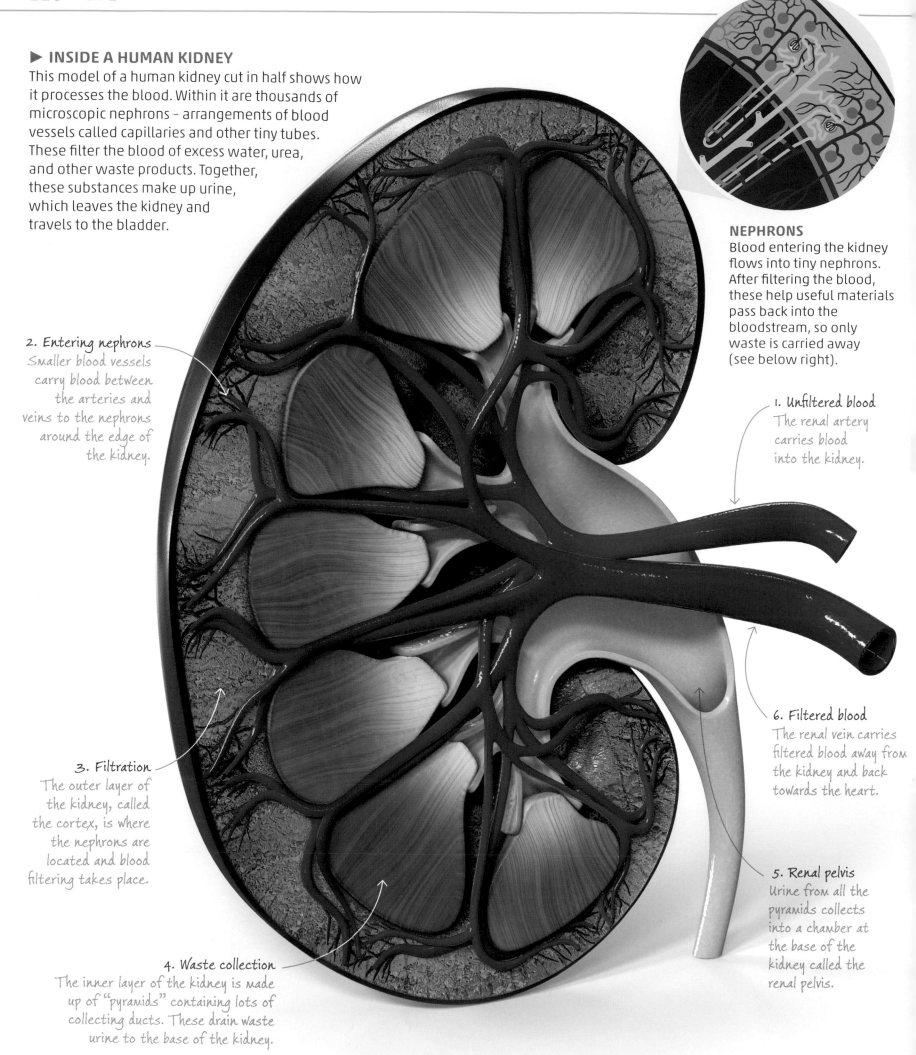

▶ INSIDE A HUMAN KIDNEY
This model of a human kidney cut in half shows how it processes the blood. Within it are thousands of microscopic nephrons – arrangements of blood vessels called capillaries and other tiny tubes. These filter the blood of excess water, urea, and other waste products. Together, these substances make up urine, which leaves the kidney and travels to the bladder.

NEPHRONS
Blood entering the kidney flows into tiny nephrons. After filtering the blood, these help useful materials pass back into the bloodstream, so only waste is carried away (see below right).

2. Entering nephrons
Smaller blood vessels carry blood between the arteries and veins to the nephrons around the edge of the kidney.

1. Unfiltered blood
The renal artery carries blood into the kidney.

3. Filtration
The outer layer of the kidney, called the cortex, is where the nephrons are located and blood filtering takes place.

6. Filtered blood
The renal vein carries filtered blood away from the kidney and back towards the heart.

5. Renal pelvis
Urine from all the pyramids collects into a chamber at the base of the kidney called the renal pelvis.

4. Waste collection
The inner layer of the kidney is made up of "pyramids" containing lots of collecting ducts. These drain waste urine to the base of the kidney.

HOW KIDNEYS WORK

Excretion is the way the body removes waste produced by chemical reactions inside cells. The kidneys are one of the body's key excretory organs, getting rid of a waste product called urea by filtering it from the blood and expelling it from the body in urine. They can produce up to 1.5 litres (3 pints) of urine every day.

A tough protective layer called the capsule surrounds the kidney.

The ureter drains urine formed inside the kidney down to the bladder.

INSIDE THE NEPHRON
When blood enters each nephron, it passes into the glomerulus – a knot of blood vessels inside a sac. Here, the blood is filtered of its dissolved substances and any excess water. These pass into a long, winding tube called a tubule. Useful substances, such as glucose, are then reabsorbed back into the blood vessels from this tube. The remaining waste products (making up urine) are carried away to the renal pelvis.

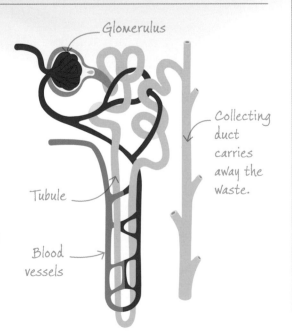

Glomerulus

Collecting duct carries away the waste.

Tubule

Blood vessels

FEMALE URINARY SYSTEM

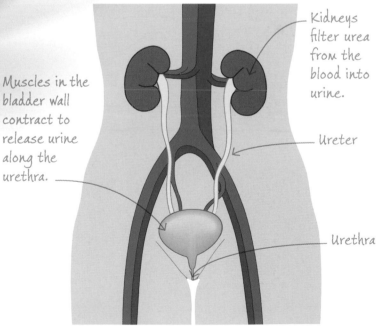

Muscles in the bladder wall contract to release urine along the urethra.

Kidneys filter urea from the blood into urine.

Ureter

Urethra

THE URINARY SYSTEM
The kidneys make up part of the human body's urinary system. The urine they produce is sent down to the bladder through tubes called ureters. It is then stored there until the bladder is full, at which point muscles squeeze to remove it by urination.

WHY PLANTS GROW TOWARDS LIGHT

Like animals, plants sense and respond to their surroundings. Since they can't move quickly like animals can, plants usually rely on their parts moving slowly as they grow. Leafy shoots must grow upwards to catch light energy to make a plant's food, while roots grow downwards to absorb water and minerals from the soil.

▶ **GROWING THE RIGHT WAY**
If a plant is toppled to one side, its roots and shoots bend to continue growing up and down. This movement towards or away from a stimulus is called tropism. Geotropism is movement in response to gravity. Phototropism is movement in response to light coming from one direction.

ROOT GROWING DOWN
Tropism can be positive or negative, depending on whether there is movement towards or away from a stimulus. Roots show positive geotropism by moving down with the pull of gravity and negative phototropism by moving away from light. Both happen because of a growth-regulating chemical called auxin found in the roots and shoots.

The plant grew from a seed planted in an upright pot, before being knocked over onto its side.

1 LEVEL ROOT
When the root is laid on its side, auxin moves away from the light and settles downwards under the pull of gravity, so levels are higher in cells along its lower surface.

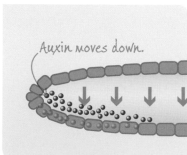

Auxin moves down.

2 BENDING ROOT
Cells in the root respond to auxin by growing more slowly. This means that cells on the upper surface are growing bigger, curving the root tip downwards.

Cells on upper side grow bigger.

When knocked onto its side, the shoot corrects itself and bends to grow upright towards the light.

Leaves spread to face the source of light, helping them to absorb its energy for use in photosynthesis.

CLIMBING PLANTS

When vines and other climbing plants coil upwards and around an upright stick, they are responding to touch – a tropism called thigmotropism.

Some climbing plants send out long coiling tendrils to grip an upright support.

SHOOT GROWING UP

Shoots usually respond to gravity and light in the opposite way to roots. Shoots show negative geotropism by moving up against the pull of gravity and positive phototropism by moving towards light. This is because the cells of shoots and roots respond differently to the chemical auxin that affects their growth.

FAST-MOVING PLANTS

Some plants can respond very quickly. A Venus flytrap can sense the action of a fly landing on it. It does this by using electrical triggers that are similar to those used by an animal's nerves, and responds by snapping the fly up as an extra source of food.

1 OPEN TRAP
The trap of the plant is a special kind of leaf that produces drops of nectar. These attract various types of insect – the plant's unwilling victims.

Auxin moves down.

1 LEVEL SHOOT
Auxin occurs in the shoots as well as in the roots. When the plant is laid on its side, auxin moves to the lower side away from the light – just as it did in the roots.

2 FLY LANDS
When a fly lands on the leaf, it bends tiny hairs on the leaf surface. When these are brushed twice, the plant senses there is something there and this triggers the trap.

Cells on lower side grow bigger.

2 BENDING SHOOT
Unlike in the root, auxin makes the cells in the shoot grow more quickly. The cells on the shaded side with higher levels of auxin divide faster, curving the shoot tip upwards.

3 TRAP CLOSES
The leaf closes along a hinge at its base, locking the insect inside. The plant will release juices to digest the dying insect, and use its nutrients to grow.

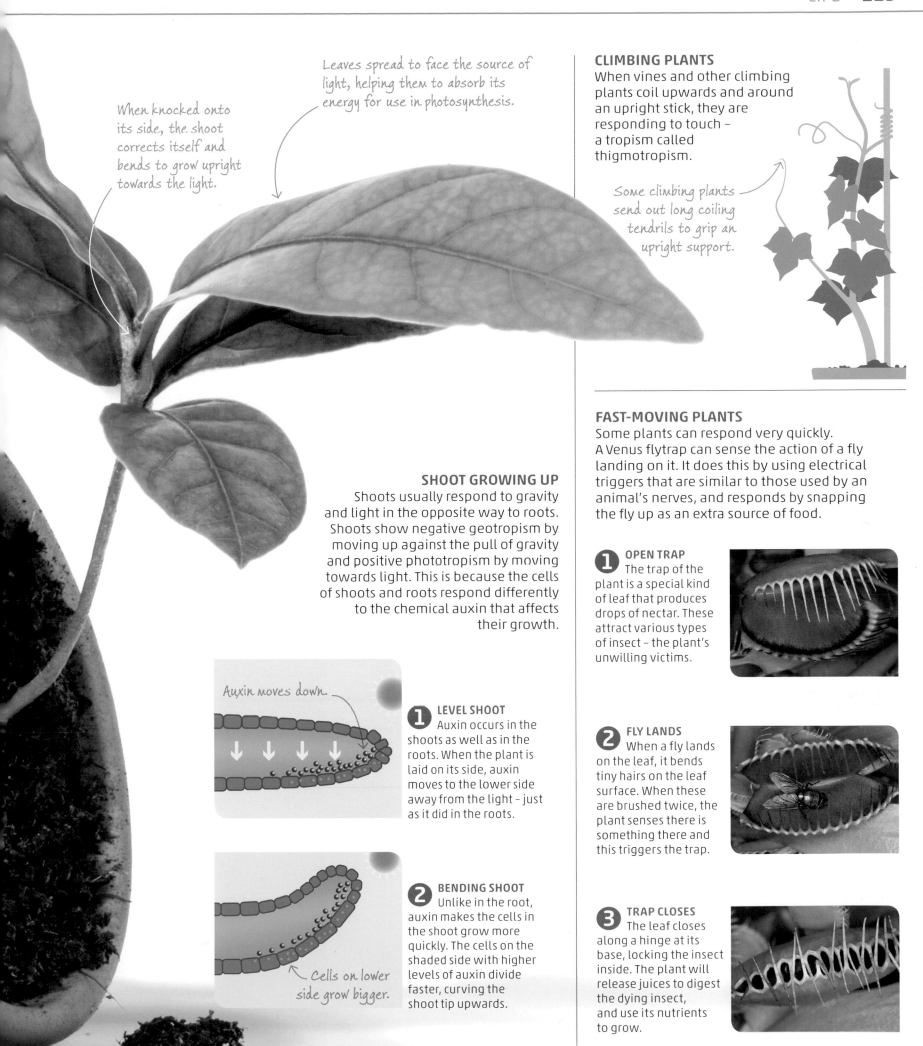

HOW EYES WORK

Animals have sense organs that help their body detect their surroundings. These organs carry cells called receptors that can pick up on changes called stimuli, and then fire electrical impulses into the nervous system. Eyes contain receptor cells that are stimulated by light, and when this happens the impulses arriving at the brain help it to form an image of the world.

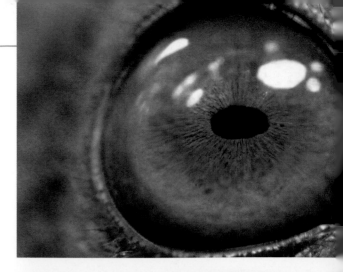

▶ DIFFERENT EYES

Animal eyes mostly all work with a similar arrangement of parts: a transparent window, or cornea, lets light through to a lens that focuses light onto the light-sensitive receptors inside. But different animals have eyes that are suited to the way they live, helping them to find their way around in their different habitats or locate their food.

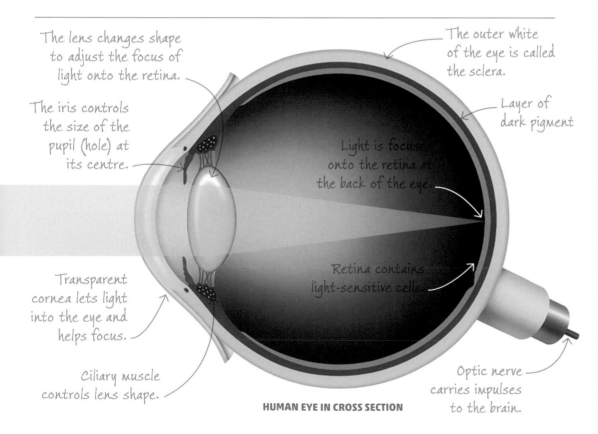

The lens changes shape to adjust the focus of light onto the retina.

The iris controls the size of the pupil (hole) at its centre.

Transparent cornea lets light into the eye and helps focus.

Ciliary muscle controls lens shape.

The outer white of the eye is called the sclera.

Layer of dark pigment

Light is focused onto the retina at the back of the eye.

Retina contains light-sensitive cells.

Optic nerve carries impulses to the brain.

HUMAN EYE IN CROSS SECTION

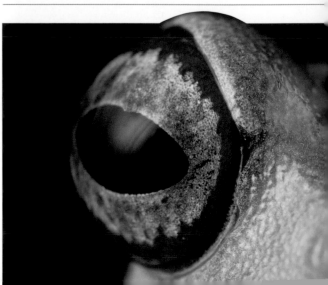

HOW THE HUMAN EYE WORKS

Like many other animals, humans have eyes that control how light reaches the light-sensitive receptor cells on the retina. A ring of muscle called an iris can open or close the pupil to let more or less light through, while the ciliary muscle can control the shape of the lens to help the eye change focus on near or far objects.

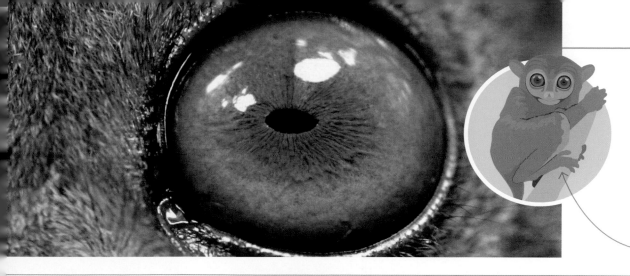

EYES FOR NIGHT-TIME
Tarsiers are tiny rainforest primates that are active at night. They need huge eyes to collect the tiny amounts of light coming from the Moon or stars. In bright light their pupils shrink to pin-points, as here. In darker conditions the pupils open very wide to let more light through.

A tarsier's eye is as big as its brain.

COMPOUND EYES
Each compound eye of a mantis shrimp is made up of thousands of tiny mini-eyes, each with its own lens for focusing light onto its own set of receptors. Although each mini-eye cannot make a clear image, together they help the mantis shrimp quickly spot movements, giving it lightning-fast reactions for attacking prey.

Each eye can rotate independently for all-round vision.

EYES FOR HUNTING
Most owls hunt at night and some during the day, but all survive by hunting fast-moving prey, such as rodents, and combine their acute vision with sensitive hearing. Like many other predators, their eyes face forwards on their heads, which helps them to judge distance as they pounce on their target.

Owl species with orange eyes hunt at dusk and dawn.

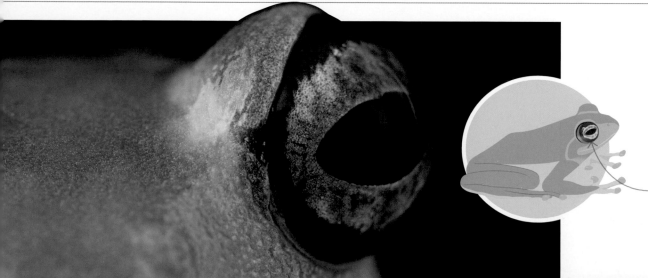

SENSING DANGER
Adult amphibians, like this Madagascan tree frog, spend some of their life on land and some in water, and their eyes work when submerged or in air. By having their eyes on the sides of the head, they have better all-round vision for spotting danger.

The bulging eyes pull into the head when the frog swallows, to help its food go down.

GROUP HUNTING

Silky sharks prey on other fish and have a complex brain that controls their behaviour, making them formidable predators in the ocean. Their sophisticated senses and nervous system help them react to their environment, but also allow them to carry out complex actions such as working together with other animals. By swimming around a shoal of fishes as a group, the sharks force their prey into a tighter bunch – making it easier to dive in and grab a mouthful.

HOW NERVES WORK

An animal's body can react to a change in environment with lightning-fast speed because it has a nervous system that carries fast electrical impulses from one part of the body to another. These impulses travel from sense organs, such as the eyes, through a network of nerves and the central nervous system, and finally to the body's muscles, which react.

NERVOUS SYSTEM

Nerves are bundles of very long neurons (nerve cells) with fibres that carry electrical impulses around the body. Other neurons are tightly packed within the brain and spinal cord and also control where these impulses travel. Together, the brain and spinal cord make up the central nervous system.

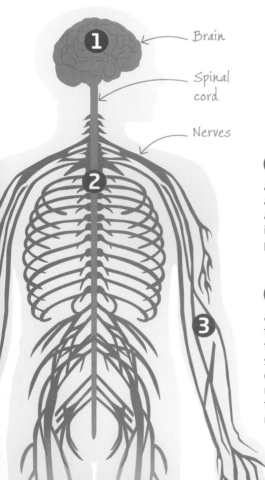

Brain

Spinal cord

Nerves

1 BRAIN
The brain is the body's control centre. It performs complex activities – making decisions, feeling emotion, and remembering events, as well as helping to control vital functions, such as heart beat.

2 SPINAL CORD
This runs through the spine and directs impulses passing to and from the brain. In cases where a quick response is needed, some impulses bypass the brain and just pass through the spinal cord.

3 NERVES
Networks of nerves are all around the body. There are two main types. Sensory nerves carry impulses from sense organs to the brain or spinal cord. From there, motor nerves carry them to muscles to create a response. Some nerve impulses travel faster than others – some reaching up to 400 km/h (250 mph).

▼ **NERVE CELL**
With their spindly fibres, neurons (nerve cells) are some of the most distinctive cells of the body. This highly magnified image shows a neuron from a region of the brain called the hippocampus. Like other brain neurons, it has branching fibres to carry electrical impulses in different directions. In contrast, neurons running through nerves in the body have long fibres that carry the impulses along fixed routes.

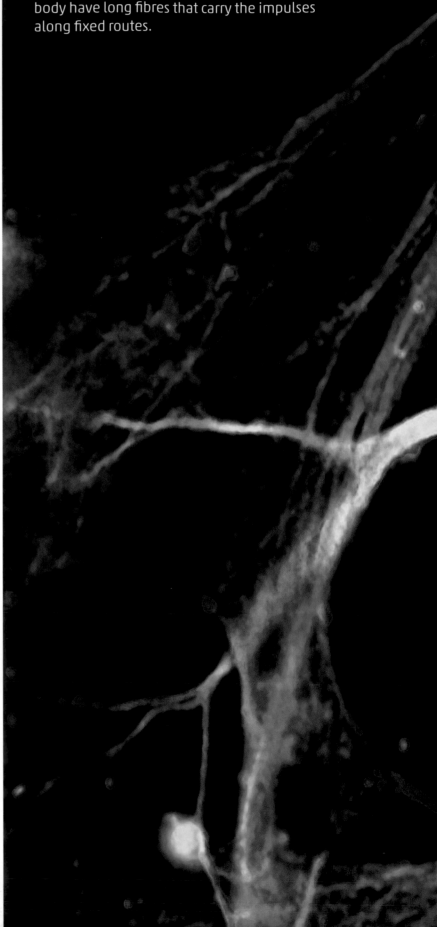

TRAVELLING SIGNALS

Masses of neurons form a huge network throughout the brain and the rest of the body, but the individual cells do not quite touch each other. Where each of their long fibres meets another neuron, there is a gap called a synapse. For the message being transmitted to get across this gap, the signal must change from an electrical one to a chemical one. This seeps across the synapse to reach the next neuron.

The cell body of a neuron contains a nucleus (its genetic control centre) and other structures needed to keep the cell alive.

Fibres branching from each brain neuron help it to communicate with its neighbours. Each cell can have thousands of these fibres.

Electrical impulse

1 IMPULSE ARRIVES
Electrical impulses travel in one direction along the long structure of a neuron until they reach the end of one of its fibres.

Branching fibres

2 SYNAPSE
The impulse then stimulates tiny sacs of chemicals to release their contents. These chemicals travel across the synapse – a tiny gap between the two cells.

Chemicals are released across the synapse.

3 NEW IMPULSE
The chemicals cross the gap and reach the other neuron. They stimulate it to generate a new electrical impulse, which continues its journey onwards around the body.

The skull, or cranium, forms a protective casing around the brain and supports the muscles that open and close the jaws.

The flexible backbone, or vertebral column, is made up of small interlocking bones called vertebrae.

▶ PREDATOR SKELETON

The 432 bones of this tiger make up a hard internal skeleton also known as an endoskeleton. Skeletons can tell us a lot about how an animal moves and how it lives. Long legs indicate the animal has big strides so can run fast, while large jaws with dagger-like teeth show it can kill other animals for their meat.

A set of bones called a girdle connects the legs to the main body.

The shoulder blade, or the scapula, connects to the front legs.

HOW SKELETONS WORK

The long breastbone sits under the ribs.

A single bone called the humerus makes up the upper part of each front leg.

A skeleton gives an animal's body its shape and supports and protects its working parts – especially the soft organs, such as the heart and brain. Many animals have hard skeletons made of bone, which connect at flexible joints. Muscles attach to the bones, and contract to pull on them and make them move.

At flexible joints, bones tipped with smooth cartilage are held together with fibres called ligaments.

Two bones, called the ulna and radius, make up the lower part of the leg.

INSIDE BONES

Bones are made of hard mineral – mainly calcium – with dense compact bone on the outside and a honeycomb-like network of spongy bone on the inside. Large bones contain a tissue called bone marrow at their centre, which produces new blood cells when old ones wear out.

Strong compact bone covers the bone marrow.

Bone marrow

Lightweight spongy bone makes up most of the bone.

Blood vessels supply food and oxygen to bone cells and help newly made blood cells circulate.

The high wrist bones show how the tiger walks on its toes.

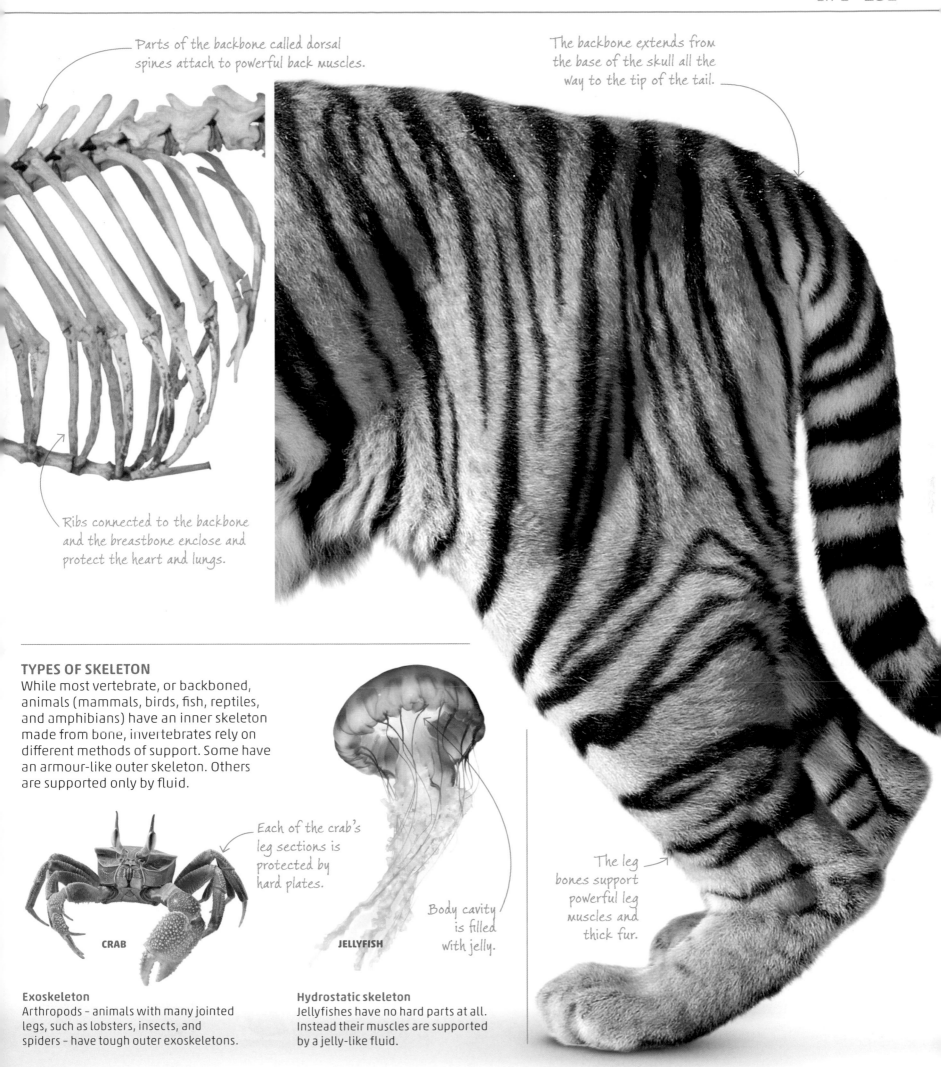

Parts of the backbone called dorsal spines attach to powerful back muscles.

The backbone extends from the base of the skull all the way to the tip of the tail.

Ribs connected to the backbone and the breastbone enclose and protect the heart and lungs.

TYPES OF SKELETON

While most vertebrate, or backboned, animals (mammals, birds, fish, reptiles, and amphibians) have an inner skeleton made from bone, invertebrates rely on different methods of support. Some have an armour-like outer skeleton. Others are supported only by fluid.

Each of the crab's leg sections is protected by hard plates.

Body cavity is filled with jelly.

The leg bones support powerful leg muscles and thick fur.

CRAB

JELLYFISH

Exoskeleton
Arthropods – animals with many jointed legs, such as lobsters, insects, and spiders – have tough outer exoskeletons.

Hydrostatic skeleton
Jellyfishes have no hard parts at all. Instead their muscles are supported by a jelly-like fluid.

HOW MUSCLES WORK

Muscles make the body move – whether it is the blink of an eye or the swing of a leg. Packages of fibres (long, thin specialized cells), muscles are all over the bodies of most animals. Some move automatically, but others – like the muscles in a horse's legs – are consciously controlled by the brain whenever the animal decides to make a movement.

Long neck muscle running from the base of the head to the top of the front leg pulls the leg forwards.

Biceps muscle helps bend the elbow joint.

Muscles running between the ribs help to raise and lower the ribcage when breathing.

Triceps muscle helps straighten the elbow joint.

Powerful hip muscles extend the leg and help the horse rear up onto its hind legs.

▶ MUSCLES FOR RUNNING

Strong muscles are needed to power the big body of a horse and enable it to reach a speedy gallop. A horse has no muscles below the knee, so its large upper leg muscles must carry out most of the work. These muscles are attached to the horse's skeleton, and only move when electrical signals are sent to them by the nervous system (see pages 228–229).

MUSCLE PAIRS

Skeletal muscles can either contract (shorten) or relax (lengthen). When they contract they pull on bones, moving part of the body. However, muscles can only pull – they can never push. This means that they must work in pairs to pull a body part both ways. In a horse's leg, extensor muscles pull on cords called tendons to straighten the limb. To bend it, the opposite muscles – flexor muscles – pull the tendons the other way.

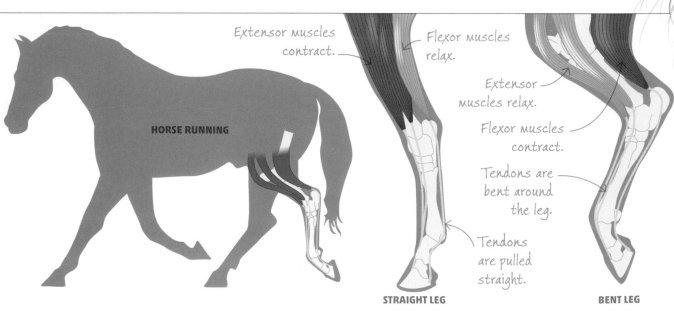

HORSE RUNNING

Extensor muscles contract.

Flexor muscles relax.

Extensor muscles relax.

Flexor muscles contract.

Tendons are bent around the leg.

Tendons are pulled straight.

STRAIGHT LEG

BENT LEG

Trapezius muscles running from the back of the neck help raise the shoulder.

When a horse runs, large amounts of lactic acid build up in its muscles. This is a byproduct of a process called anaerobic respiration (see page 213).

Cheek muscles open and close the jaws.

Most muscles that work the legs are packed high up, close to the body, to leave the long legs more lightweight.

Long tendons in the horse's leg reach right down to the toe. Tendons are cords that connect muscle to bone.

TYPES OF MUSCLE

An animal's body contains three types of muscle – each with a unique pattern of muscle fibres. Skeletal muscles are the only ones that an animal can voluntarily control. Other muscles work automatically to keep the body functioning.

Muscle cell nucleus

SKELETAL MUSCLE

Muscles attached to the skeleton are also called striated muscles because their long fibres have a stripy pattern. These muscles are moved voluntarily to make the body change position or move around.

SMOOTH MUSCLE

Smooth muscle is an involuntary muscle found in the walls of many organs and contains shorter muscle cells packed into sheets. When it contracts, it squeezes the organs' walls, such as those in the intestines.

CARDIAC MUSCLE

The walls of the heart's chambers contain a branching network of muscle fibres, called cardiac muscle. Like smooth muscle, this does not get tired, and works automatically to keep the heart beating for an entire lifetime.

Colourful petals attract pollinating insects.

Scattered pollen

The broad stigma collects pollen from a visiting bee that has just come from another pollen-releasing flower.

The bee packages some of the pollen into a bundle on its hind legs to take back to its hive as food.

Pollen is released from sac-like anthers, which split apart after the flower opens.

Each of the flower's hundreds of eggs is contained in tiny white capsules called ovules.

As the bee enters the flower, pollen released from the anthers rubs onto the insect's hairy body.

The bee's long tongue seeks out the sugary nectar.

HOW FLOWERS WORK

MAKING SEEDS

A flower's eggs need to be fertilized so that they can develop into seeds, from which new plants will grow. For this to happen, male sex cells in the pollen grains from another flower must fuse with the flower's female egg cells.

Many kinds of plants use flowers to reproduce.
These bright blooms contain sex cells in the form of tiny pollen grains and even smaller eggs. Plants must rely on insects, other animals, or the wind to transfer the pollen grains from plant to plant and start the reproductive process. Not all plants reproduce this way. Ferns release spores, and conifers have sex organs in woody cones.

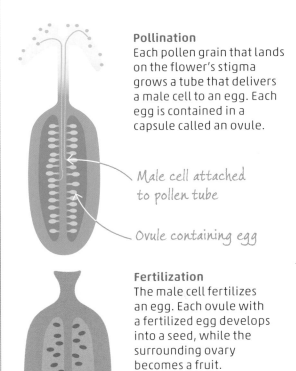

Pollination
Each pollen grain that lands on the flower's stigma grows a tube that delivers a male cell to an egg. Each egg is contained in a capsule called an ovule.

Male cell attached to pollen tube

Ovule containing egg

Fertilization
The male cell fertilizes an egg. Each ovule with a fertilized egg develops into a seed, while the surrounding ovary becomes a fruit.

Seed

Fruit

◄ BEE POLLINATION
The colourful petals and scent of this *Lisianthus* flower, seen here in cross-section, attract insects, such as bees. As a bee feeds on the flower's nectar, pollen grains rub onto its body. The bee then carries these to another flower of the same species where they brush off and pollinate the plant.

The sepals support the flower's petals.

The stigma is a platform for collecting pollen.

PARTS OF A FLOWER
A flower has everything it needs for reproduction. Most flowers, including this *Lisianthus*, contain both male and female parts.

The style connects the stigma to the ovary.

Pollen is produced in a sac called an anther.

Flower petals can come in many bright colours.

Nectary gland at base produces sweet nectar.

Ovary is a swollen base containing eggs.

SEPALS
Leaf-like structures around the outside of the flower protect the flower bud before it opens.

PETALS
Colourful petals attract insects, and produce nectar at their base to feed visiting pollinators.

CARPEL
This female sex organ collects pollen on its stigma to fertilize the eggs in the ovary.

STAMENS
These male sex organs produce tiny grains called pollen. Each grain contains a male sex cell.

HOW SEXUAL
REPRODUCTION
WORKS

Most animals, including humans, reproduce sexually, producing offspring that are not identical to them, but that instead contain a mixture of genetic information from two parents. Sexual reproduction begins when two single cells – an egg and a sperm – join together.

▶ **NEW HUMAN LIFE**
Human reproduction takes place inside the female body. It brings together the smallest human cell with one of the biggest: a tiny long-tailed sperm and a larger round egg. Once the male sperm cell is inside the female body, it enters the egg in a process known as fertilization. The fertilized egg then divides, producing all the cells of the new body as it develops.

1 FERTILIZATION
When humans reproduce, many sperm travel into the female body. But only one will fertilize the egg by pushing its head through the egg's outer cell membrane. The sperm and egg each contain half the genetic material (DNA) of a normal cell. When they join together, they form a complete set of genetic information needed for building a new body.

The sperm's half of the DNA is contained in its head.

The sperm uses its tail to propel itself towards the egg.

The 0.1-mm- (0.004-in-) wide egg is so much bigger than the sperm as it contains nutrients required after fertilization.

The fertilized egg (zygote) contains all the genetic information needed to produce a new human.

1 CELL

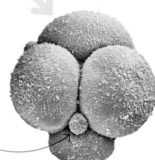

After copying its DNA the cell splits down the middle.

2 CELLS

② CELLS DIVIDE
The fertilized egg, now called a zygote, begins to divide by a process called mitosis (see pages 242–243). Each time it divides, its mixture of DNA gets copied, so each newly created cell is genetically identical. One cell divides into two, then each of these cells divides to make four.

Tiny cells made with the original egg break down and do not become part of the embryo.

4 CELLS

③ GROWING EMBRYO
Cells continue dividing – four into eight, eight into sixteen and so on – to produce a ball called an embryo. As the embryo continues to grow, different cells use the specific instructions contained in their DNA to develop into the organs and structures of the body.

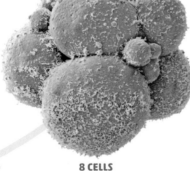

8 CELLS

Several days after fertilization, this ball of cells will implant itself in the lining of the woman's uterus.

16 CELLS

The placenta attaches to the uterus's wall.

The umbilical cord connects the baby to the placenta.

GROWING INTO A BABY
After about eight weeks, the developing embryo looks like a tiny human and is called a foetus. It is nourished inside the uterus by the placenta, which passes nutrients from the mother to the baby. Around nine months after fertilization, it will be ready to be born.

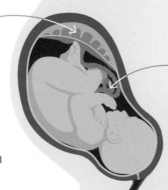

FULLY DEVELOPED FOETUS READY TO BE BORN

MEIOSIS
Normal cell division (mitosis) results in genetically identical cells. However, sex cells – sperm and eggs – are produced in a different way, to make cells that are genetically different and have half the usual amount of genetic material.

Duplicated chromosomes

① CHROMOSOMES
DNA is packaged into structures called chromosomes, of which humans have 46. To begin meiosis, the chromosomes in a cell copy themselves to become x-shaped.

② MIXING DNA
The copied chromosomes swap sections of their DNA with other similar-sized chromosomes to create a new unique mix of genetic information.

③ DIVISION BEGINS
The cell divides in two, with pairs of similar chromosomes separating so that each new cell has half the chromosome number.

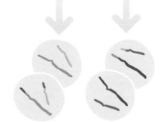

④ NEW SEX CELLS
Each new cell splits again. These final four cells now contain just 23 chromosomes – half the amount of genetic material needed to make a new organism.

Fertilized eggs are surrounded by protective soft jelly.

TYPES OF FERTILIZATION
In animals such as humans, fertilization takes place inside the body of a female animal. Other animals, such as frogs, carry out external fertilization. The males and females release their sperm and eggs into water, where they join together and grow.

1 HATCHING INTO THE WORLD
For 55 days mother and father penguin incubate their egg as the chick grows inside, keeping it warm under their bellies. When the chick has outgrown the egg it uses its bill and feet to break free of the shell.

A pointed shape prevents the egg from rolling away.

READY TO HATCH

The chick cuts through the shell using a small bump on its bill called an "egg tooth".

HOW ANIMALS DEVELOP

An animal starts its life as a single-celled fertilized egg. This egg divides over and over again, growing and developing until the animal is ready to be born. As its growth continues after birth, a young animal's body begins to take on the shape and structure of an adult until, eventually, it will be able to reproduce for itself.

NEWLY HATCHED

A newly hatched chick has its eyes closed – they open after a few hours.

2 THE YOUNG CHICK
A penguin chick has no feathers when it hatches. Until they grow the chick spends its time huddled under the warm belly of its parents. The parents take it in turns to swim out to sea on fishing expeditions to bring back food.

ONE DAY OLD

Within days the chick develops the strength to stand upright.

The first feathers to grow are brown and fluffy down feathers, which help to lock in body warmth.

Chicks grow fat on a diet of fish, and may weigh more than their parents.

GROWING OLDER

▶ HATCHING AND GROWING

All birds begin their development inside a hard-shelled egg. Once it is strong enough to hatch, this helpless King penguin chick starts life completely dependent on its parents, who provide the chick with the food and warmth it needs to make it into adulthood. Many other baby animals are also cared for by parents.

METAMORPHOSIS
In some animals the body changes dramatically, so that young and adult stages look completely different. This is called metamorphosis. Insects metamorphose from larva to their adult forms.

Butterfly eggs are often laid in clusters.

The pupa hangs in a safe place until the butterfly is ready to hatch.

EGG
Butterfly eggs can be round or oval in shape. Each one contains a tiny caterpillar.

CATERPILLAR
After hatching, the caterpillar grows quickly and eats as much as it can.

PUPA
When it is large enough, the caterpillar spins a cocoon called a pupa around itself.

ADULT
By the time it emerges from its cocoon the caterpillar has turned into a butterfly.

3 NEARLY ADULT
A moult marks the time when a penguin changes into an adult. This is when the bird swaps its fluffy juvenile feathers for feathers that are better for swimming in the ocean. As young penguins gain independence, their parents feed them less and less.

4 FULLY GROWN
The adult plumage of a King penguin has tiny stiff feathers that act like a streamlined wetsuit when hunting fish in the ocean. It also develops the colours to attract a mate, having reached a stage where it can produce babies of its own.

A long, strong bill will soon be used for catching fish.

Small, stiff adult feathers make the body surface smooth.

Orange feathers indicate this penguin is old enough to mate.

All cells in the plant contain identical DNA.

HOW CLONING WORKS

1 **PARENT PLANT**
An *Echeveria* plant grows as a rosette of diamond-shaped leaves connected to a short, thick stem at the centre. To clone the plant, one of these leaves is carefully cut away from the stem.

Making identical copies of living things is called cloning. These new organisms – called clones – share the exact same DNA as their parent. Sometimes cloning happens naturally, such as when new plants grow from the fallen leaves of old ones. But, today, scientists also have techniques for making clones in a lab.

The leaf contains the same DNA as the parent plant.

A new rosette of leaves grows around the stem of the young clone.

The young stem grows from the base of the old leaf cutting.

Roots grow downwards from cells around the base of the leaf stalk.

2 **ROOTS GROW**
When the leaf is placed on damp soil or tissue paper, it only takes a few days for roots to grow from its cut end. This part of the leaf is called the meristem and contains lots of rapidly dividing cells – making it the ideal place for a new plant to sprout from.

Roots branch out to anchor the cutting into the soil and find water and nutrients.

The old leaf will eventually wither and die.

CLONING IN THE LABORATORY
Using cuttings for cloning does not work for many plants, so scientists instead rely on the more difficult technique of cloning them in a lab. They use tiny samples of cells, and grow them in carefully controlled surroundings.

1 TAKING SAMPLES
Small pieces of plant, called explants, are removed from the parent plant using a sharp blade. Any part of the plant can be used, but young or rapidly growing parts work the best.

2 PREPARING THE EXPLANTS
The explants are sterilized, or cleaned, with special chemicals that prevent microbes from growing. The explants are then added to a dish of sterile jelly.

3 CLONES GROW
The jelly contains nutrients and chemicals that make the cells in the explant divide. Each explant develops into a tiny new plant with its own roots and shoots.

◀ CLONING A SUCCULENT
Echeveria is a type of succulent plant – a plant with thick, fleshy parts that help it survive in dry environments. Clones, or copies, of the plant can be produced by taking a cutting from one of its leaves. When planted, this then sprouts its own new roots and shoots. Because this cutting has cells that come from the original "parent" plant, both the cutting and the parent are genetically identical.

CLONING ANIMALS
Single animal cells do not easily grow into a whole organism, making animals harder to clone than plants. In 1996, the first mammal was cloned – Dolly the sheep. To do this, the cell nucleus of a "parent" sheep was injected into the egg cell of another sheep. After Dolly's death, she became a museum exhibit.

All cells in the young plant will still contain the exact same DNA as its original parent.

3 A CLONED PLANT
After roots emerge, a new shoot with tiny leaves of its own grows upwards from the base. The entire young plant – a clone of the original plant – can then be potted in compost.

GROWING ROOTS
When a red onion is placed over a glass filled with water, its roots will grow down to reach the water source. The end tips of these growing roots contain many dividing cells.

New white roots grow out from the base of an onion when it is supported over water.

The ends of the long roots can be cut and squashed onto a microscope slide.

Mitosis happens in the end 5 mm (0.2 in) tip of each onion root.

X80 MAGNIFICATION

HOW CELLS DIVIDE

As plants and animals grow they produce new cells in a process called mitosis. These are made when old cells divide in two. Before this can happen, the old cells need to copy their DNA – the genetic information that helps to make each organism unique.

▶ **CELL DIVISION UNDER A MICROSCOPE**
In animals, mitosis happens all over the body, but in plants it is concentrated at the tips of shoots and roots, where the plant is growing up and down. By staining the cells of a root tip with a purple dye that sticks to DNA, the cell division can be seen under a microscope.

Higher up the root tip, fewer cells are dividing.

Mitosis happens in the region just behind the tip of the root – an area called the apical meristem.

A protective root cap at the very end of the root contains tough, protective cells that are not dividing.

Here, the chromosomes are thickening and shortening to make them easier to move about.

UNDER THE MICROSCOPE
This image shows a piece of root tip after it has been cut off and squashed on a microscope slide to make it flat. Adding a purple stain to the root has highlighted the DNA-containing nucleus of each cell in a vivid colour.

The two sets of chromosomes have moved apart in this cell.

X600 MAGNIFICATION

DIVISION IN ACTION
DNA is packaged into threads called chromosomes. At a higher magnification, the chromosomes show up inside the dividing cells. The cells visible here are all in varying stages of mitosis, with some nearly ready to divide and become two new cells.

Before a cell divides, its DNA appears as a dark smudge inside the cell's nucleus.

The two new daughter cells each contain copies of every chromosome.

Original parent cell

STAGES OF MITOSIS
A crucial part of a cell's lifecycle, cell division is made up of several stages. Firstly, DNA is replicated within each cell as it grows and develops. Then the cell begins the multi-step process of dividing in two.

1 WHOLE CELL
Each chromosome makes a copy of itself before mitosis begins.

6 CELL SPLITS
Protective cell walls form around the two new cells.

2 PREPARING
The DNA in the cells changes into a form that allows it to divide more easily.

Aligned chromosomes

Separating chromosomes

5 READY TO SPLIT
The copied sets of chromosomes reform into two separate nuclei.

3 LINING UP
The copied chromosomes line up along the cell's middle.

4 SEPARATING
The copies separate and move apart.

The DNA in each cell's nucleus shows up as a little purple spot.

HOW DNA WORKS

All the instructions needed to make a living thing start with a remarkable substance called DNA (deoxyribonucleic acid). There is a package of DNA inside every cell, containing a set of instructions on how to build all the parts in a body and keep them working properly.

▼ EXTRACTING DNA
DNA is not just found inside animals, but inside all living things, like the fruit of a strawberry plant. Some simple equipment can be used to extract this DNA from cells and view it with the naked eye.

Fresh strawberries

Water

200

Washing-up liquid

Table salt

① PREPARING THE MIXTURE
DNA is contained inside the nucleus of each strawberry cell, but is not easily accessed. Soapy detergent is needed to break up the oily membranes around each nucleus, and salt helps to pull the DNA away from other substances inside the cells.

The solid pulpy parts of the strawberries do not pass through the sieve.

Strawberries are crushed with water, soap, and salt in a sandwich bag.

Liquid contents of the cells, including DNA, pass through the sieve.

125
100
50

② BREAKING THE CELLS
The strawberries are squeezed to a pulp with the salt and detergent to break open the cells. The mixture is then sieved so that the contents of the cells, including DNA, separate from the solid seeds and pith.

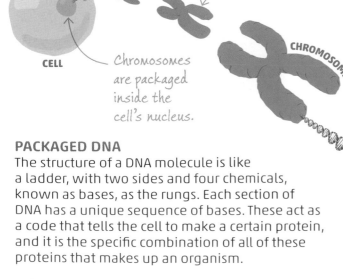

CELL

Chromosomes are packaged inside the cell's nucleus.

To fit inside the nucleus, DNA is arranged into bundles called chromosomes.

CHROMOSOME

Adenine

Cytosine

Guanine

Thymine

Two sets of bases always pair with each other.

DNA

The "backbone" of DNA is made up of blocks of sugar and phosphate.

PACKAGED DNA
The structure of a DNA molecule is like a ladder, with two sides and four chemicals, known as bases, as the rungs. Each section of DNA has a unique sequence of bases. These act as a code that tells the cell to make a certain protein, and it is the specific combination of all of these proteins that makes up an organism.

3 SEPARATING THE DNA
To make the DNA separate out from the remaining mixture, ice-cold isopropyl alcohol is then poured onto the surface. The DNA soon becomes visible as thick white bundles. These can be picked out of the mixture in clumps – each one containing many molecules of strawberry DNA.

The **DNA** double helix

Too small to be visible even under a microscope, the DNA molecule's structure resembles a spiralling ladder – a shape known as a double helix.

Pure DNA, looking like white slime, can be picked up with tweezers.

The cold temperature of the isopropyl alcohol helps the DNA to solidify out of the soapy mixture.

DNA does not dissolve in the colourless alcohol, so instead separates out into solid threads.

The rest of the cell's contents, including cytoplasm and red pigment, stay at the bottom of the beaker.

125

100

75

50

HOW INHERITANCE WORKS

Offspring inherit characteristics from their parents through the genes that are passed on in sex cells. Genes are packages of DNA linked together on structures called chromosomes inside most body cells. Each gene acts like a set of instructions that affects what the cells do, and so they determine inherited characteristics, such as eye colour, blood group, and height.

CHROMOSOME PAIRS
Humans have 46 chromosomes in their cells, but wallabies have 16. The chromosomes come in pairs that carry similar sorts of genes, and one of these pairs determines sex. Two albino genes together always produce an albino wallaby, like this baby. Two brown genes or a mix of brown and albino genes will produce a brown wallaby, like the mother.

Genes occur in pairs, which are carried on similar chromosomes. This pair of chromosomes contains genes that affect the wallaby's colour.

These two albino genes mean the wallaby's cells cannot produce pigment.

This pair of sex-determining chromosomes has one shorter Y chromosome, which is only found in males.

▶ GENES AND CHARACTERISTICS
Wallabies are Australian marsupials that are similar to kangaroos but smaller. Most wallabies have the brown-grey coloured coat like this mother wallaby, but her baby's coat is completely white. This is because he has inherited two sets of albino genes from his parents. These genes cannot make the pigment required to produce colour. Even the baby's eyes lack pigment, so its blood vessels make them appear pink.

INHERITING ALBINO GENES

Genes occur in pairs in body cells, but when sperm and egg cells are made these gene pairs separate (see page 237). During fertilization they come together to create the offspring's new gene pairs. Brown genes are dominant and white are recessive. This means a baby needs two recessive white genes in its cells in order to be born albino, so it must inherit a white gene from both of its parents.

Gene pairs separate when sex cells are made.

Each body cell contains a pair of colour genes.

When sex cells fuse, genes come together as pairs again.

1 **PARENTAL GENES**
Each parent has a copy of both a brown and an albino colour gene in every normal cell in its body.

2 **GENE PAIRS SPLIT**
The parents' sperm and egg cells hold either a brown or an albino gene, because gene pairs split when sex cells are made.

3 **GENES COME TOGETHER**
Sperm and egg cells fuse randomly at fertilization. If both sex cells contain an albino gene, the baby will be albino.

If both parents carry the albino gene there is a 25 per cent chance of getting an albino baby.

INHERITING SEX

The types of chromosomes in the sex cells that come together at fertilization affect whether offspring will be male or female. If the sex chromosomes are identical (two X chromosomes) they produce a female. If they are different (X and Y chromosomes) they produce a male. All egg cells carry X chromosomes but sperm cells may contain either an X or a Y chromosome. This means that the father's sex cells determine the sex of the offspring.

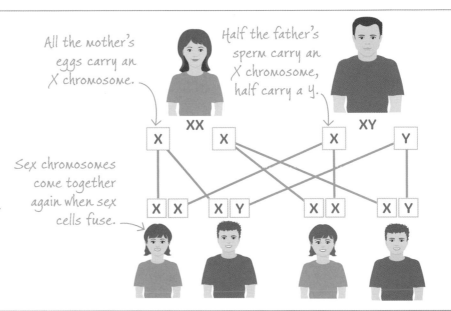

All the mother's eggs carry an X chromosome.

Half the father's sperm carry an X chromosome, half carry a Y.

XX

XY

Sex chromosomes come together again when sex cells fuse.

HOW GENES WORK

Human cells contain about 21,000 kinds of gene. Each gene is on a section of a chromosome and controls part of a cell's activity. It does this by instructing the cell to make a particular kind of protein. Some proteins make up body structures such as skin, others are enzymes that control cell activities. The same genes are found in all cells, but are only activated in certain parts of the body – so eye colour genes, for instance, only affect eyes.

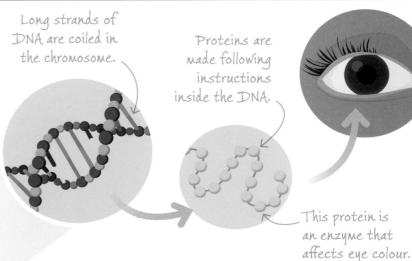

Long strands of DNA are coiled in the chromosome.

Proteins are made following instructions inside the DNA.

This protein is an enzyme that affects eye colour.

1 **LOCATION OF A GENE**
Each gene occupies a fixed position on a particular chromosome inside the cell.

2 **MAKE-UP OF A GENE**
The gene is a section of the DNA double helix that contains information to make a protein.

3 **GENES AND CHARACTERISTICS**
The eye colour gene instructs cells in the eye to build an enzyme that makes eye pigment.

HOW
EVOLUTION
WORKS

Organisms alive today have descended from different species that lived in the past. Over many generations, entire populations of living things have changed their characteristics by a process called evolution. Many tiny changes add up to produce completely new species.

▶ PEPPERED MOTH

New characteristics appear in a population through a process called mutation. This happens when genes get randomly miscopied during reproduction. The peppered moth is a common insect species that exists in two colour varieties. The darker variety (below) evolved when an existing gene for light speckled colour (right) changed into a form that made the moths black.

Moths use their feathery antennae as scent receptors.

The dark wings are caused by a pigment called melanin.

NATURAL SELECTION
Much of evolution happens by natural selection. This is where individuals with certain inherited characteristics are more likely to survive and breed, and pass on these characteristics to offspring. The peppered moth went through a process of natural selection during the Industrial Revolution.

1 LIGHT MOTHS THRIVE
Before the Industrial Revolution tree trunks were covered with grey lichen that flourished in clean, unpolluted air. This meant light-coloured moths were less likely to be seen by insect-eating birds, so they were more common than the black ones, which were easily seen and eaten.

2 DARK MOTHS THRIVE
During the Industrial Revolution polluting smoke killed lichen and blackened trees with soot, hiding darker moths so more of the light-coloured ones were eaten by birds. Today, with cleaner air, light moths are common again – especially in the countryside away from cities.

Moth wings are covered with tiny scales that give them their colour.

Light moths need both of the genes that affect colour in their body cells to be capable of creating light pigment.

Like other moths, these insects hold their wings out flat when perched on a surface.

As with all species, the genes in this moth's body cells are linked in pairs. Only one of the genes in the colour pair needs to be able to create black pigment for the moth to be black.

NEW SPECIES
Over many generations, organisms can evolve so much that they end up becoming an entirely new species. Two million years ago the Galapagos Islands were colonized by some finches from nearby South America. Conditions on the separate islands were not identical and suited finches who had mutated slightly different beaks. Over time, the finches evolved into entirely different species, as those whose beaks were best suited for getting food on their island survived and produced more offspring than those whose beaks had not adapted. Today, 17 different species of finch live on the Galapagos Islands, all descended from the same ancestors.

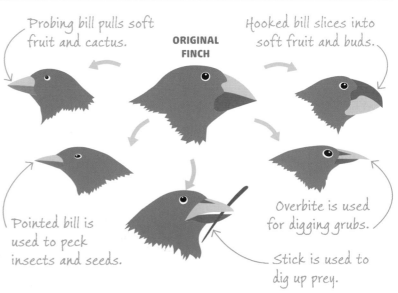

Probing bill pulls soft fruit and cactus.

ORIGINAL FINCH

Hooked bill slices into soft fruit and buds.

Pointed bill is used to peck insects and seeds.

Overbite is used for digging grubs.

Stick is used to dig up prey.

EVOLUTION FROM A COMMON ANCESTOR

LIVING TOGETHER

Zebras are just one of the many creatures found in the tropical grasslands of Africa, a region that contains more large animals than most other parts of the world. Large numbers of an individual species are called a population. When different species live together in the same environment, they are known as a community. Zebras are part of a network of food chains within their community, often falling prey to large carnivores, such as lions.

HOW MOULD WORKS

Mould is a fungus – often seen growing on old food, such as this bread. In doing so, it helps to recycle material that would otherwise go to waste. Mould is a decomposer, which means that it feeds on waste or dead material. It digests the bread and in this way helps to release nutrients into the surroundings that can go on to be used by other living things.

Spores land on the bread and grow into threads.

GETTING FOOD
Mould begins life as tiny spores, which are carried in the air to the bread. They grow into threads called hyphae, and can spread into a huge network. The threads release chemicals that break the bread down into nutrients – some of which are used by the mould and others which are released into the environment.

Lots of mould threads make up a network called a mycelium.

RECYCLING NUTRIENTS
Without decomposers, dead and waste material would build up and the nutrients in them would be lost. By feeding on dead organisms, decomposers release products such as carbon dioxide and minerals back into the air and soil. Both these products are then taken in by plants and used to help them grow.

Decomposers are not always fungi, but can also be animals too.

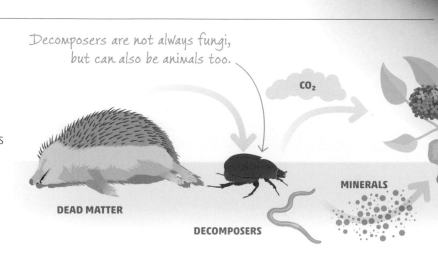

CO$_2$

MINERALS

DEAD MATTER

DECOMPOSERS

The plant reuses the decomposer's waste materials.

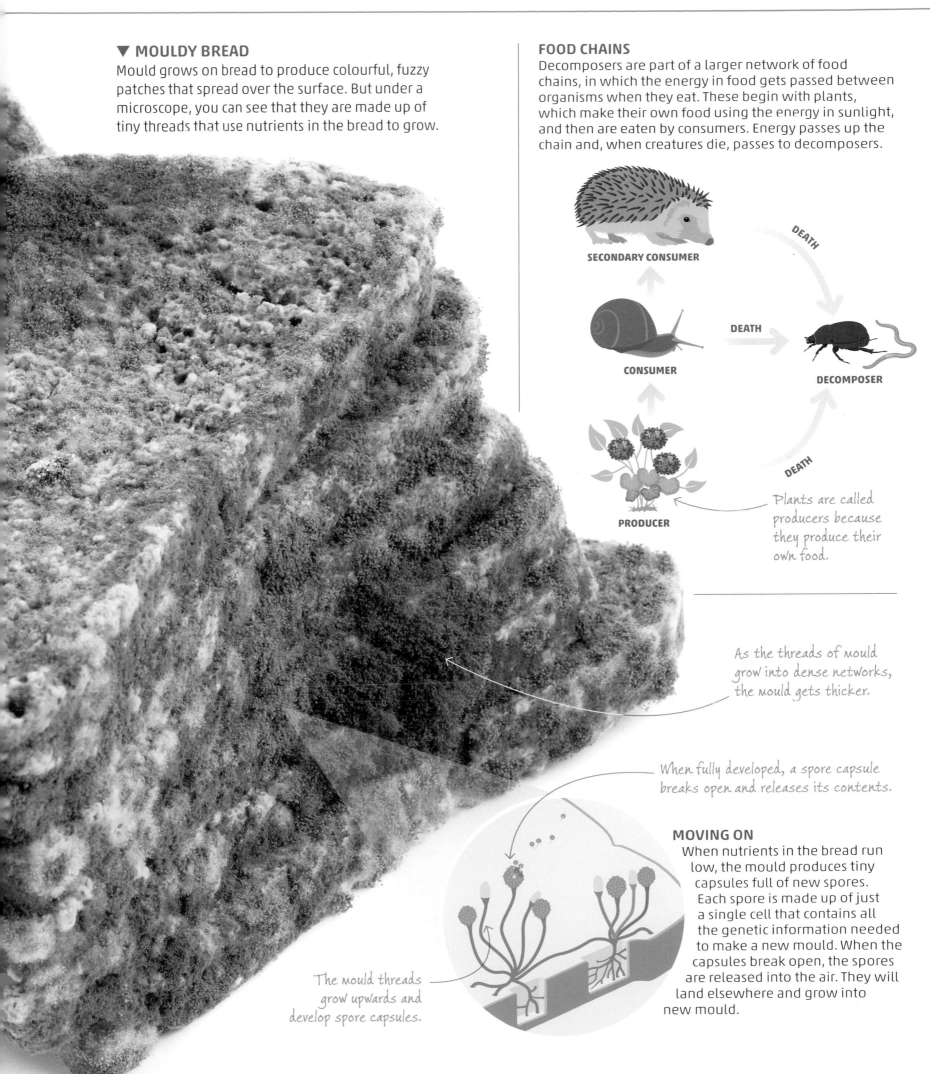

▼ MOULDY BREAD
Mould grows on bread to produce colourful, fuzzy patches that spread over the surface. But under a microscope, you can see that they are made up of tiny threads that use nutrients in the bread to grow.

FOOD CHAINS
Decomposers are part of a larger network of food chains, in which the energy in food gets passed between organisms when they eat. These begin with plants, which make their own food using the energy in sunlight, and then are eaten by consumers. Energy passes up the chain and, when creatures die, passes to decomposers.

SECONDARY CONSUMER

DEATH

CONSUMER

DEATH

DECOMPOSER

DEATH

PRODUCER

Plants are called producers because they produce their own food.

As the threads of mould grow into dense networks, the mould gets thicker.

When fully developed, a spore capsule breaks open and releases its contents.

MOVING ON
When nutrients in the bread run low, the mould produces tiny capsules full of new spores. Each spore is made up of just a single cell that contains all the genetic information needed to make a new mould. When the capsules break open, the spores are released into the air. They will land elsewhere and grow into new mould.

The mould threads grow upwards and develop spore capsules.

Our home planet is a ball of **rock and metal**, covered by oceans of **liquid water** and surrounded by protective layers of gas called the **atmosphere**. Formed **4.5 billion years** ago, the Earth is **constantly changing** at a very slow rate. Scientists study the **movements** and **cycles** that take place on Earth to understand how it has changed over time and to predict how it might change in the future.

EARTH

HOW THE
EARTH
WORKS

The Earth is the third planet from the Sun.
Its metal core is so hot that it can melt the
rock around it, but across its surface the
solid crust of the Earth has oceans of liquid
water and a breathable atmosphere above.
These conditions make the Earth unique as
the only known planet to support life.

▶ THE BLUE PLANET
Seen from space, the Earth is mainly blue – with
three-fifths of its surface covered by oceans. The rest is solid
land, stretching from the ice-covered poles to the warm
equator thick and green with vegetation. The swirling
atmosphere is the source of the planet's daily weather.

LIVING PLANET
Life began on Earth 3.8 billion years ago, less than a billion
years after the Earth itself was formed. From simple single-celled
organisms in the early oceans, life has evolved and diversified
so that living things are found in every part of our planet – from
the deepest ocean trenches to the highest mountain peaks.
Light energy from the Sun is used by plants to drive food chains.
Flowing water and oxygen support plant and animal life.

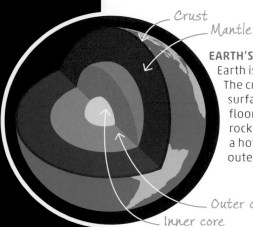

Crust
Mantle
Outer core
Inner core

EARTH'S LAYERS

Earth is made up of distinct layers. The crust, the thinnest layer, is the solid surface rock of continents and ocean floor. Below this is a thick layer of solid rock called the mantle. At the centre is a hot metal core, consisting of a molten outer core and a solid inner core.

MIX OF ELEMENTS

The rocks that form the crust and mantle contain a mixture of different chemical elements, but the most common are silicon and oxygen. Rocks containing magnesium and aluminium are also abundant. The core is mostly made of iron, with some nickel and sulfur.

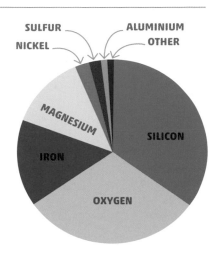

SULFUR
NICKEL
ALUMINIUM
OTHER
MAGNESIUM
SILICON
IRON
OXYGEN

ELEMENTS IN THE EARTH

TECTONIC PLATES

Earth's surface is solid rock, but it is broken into shapes called tectonic plates that fit together like the pieces of a jigsaw puzzle. Each plate is made of a piece of the crust and the strong topmost part of the mantle, sticking to it just underneath.

Earth's tectonic plates are constantly moving but at a very slow rate.

PLATE MOVEMENT

Heat rising from the core flows through the very slow-moving rock of the mantle. Heat currents move the tectonic plates sitting on the surface. Some plates spread apart when hot rock rises between them. Other plates collide, with one plate sinking beneath the other. These processes can cause earthquakes and volcanoes.

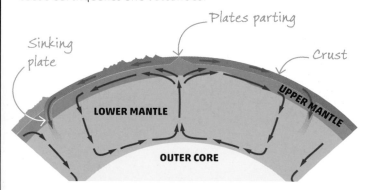

Plates parting
Sinking plate
Crust
UPPER MANTLE
LOWER MANTLE
OUTER CORE

HOW ROCKS FORM

Earth's crust contains many different kinds of rock made up of crystallized chemicals called minerals. Some rocks are produced quickly by volcanic eruptions; others are formed over thousands of years by the movements of Earth's plates.

▶ TYPES OF ROCK

Igneous, sedimentary, and metamorphic are the three key types of rock. Igneous rock forms when magma (molten rock) cools and turns solid. When magma is trapped in the crust, the igneous rocks are called intrusive. If the magma reaches Earth's surface before it cools, the rock is known as extrusive. Sedimentary rock is made when tiny mineral particles from other rocks are cemented together by pressure. Metamorphic rocks form when other rocks are altered by pressure from the movements of the crust or heat from inside the Earth.

THE ROCK CYCLE

The materials found in rock are recycled over and over again, as rocks change from one kind into another. Rocks can be melted by heat inside the Earth, worn away by weathering on the surface, or altered due to pressure. These processes are linked in a continual cycle, which takes place over the course of many millions of years.

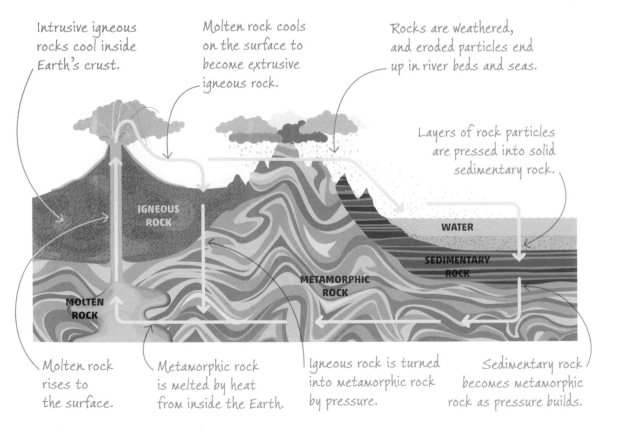

Intrusive igneous rocks cool inside Earth's crust.

Molten rock cools on the surface to become extrusive igneous rock.

Rocks are weathered, and eroded particles end up in river beds and seas.

Layers of rock particles are pressed into solid sedimentary rock.

IGNEOUS ROCK

WATER

SEDIMENTARY ROCK

METAMORPHIC ROCK

MOLTEN ROCK

Molten rock rises to the surface.

Metamorphic rock is melted by heat from inside the Earth.

Igneous rock is turned into metamorphic rock by pressure.

Sedimentary rock becomes metamorphic rock as pressure builds.

GRANITE
The cliffs of Yosemite National Park, USA, are granite, a type of intrusive igneous rock. The magma that forms intrusive igneous rock cools slowly and large mineral crystals form. These minerals are visible in the rock.

Granite is dappled with minerals that grow as the rock forms.

MARBLE
This river bed in Norway is made from marble. When a sedimentary rock is altered by heat and pressure, new mineral crystals grow. The minerals create unusual shapes and colourful veins, which can be seen when the rock has transformed into the hard metamorphic rock of marble.

Marble is known for its coloured veins of mineral.

SANDSTONE
Cappadocia in Turkey is blanketed with a sedimentary rock called sandstone. The rock has colourful stripes because it is made from layers of different sand particles. Pressure on the layers presses them together to form solid rock but the grainy texture remains.

Sandstone has a grainy appearance.

BASALT
Basalt is an extrusive igneous rock. Basalt often covers a wide area because it flows to the surface through a volcano. It is sometimes arranged in giant columns, like this cliff in Iceland, which are caused by deep cracks appearing as the rock cools.

Basalt mineral crystals are only visible under a microscope.

WHAT IS A MINERAL?

Minerals are naturally occurring solid forms of chemicals – either single elements or compounds. Many minerals form as large crystals in distinctive shapes, some of which can be cut and polished into gemstones. The six most common crystal shapes are shown here.

TOPAZ
Minerals vary in their hardness. The softest, talc, can be scratched with a fingernail. Harder minerals, such as topaz, can be cut and polished into gemstones. Topaz is coloured blue, pink, or yellow, depending on the exact quantities of the different elements it contains. Topaz crystals are a prism shape, called orthorhombic, which can form in columns or flatter prisms.

AMAZONITE
Amazonite is a compound of potassium, aluminium, silicon, and oxygen. It forms crystals in a shape known as triclinic, which look like slanted cubes. Like all minerals, its shape is fixed by the way its atoms are arranged (see pages 22–23). As crystals grow, more atoms join the same system, until the shape is visible.

TRICLINIC

ORTHORHOMBIC

WULFENITE
Minerals that contain useful metals are called ores. Wulfenite is an ore of lead and molybdenum (a metal used to make steel). They react with oxygen to form a compound, which produces crystals in a rectangular prism shape known as tetragonal.

TETRAGONAL

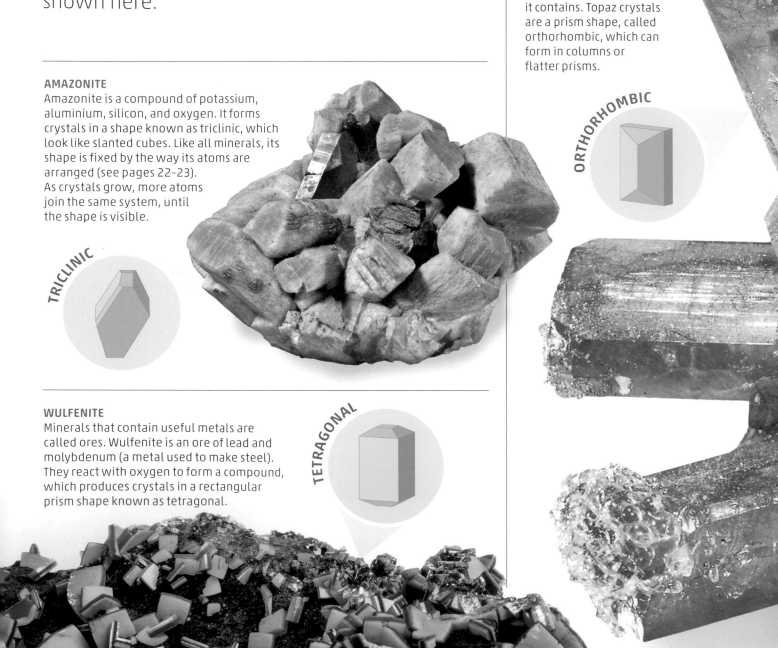

These wulfenite crystals are yellow because they contain traces of chromium.

The pinkish tinge of this topaz is due to tiny quantities of the element chromium.

MONOCLINIC

QUARTZ

Although made from just two elements, silicon and oxygen, the crystal structure of quartz varies to give many different forms including sand and rose quartz gemstone. The specimen of orange quartz below, which has formed next to a black tourmaline crystal, has a hexagonal shape known as trigonal.

TRIGONAL

Azurite minerals were used to make blue pigments in the past.

AZURITE

Extraordinary colours in minerals are due to metal elements, which have combined in particular ways. The deep blue of azurite is due to copper combined with carbonate (a carbon and oxygen compound). Azurite crystals grow in flat columns called monoclinic crystals.

Orthorhombic crystals can grow in groups forming long columns.

PYRITE

Perfect cubes of pyrite form when a mineral compound of iron and sulfur is free from impurities. The cubic arrangement of atoms is preserved even on a large scale. Pyrite looks like a precious metal, so it is sometimes called fool's gold.

CUBIC

Although it can look like gold, pyrite is much less dense than real gold.

Sediment layers covered the seabed. Heat and pressure turned the sediment into rock.

4 TURNING TO ROCK
Over time, sediment layers cemented the shell into the rock. At the same time, ocean water seeped through the rock and replaced the minerals in the shell with rock minerals. This eventually turned the shell into a rocky fossil.

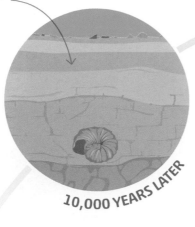

10,000 YEARS LATER

5 EXPOSURE
Millions of years later, slow movements of Earth's crust brought the layer of rock containing the fossil near to the surface. Here wind, rain, or ice eroded the rock to expose the fossilized ammonite inside.

HOW FOSSILS FORM

Prehistoric plants and animals lived millions of years ago, yet some have left evidence of their existence in rocks. These remains are called fossils, preserved because of the particular ways these organisms decayed.

3 BURIAL
Drifting sediment on the seabed quickly covered the dead ammonite's shell, stopping it from breaking down further. Traces of soft parts can sometimes be found if this process began before they decayed.

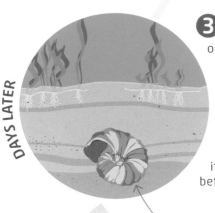

DAYS LATER

The ammonite was buried under many layers of sediment.

2 DEATH
When it died, this ammonite sank to the bottom of the ocean and its soft parts quickly decayed. This left only the hard shell, which was covered with sediment.

▶ RELICS FROM ANCIENT SEAS
Ammonites were creatures that lived in prehistoric oceans. First appearing 400 million years ago, they became extinct 65 million years ago at the same time as the dinosaurs. They were related to octopuses and squids, but had hard coiled shells. Fossils of these shells have been found in rocks all over the world. This type of fossil is known as a body fossil.

1 SWIMMING THE SEAS
Ammonites swam in prehistoric oceans. These creatures were the ancestors of modern-day octopuses and they were active hunters.

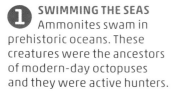

MILLIONS OF YEARS AGO

Ammonites might have used tentacles to hunt their prey.

The ammonite lived in the outermost chamber of the shell, leaving the old chambers empty as the shell grew.

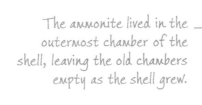

6 FOSSIL REVEALED
Palaeontologists (scientists who study prehistoric organisms) carefully separated the ammonite fossil from the rest of the rock. It can be studied to help them understand how ammonites once lived.

This *Hoplites dentatus* ammonite is only a few centimetres wide.

The ridged structure of ammonite shells marks the edges of gas chambers inside.

Gas chambers were created as the ammonite grew. Each ridge was once the end of the coiled shell.

FOSSIL TYPES

When they die, most living organisms do not form fossils but simply decay. Fossils can take many different forms because of variations in how the organism decayed and how the fossil formed. Some fossils are impressions left from a body or track, such as trace and mould fossils. Other fossils show the entire organism preserved with very little decay, known as true form fossils.

TRACE FOSSILS
Trace fossils are the preserved tracks or impressions left by organisms. The traces are left in mud then quickly covered with sediment, which preserves the trace in rock.

MOULD FOSSIL
When an organism, such as this trilobite (an extinct sea creature related to insects and crabs), decays after it is encased in sediment it can leave a gap. A mould of its shape is left in the rock.

TRUE FORM FOSSIL
An organism can be trapped in ice or amber (a sticky tree sap). The entire organism, including any soft parts, is preserved so these fossils are known as true form fossils.

HOW VOLCANOES WORK

The centre of Earth is extremely hot, reaching temperatures of 5,500°C (9,932°F). This heat builds in spots and melts some of the solid rock below Earth's surface. This molten rock, called magma, collects in chambers and, in places where there are cracks or weak spots, escapes through the vent of a volcano, sometimes explosively.

INSIDE A VOLCANO

Liquid magma escaping from a volcano is called lava. When lava is ejected from the volcano, the rocky material collects around the edge, forming a cone of rock. Clouds of ash and poisonous gases rise from the volcano into the atmosphere.

A magma chamber gets so hot the rock melts and erupts through Earth's lower crust.

Lava runs down the side of the volcano before cooling back to rock.

Rising lava flows through smaller gaps as well as the main vent.

TYPES OF LAVA

Volcanoes have different shapes due to the type of lava they erupt. Cone-shaped volcanoes form through explosive eruptions of thick, sticky lava. This lava flows a short distance and cools into a high mound. Runny lava spreads thinly over a large area and creates flatter volcanoes. Ash-filled lava creates small, wide cones.

▶ VOLCANO IN A BEAKER

A simple arrangement of water, sand, and wax in a glass beaker shows what happens in a volcanic eruption. When heated by a Bunsen burner, the layer of hard red wax at the bottom melts like magma. As the heat builds, the wax erupts through the weak material of sand and water to the surface.

The water represents Earth's upper crust.

WATER

Sand acts as Earth's lower crust.

SAND

Wax shows what happens to Earth's upper mantle.

WAX

1 SURFACE LAYERS
The different layers in the beaker represent the layers of Earth's surface. Water represents the crust closest to Earth's surface where the rock is coolest, and the sand acts as the lower crust. The hard, red wax at the bottom of the beaker is Earth's solid upper mantle.

Wax spreads over the surface of the water and hardens.

Some wax becomes solid before it reaches the surface. In volcanoes, magma trapped below the surface cools and solidifies to form rocks called intrusions.

Hot melted wax, like magma, rises up.

The wax breaks through weak points in the sand.

The concentrated heat from below melts the solid wax.

② ERUPTION
A Bunsen burner flame placed underneath the beaker melts the wax. The melted wax erupts through the layers of sand and water because it has a lower density than the substances around it. A flowing column of wax forms as the wax moves through the cooler materials. When the wax reaches the cold surface of the water it hardens, just like magma turning back to solid rock on Earth's surface.

HOW EROSION WORKS

Over time, the forces of nature break down even the hardest rocks into tiny particles. Wind, waves, or running water can transport these particles great distances. This process is called erosion.

WEATHERING

The particles that wash away during erosion were once solid rock. Rock particles form when natural processes, known as weathering, break the rock into small pieces.

RAINFALL
Rain dissolves minerals in rocks causing them to break down. Acid in polluted rain can also weather rocks.

ICE
When water in rock crevices freezes, the ice expands. The rock is pushed apart, cracks, and separates.

SUNSHINE
Sunshine warms rocks, causing them to expand. These rocks push outwards and crack the rocks around them.

ROOTS
Plants with strong roots can cause rocks to crack and crumble as the roots grow longer and wider.

WAVE EROSION
Crashing waves erode the rock along a coastline. The force of the waves creates cracks in the rock which get wider over time. This forms large caves or archways which eventually crumble away. Waves and currents carry the rock debris along the shoreline so only the columns remain. These columns of rock are called sea stacks.

The grass has branching roots which hold soil particles together.

SOIL WITH PLANTS

Water not used by the plants runs through the mouth of the bottle and into the beaker.

The water is clear because the plant roots stop the soil particles from being washed into the beaker.

▲ SOIL EROSION
Soil erosion is when particles of soil are carried away by running water. Pouring water into these bottles shows how soil erosion happens on different soils. The roots of the plants in the bottle on the left help to keep soil particles in place, avoiding erosion. Debris and dead leaves in the central bottle help to reduce erosion but do not prevent it completely. In the bottle on the right, the loose, exposed soil erodes quickly and particles soon wash away.

Water is poured onto each bottle in a fine shower from a watering can.

SOIL WITH DEBRIS

LOOSE SOIL

Some soil particles are washed into this beaker, but most are held back by the dead leaves.

Lots of soil particles are washed into the beaker from the loose soil.

SOIL DRAINAGE

The type of soil in an area depends on the rocks and plant materials that form it. Particle sizes in the soil determine how well water drains away. A soil with plenty of humus holds water like a sponge, sandy soil drains quickly, and clay soil drains poorly. The minerals and drainage of the soil affect the kinds of plants that can grow there.

PEAT BOGS
In low-lying, poorly drained areas, partially decayed plants build up into thick wet layers called peat. The water-logged soil slows down the rotting of dead material. This creates an acid environment where specialist plants such as sphagnum moss may thrive.

CLAYPANS
The very fine particles of clay hold water and stop it from soaking away. When heated by the sun, however, the clay soil dries quickly and bakes to a hard rock-like consistency. Claypans are low-lying areas with high clay content that do not drain well.

SAND DUNES
Sand dunes have very little rotted plant material to absorb water and hold the tiny particles together. This means that only a few hardy plants that can tolerate drought, such as marram grass, can grow. The roots of these plants help keep the dune together.

HOW SOIL WORKS

Soil is more than the dirt beneath our feet: it is a mixture of tiny particles of rock, and fragments of dead plants and animals. Although it looks lifeless, soil contains billions of living microbes, animals, and plants that depend on it for water and nutrition.

▶ SOIL TESTING
When plants and animals die, fragments of their bodies rot to form a natural compost called humus, which mixes with particles of rock to create soil. These rock particles are called sand, silt, or clay depending on their size. The composition of soil can be seen by mixing it with water.

Dead animals and plants decompose and release minerals into the soil.

Plants absorb water and minerals from the soil through their roots.

Air gaps in the soil provide oxygen for roots and other living things.

Roots anchor plants to the ground and help to hold soil together, preventing it from being washed away.

SOIL
Living things help to create soil as well as depending on it for nutrition. Microbes, animals, and plant roots live in the spaces between rock particles using the nutrients released from the humus. Some plants thrive where nutrition is limited, while others need a rich soil.

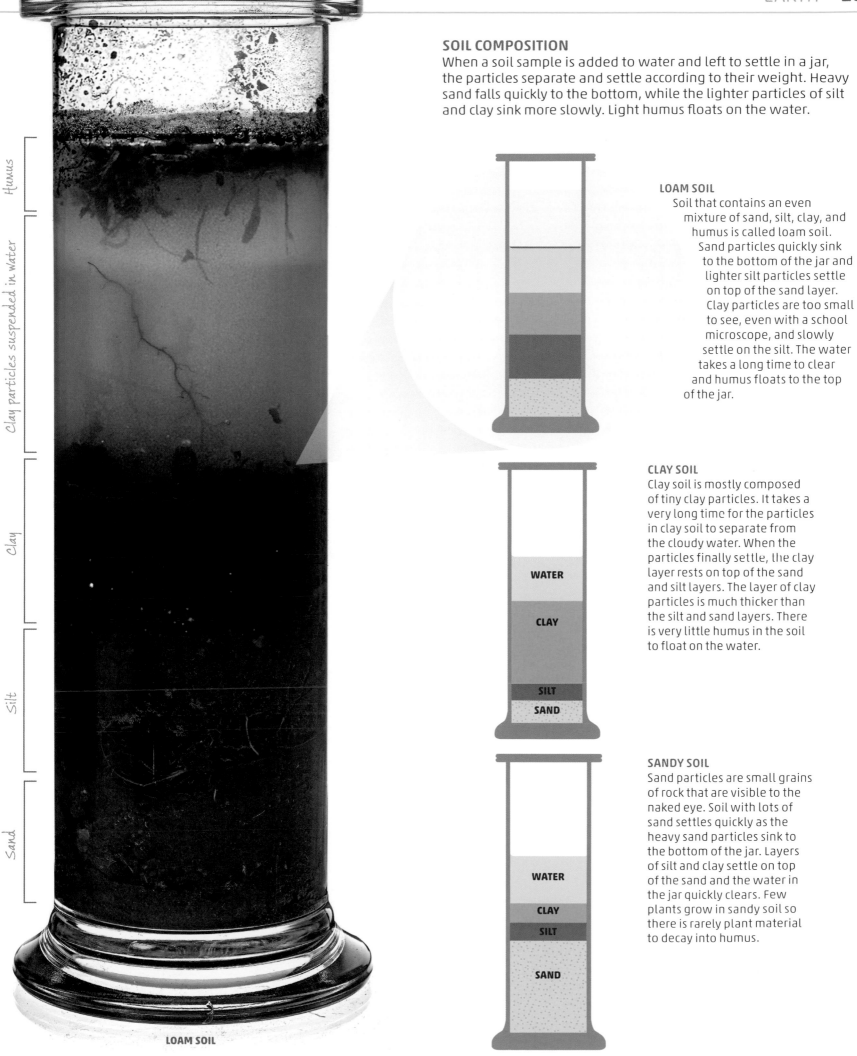

SOIL COMPOSITION

When a soil sample is added to water and left to settle in a jar, the particles separate and settle according to their weight. Heavy sand falls quickly to the bottom, while the lighter particles of silt and clay sink more slowly. Light humus floats on the water.

LOAM SOIL

Soil that contains an even mixture of sand, silt, clay, and humus is called loam soil. Sand particles quickly sink to the bottom of the jar and lighter silt particles settle on top of the sand layer. Clay particles are too small to see, even with a school microscope, and slowly settle on the silt. The water takes a long time to clear and humus floats to the top of the jar.

CLAY SOIL

Clay soil is mostly composed of tiny clay particles. It takes a very long time for the particles in clay soil to separate from the cloudy water. When the particles finally settle, the clay layer rests on top of the sand and silt layers. The layer of clay particles is much thicker than the silt and sand layers. There is very little humus in the soil to float on the water.

WATER

CLAY

SILT

SAND

SANDY SOIL

Sand particles are small grains of rock that are visible to the naked eye. Soil with lots of sand settles quickly as the heavy sand particles sink to the bottom of the jar. Layers of silt and clay settle on top of the sand and the water in the jar quickly clears. Few plants grow in sandy soil so there is rarely plant material to decay into humus.

WATER

CLAY

SILT

SAND

Humus

Clay particles suspended in water

Clay

Silt

Sand

LOAM SOIL

HOW GLACIERS WORK

Over centuries, the vast amount of snow that builds up in icy polar regions or high in mountains freezes solid to form huge lumps of ice called glaciers. These gradually move under their own weight, carving out valleys and eroding the surface of the land, carrying rocky debris along with them.

GLACIAL LANDFORMS

The weight of a glacier is heavy enough to scrape away the rocks beneath it. The erosion caused by the movement of a glacier can change the shape of the land, making valleys wider and deeper. As a glacier moves it pushes rocks along in front of it, leaving behind banks of stones called moraines when it melts.

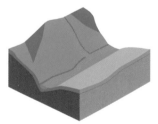

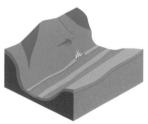

V-SHAPED RIVER VALLEY
As a river flows, it carves a narrow channel. The river's banks gradually erode, producing a valley with a V-shape.

GLACIAL EROSION
A glacier travels down the valley. The ice erodes the sides of the valley, carving it into a wider and deeper shape.

U-SHAPED VALLEY
After thousands of years the glacier melts, leaving behind a U-shaped valley, with a flat floor and steep sides.

MELTING GLACIERS

Global warming caused by polluting gases in the atmosphere is making glaciers melt faster in certain parts of the world. Meltwater from glaciers flows into the ocean, where it adds to the total volume of water, raising sea levels. Scientists think that higher sea levels could threaten many towns and cities that lie along coastlines.

◄ **MOUNTAIN GLACIER**
Glaciers can grow to enormous sizes – up to 1.5 km (0.9 miles) thick – and, across the world, they collectively lock up 99 per cent of the Earth's fresh water. Most glaciers are concentrated in the Arctic and Antarctic where they make up huge ice sheets that cover the land, but they are also found in high mountain ranges where snow gathers. This image shows the Briksdal glacier in the mountains of Norway.

HOW A GLACIER FORMS
Glaciers are made when snow accumulates faster than it melts. This means that multiple layers of snow can build on top of each other. It can take hundreds or even millions of years for glaciers to form this way.

Snow falls and builds up in layers.

1 ACCUMULATION
When conditions are cold enough, falling snow gathers without melting. This may happen high in the mountains. The weight of the new snow on top compacts the snow underneath, which compresses into solid ice.

Solid, moving ice

2 FLOW
The block of compacted snow and ice gradually moves downhill under the pull of gravity. It can cover about 1 m (3 ft) every day. The sides of the glacier scrape against the land and lumps of rock can be carried along with it, trapped in the ice.

Melting ice

3 ABLATION
When the glacier gets further down the mountain and begins to warm up, its edges start to melt. The area where this happens is called the ablation zone and it is often marked by the rocky debris released from the melting ice.

HOW THE WATER CYCLE WORKS

The total amount of water on the Earth stays about the same, but water changes states when it evaporates or freezes. This means water is always moving between the oceans, the air, and the land as it gets recycled over and over again.

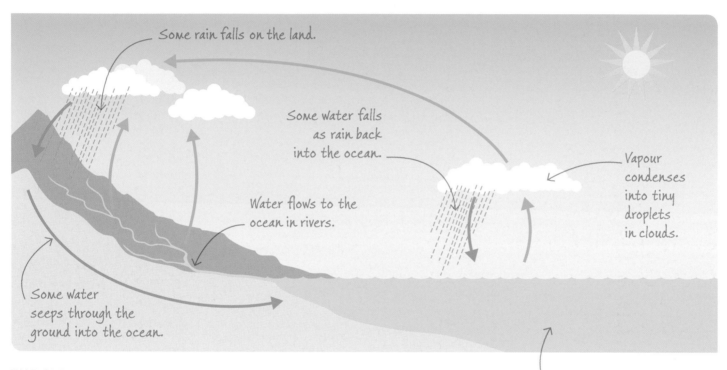

Some rain falls on the land.

Some water falls as rain back into the ocean.

Water flows to the ocean in rivers.

Vapour condenses into tiny droplets in clouds.

Some water seeps through the ground into the ocean.

THE GLOBAL WATER CYCLE
The global water cycle is driven by the Sun's heat, which evaporates water to make vapour in the air. The vapour condenses into tiny droplets in clouds, which fall as rain or snow. Some water collects into rivers and some seeps underground, but all water is eventually recycled back to the ocean.

Most of the water vapour in the air comes from evaporated water from the ocean.

TRANSPIRATION
Water vapour in the air also comes from water that evaporates from the leaves of plants. This process is called transpiration. So much water vapour is given off by the trees in a rainforest that it creates low clouds that gather in rainforest valleys.

▶ A MINI WATER CYCLE
The water cycle can be shown on a very small scale in a glass bowl with a miniature ocean, an island of stones, and an atmosphere sealed with cellophane. The ice on the cellophane helps to condense water that has evaporated under the heat of the lamp. The condensation drips like rain into a river, trickling down the rock, and back into the ocean-like pool.

Ice on the cellophane cools the rising vapour, making it condense into droplets.

A lamp warms the water to make it evaporate.

A sheet of cellophane keeps the water vapour trapped inside.

When cooled water drops grow big enough, they fall under the effect of gravity, just like rain.

Water evaporates from the pool of water into the air, forming water vapour.

Falling drops collect on the rock and trickle back to the pool of water at the bottom of the bowl.

IGUAZU FALLS

The Iguazu river flows over a 300-million-year-old volcanic rock, flattened by erosion, and pours over the edge. At peak flow, more than 10 million litres (17.5 million pints) of water per second plunge down the 70 m (230 ft) drop of Iguazu Falls, on the border of Argentina and Brazil. Fresh water like this accounts for less than three per cent of Earth's water, which is mostly found as salt water in the oceans.

HOW WEATHER WORKS

Weather refers to the way that the atmosphere, the layer of gases surrounding the Earth, is behaving at any particular time and place. Changes in humidity, temperature, and air pressure (the weight of the air resting on the Earth) influence the weather on the ground. The average weather pattern in different parts of the world is called climate. In general, climates are warmer near the equator and colder at the poles.

▶ **EXTREME WEATHER**

Storms can happen when conditions in the atmosphere are disturbed. They are especially likely when the air pressure is unstable. Storms cause strong winds, heavy rain, and lightning strikes. Extreme weather can damage property, cause flooding, and even threaten lives.

WEATHER CONDITIONS

As the Sun's energy heats different parts of the Earth it influences the way that air moves and causes changes in atmospheric pressure that affect the weather. As air descends, it causes high pressure. Air flowing upwards causes low pressure.

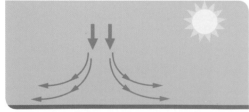

HIGH PRESSURE
In high-pressure areas the descending air is dry and causes clear, sunny, settled weather. Winds are likely to be very light.

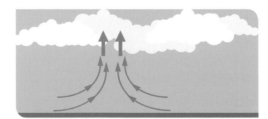

LOW PRESSURE
As air flows into a region of low pressure, it is forced upwards and begins to cool. Its moisture then condenses into rain clouds.

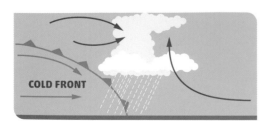

COLD FRONT
When heavier cold air advances into lighter warm air, it pushes the warm air upwards, causing it to condense and form rain clouds.

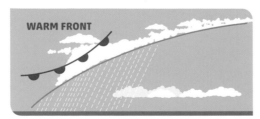

WARM FRONT
As advancing warm air rises above cold air it condenses to form light rain or fog. Behind the front is an area of warmer, high-pressure air.

WHY LIGHTNING STRIKES

Storm clouds are filled with ice crystals and droplets of water that form when rising water vapour condenses in the air. As these tumble about in the moving air, they create a build-up of static electricity (see pages 156–157) that can discharge as a bolt of lightning.

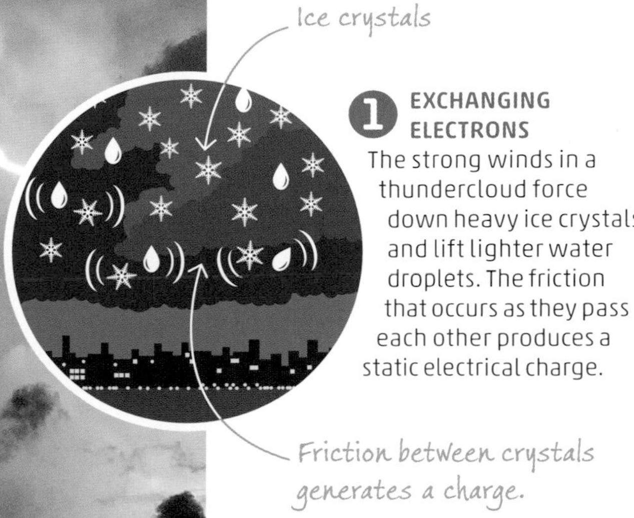

Ice crystals

1 EXCHANGING ELECTRONS

The strong winds in a thundercloud force down heavy ice crystals and lift lighter water droplets. The friction that occurs as they pass each other produces a static electrical charge.

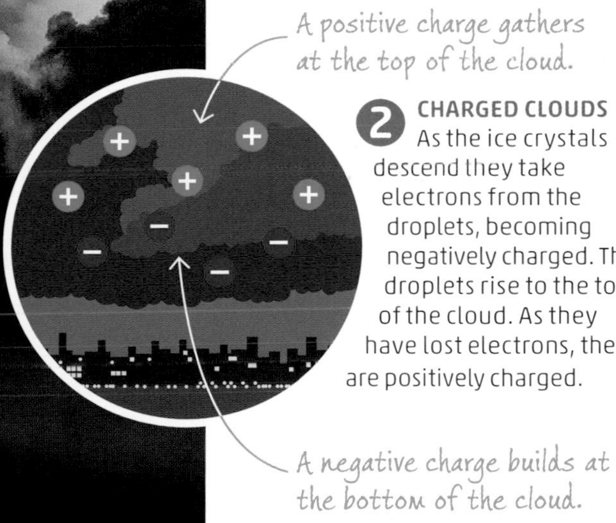

Friction between crystals generates a charge.

A positive charge gathers at the top of the cloud.

2 CHARGED CLOUDS

As the ice crystals descend they take electrons from the droplets, becoming negatively charged. The droplets rise to the top of the cloud. As they have lost electrons, they are positively charged.

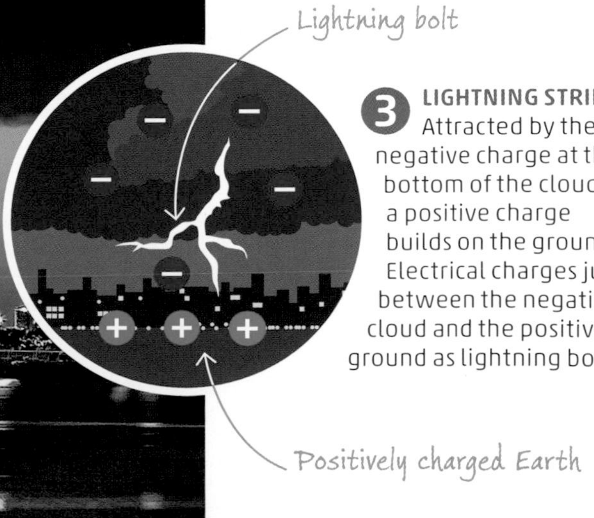

A negative charge builds at the bottom of the cloud.

Lightning bolt

3 LIGHTNING STRIKE

Attracted by the negative charge at the bottom of the cloud, a positive charge builds on the ground. Electrical charges jump between the negative cloud and the positive ground as lightning bolts.

Positively charged Earth

HOW THE GREENHOUSE EFFECT WORKS

Gases in the atmosphere, including carbon dioxide, methane, and water vapour, help to keep Earth warm. Heat from the Sun is trapped by these gases, known as greenhouse gases, in a process called the greenhouse effect. Without greenhouse gases Earth would be too cold to support life.

Some radiation reflects off the glass.

❶

Radiation comes from a source of heat and light.

Plants use some of the incoming light for photosynthesis.

❷

Stones, soil, and plants warm up as they absorb the radiation.

▶ **GREENHOUSE BOTTLE GARDEN**

A bottle garden is a model of how Earth's greenhouse effect works. The Sun's rays, which contain a mixture of ultraviolet, light, and infrared radiation (see pages 136–137), enter the bottle garden and are absorbed by the soil and plants inside. These warm up, and warm the air above them. The glass sides of the bottle stop the warm air escaping, and so the whole bottle warms up. Unlike the glass of the bottle garden, the greenhouse gases around Earth are mixed throughout the atmosphere, they do not form a distinct layer.

❶ **INCOMING RAYS**
The Sun's rays hit the bottle garden. Some are reflected or absorbed by the glass, but the rest pass through. In a similar way, most of the sunlight that hits Earth's atmosphere passes straight through.

❷ **WARMING UP THE SOIL**
The radiation is absorbed by the soil, water, and other things inside the bottle, which warm up. In the real world, energy from the Sun is absorbed by the land and oceans, which get warmer.

❸ **EMITTING INFRARED**
Like all warm objects, the soil emits infrared radiation. This type of radiation can be absorbed by greenhouse gases in the air, so the air warms up. This happens in the bottle garden and in the real world.

Some heat escapes through the glass.

Trapped heat warms the air, plants, and soil inside the bottle.

④

The warm garden emits heat.

③

⑤

GLOBAL WARMING
Greenhouse gases occur naturally in the atmosphere, but human activity, such as burning fossil fuels that produce carbon dioxide and farming cattle that produce methane, is adding to their levels. This means more heat is trapped on Earth, causing global warming – the increase of Earth's average temperature.

Shrinking polar ice cap

1980

2018

MELTING ICE
Global warming is causing the sheets of ice that cover the Arctic and Antarctic to melt. When ice on land melts, it increases the amount of water in the oceans, so sea levels rise, threatening coastal communities.

SEVERE WEATHER
Our weather depends on the temperature of the atmosphere and oceans. Global warming is likely to increase the number of severe events such as hurricanes, flooding, and heatwaves.

④ **INFRARED ESCAPES**
Some of the infrared is able to pass back out through the glass, and warms the air beyond the bottle garden. On Earth, some of the infrared emitted by the land and sea escapes into space.

⑤ **WARMING THE ATMOSPHERE**
The glass bottle traps the warm air. In the atmosphere, the warm gases radiate more infrared, and some of this is absorbed by the land and sea again. Earth and the atmosphere both get warmer.

HOW SEASONS WORK

Each year the temperate regions of the Earth (the areas above and below the Tropics) go through a cycle of seasons. Different areas of the Earth experience the seasons at different times of year. Regions above the equator (the northern hemisphere) go through summer when it is winter in regions below the equator (the southern hemisphere) and vice versa.

▶ ORBITING THE SUN

Earth travels around the Sun in an orbit that takes 365.25 days. At the same time, it rotates on its axis (an imaginary line between the North and South poles) every 24 hours, causing the change from day to night. This axis is tilted at an angle of 23.5 degrees, which means that different hemispheres tilt towards the Sun at different times of year. When a hemisphere tilts towards the Sun it goes through summer. This model uses a lamp to represent the Sun and two globes to show how the tilt of the Earth affects the seasons.

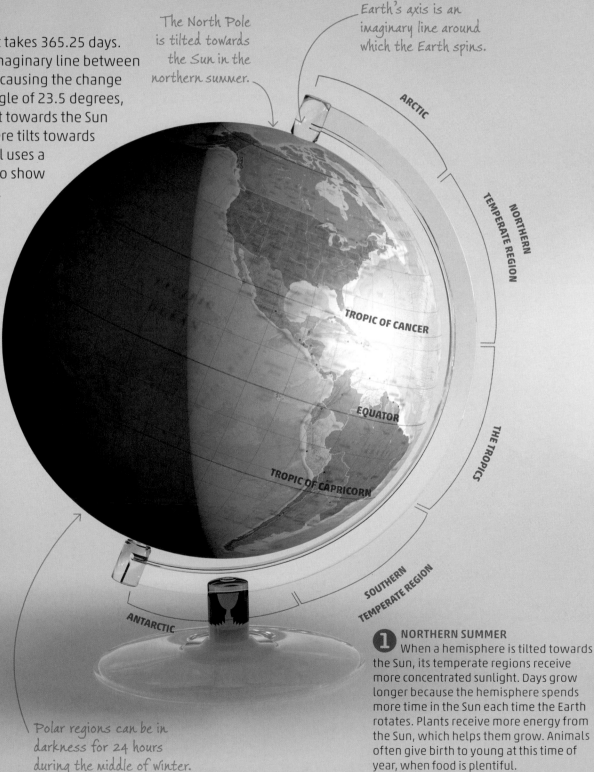

The North Pole is tilted towards the Sun in the northern summer.

Earth's axis is an imaginary line around which the Earth spins.

ARCTIC

NORTHERN TEMPERATE REGION

TROPIC OF CANCER

EQUATOR

THE TROPICS

TROPIC OF CAPRICORN

SOUTHERN TEMPERATE REGION

ANTARCTIC

Sunlight is less concentrated when it spreads over a larger area.

Sunlight is more concentrated when it spreads over a smaller area.

CONCENTRATED SUNLIGHT

The Sun always provides the same amount of energy, but when its rays hit the Earth's surface at an angle, that energy is spread out over a larger area. This means that the energy is less concentrated – the surface receives less solar energy per square metre.

Polar regions can be in darkness for 24 hours during the middle of winter.

① NORTHERN SUMMER
When a hemisphere is tilted towards the Sun, its temperate regions receive more concentrated sunlight. Days grow longer because the hemisphere spends more time in the Sun each time the Earth rotates. Plants receive more energy from the Sun, which helps them grow. Animals often give birth to young at this time of year, when food is plentiful.

PATH AROUND THE SUN

As the Earth orbits around the Sun, the hemisphere that is tilted towards the Sun changes. This happens because, even though the Earth is moving, the tilt of its axis always remains fixed. It is summer in the hemisphere that is tilting towards the Sun and winter in the hemisphere that is tilting away from it. In March and September the axis is not pointing towards the Sun at all so day and night are of equal length in both hemispheres.

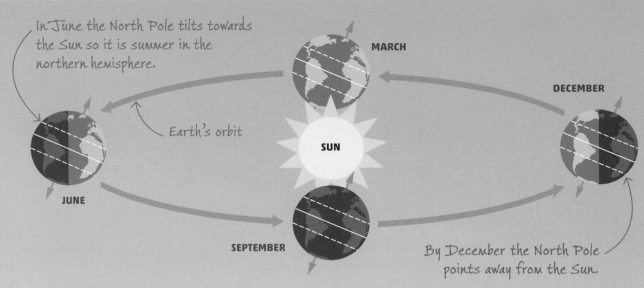

In June the North Pole tilts towards the Sun so it is summer in the northern hemisphere.

MARCH

DECEMBER

Earth's orbit

SUN

JUNE

SEPTEMBER

By December the North Pole points away from the Sun.

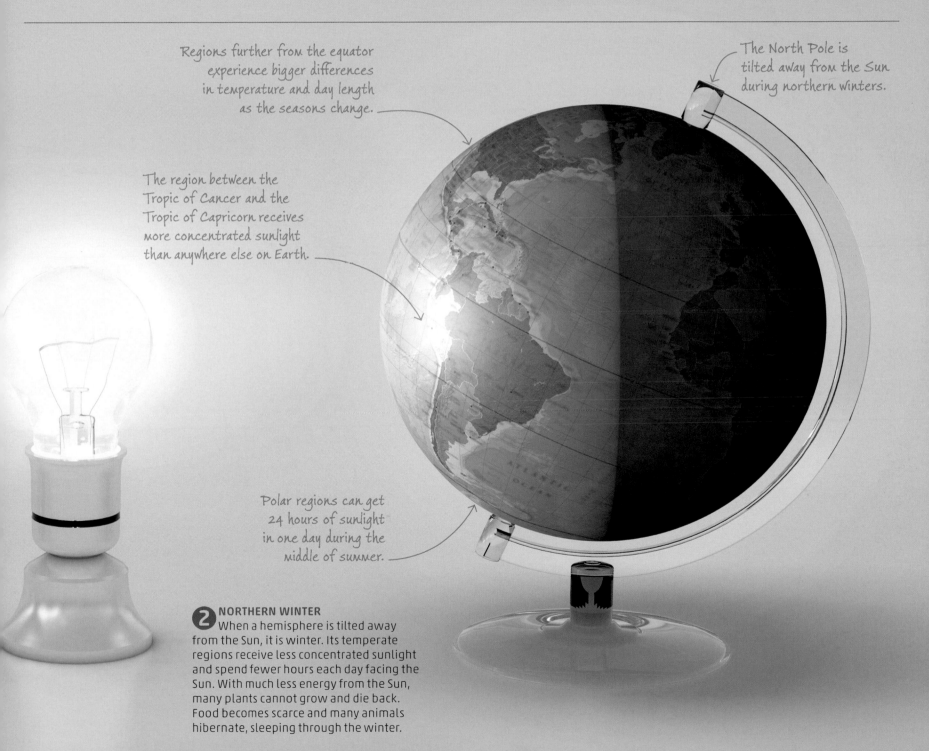

Regions further from the equator experience bigger differences in temperature and day length as the seasons change.

The North Pole is tilted away from the Sun during northern winters.

The region between the Tropic of Cancer and the Tropic of Capricorn receives more concentrated sunlight than anywhere else on Earth.

Polar regions can get 24 hours of sunlight in one day during the middle of summer.

❷ NORTHERN WINTER

When a hemisphere is tilted away from the Sun, it is winter. Its temperate regions receive less concentrated sunlight and spend fewer hours each day facing the Sun. With much less energy from the Sun, many plants cannot grow and die back. Food becomes scarce and many animals hibernate, sleeping through the winter.

HOW THE SUN WORKS

The Sun is a colossal ball of hot, electrically charged gas known as plasma, fuelled by nuclear reactions constantly taking place in its core. The Earth and other planets orbit the Sun, which is the centre of our Solar System.

The corona is a glowing layer of plasma surrounding the Sun.

THE STRUCTURE OF THE SUN

The Sun has several layers and no solid surface. The hottest of these layers is the core, where nuclear reactions produce the energy that powers the Sun. Energy from the core travels through the radiative and convective zones to the solar atmosphere. This part of the Sun is made up of the photosphere (the layer visible to the naked eye), the chromosphere, and the corona.

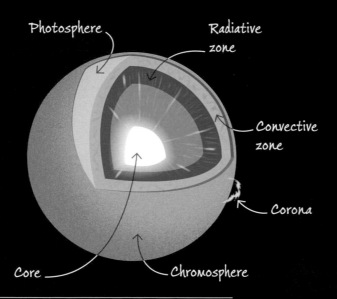

Photosphere

Radiative zone

Convective zone

Corona

Core

Chromosphere

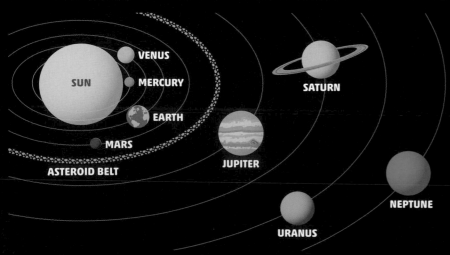

VENUS

SUN

MERCURY

EARTH

MARS

ASTEROID BELT

SATURN

JUPITER

NEPTUNE

URANUS

THE SUN'S FAMILY

The Sun is the centre of our Solar System: a system of eight planets and other objects held together by the pull of the Sun's gravity. The planets follow roughly circular orbits around the Sun. The innermost planet (Mercury) travels around the Sun in 88 Earth days, and the outermost (Neptune) takes 165 Earth years to complete its orbit. Other objects in the Solar System include asteroids and dwarf planets such as Pluto.

This coronal mass ejection occurred in August 2012. These events can send billions of tonnes of material racing through space.

Coronal loops are hot, bright arcs that rise above the Sun's surface. Plasma flows along these loops.

▶ SOLAR OUTBURST
This UV image of the Sun shows the corona as a bright, shifting layer of plasma. Sometimes, enormous bursts of hot plasma called coronal mass ejections are flung from the Sun's surface into space. These ejections can be so powerful that they interfere with electrical equipment on Earth.

HOW
STARS
FORM

New stars form when huge clouds of hydrogen and helium collapse. Over millions of years gravity causes the material to clump together, becoming hotter and denser. When the young star's core is hot and dense enough nuclear fusion begins: hydrogen nuclei are crushed together, forming helium and releasing huge amounts of energy, and the star begins to shine.

▶ STELLAR NURSERIES
Clusters of stars form in enormous clouds known as "stellar nurseries". The bright blue stars in this image are a cluster of young stars, named NGC 602, located 200,000 light-years away from Earth. Radiation from the new stars is eroding the cloud that gave birth to them and triggering more star formation on its edges.

TYPES OF STAR
Stars that burn hydrogen fuel in their core are all called main sequence stars, but they vary in their size and brightness. When stars begin to run out of fuel they stop being main sequence stars. An average-sized star, like the Sun, expands into a red giant as it dies and then shrinks to a white dwarf. A large star may grow into a supergiant and then end in a dramatic explosion called a supernova.

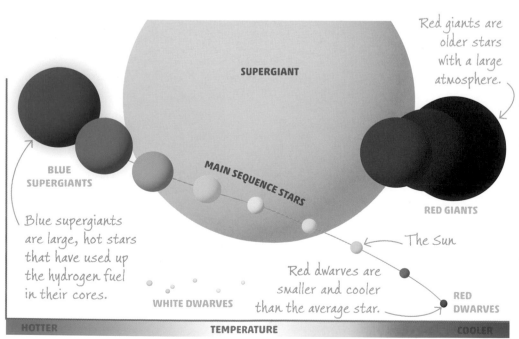

Red giants are older stars with a large atmosphere.

SUPERGIANT

BLUE SUPERGIANTS

MAIN SEQUENCE STARS

RED GIANTS

Blue supergiants are large, hot stars that have used up the hydrogen fuel in their cores.

The Sun

Red dwarves are smaller and cooler than the average star.

WHITE DWARVES

RED DWARVES

BRIGHTER

LUMINOSITY

DIMMER

HOTTER　　　　TEMPERATURE　　　　COOLER

STAR BIRTH

The vast, seemingly empty space between the stars and galaxies actually contains scattered particles of gas and dust. In places where this material clumps together, it eventually forms huge, dense clouds called nebulae. If a trigger event disturbs the nebula, stars may begin to form.

1 NEBULA
A nebula is a dense, cold cloud made mainly of hydrogen. When a nebula is disturbed, for example by a supernova explosion or an encounter with a passing star, it may be destabilized and start to collapse.

Nebulae are huge clouds of gas and dust.

2 PROTOSTAR
When a nebula collapses it breaks into fragments. Inside these fragments hot, dense cores called protostars form. The protostars grow by pulling in material from the cloud around them, getting ever denser and hotter.

Gravity pulls material into the protostar's core.

3 SPINNING DISC
The growing mass at the centre draws in more and more material. The surrounding gas and dust start to rotate around the protostar, flattening into a spinning disc.

The spinning disc creates strong winds that form large gas jets.

4 NEW STAR
Eventually the heat and pressure in the core are so great that nuclear fusion begins. The energy released balances the inward pull of gravity and makes the star stable. It may shine for billions of years, until all its hydrogen is used up.

Remaining material may become planets and moons.

ANDROMEDA

A galaxy is a vast collection of stars, gas, and dust, held together by gravity. Andromeda is the nearest major galaxy to our own Milky Way, and is visible from Earth as a bright smudge in the night sky. At 2.5 million light-years away, it is the most distant object that can be seen with the naked eye. Viewed through a powerful telescope it comes sharply into view. It is a spiral galaxy – with a bright centre and spiral arms – thought to contain about one trillion stars.

There are many different ways of **analyzing the world** around us – from **classifying elements** and uncovering the workings of **atoms** to tracking the **history of Earth**, how **life** evolved, and how the **human body** functions. Scientific **laws** describe the way the Universe works, while **standard units of measurement** allow scientists to collect accurate results.

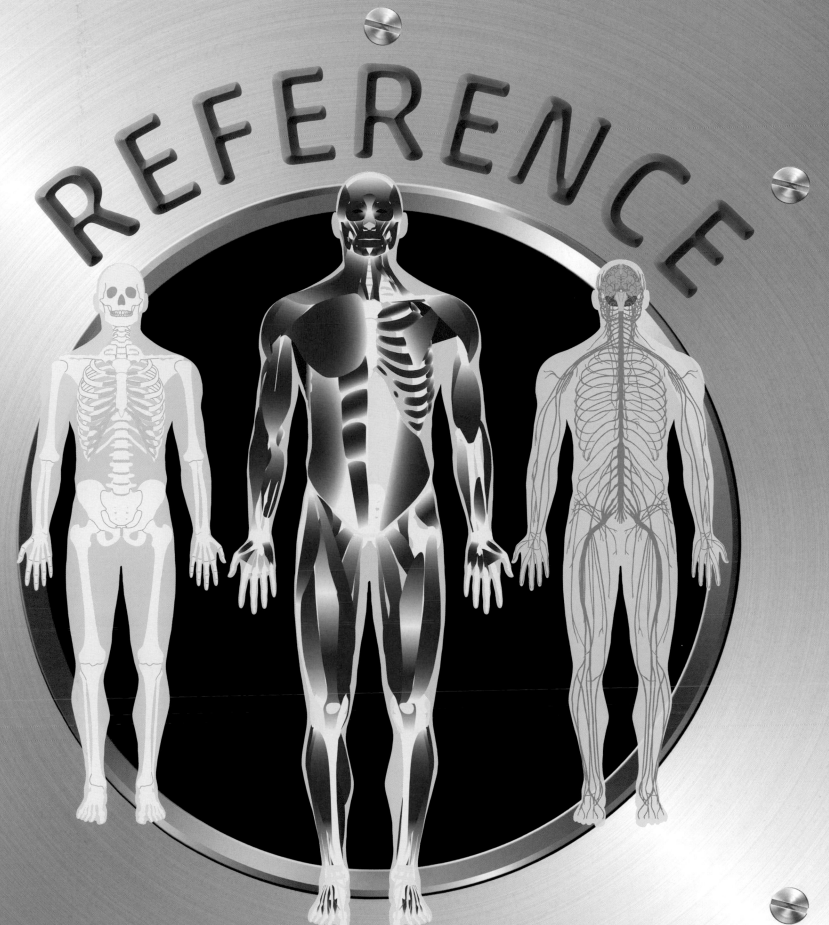

REFERENCE

THE PERIODIC TABLE

The periodic table is used to organize all the elements known to science. An element is the purest form of a substance, which means it cannot be separated into different substances. The table has 118 elements – 92 are found in nature and 26 have been artificially made.

SORTING THE ELEMENTS

Elements in the periodic table are arranged in rows and columns depending on the number of protons and electrons they have. Arranged in this way, scientists can see patterns because elements in the same column (known as a group) react in a similar way. The periodic table was first devised by Russian chemist Dmitri Mendeleev in 1869.

KEY

- ALKALI METALS
- ALKALINE EARTH METALS
- TRANSITION METALS
- LANTHANIDE METALS
- ACTINIDE METALS
- OTHER METALS
- METALLOIDS
- OTHER NON-METALS
- HALOGENS
- NOBLE GASES

Hydrogen has the simplest atoms of any element with only one proton and one electron.

1	1.0
H	
HYDROGEN	

Transition metals are good at conducting heat and electricity. Copper is used as wires in electrical items.

3 6.9 **Li** LITHIUM	4 9.0 **Be** BERYLLIUM

11 23.0 **Na** SODIUM	12 24.3 **Mg** MAGNESIUM

19 39.1 **K** POTASSIUM	20 40.1 **Ca** CALCIUM	21 45.0 **Sc** SCANDIUM	22 47.9 **Ti** TITANIUM	23 50.9 **V** VANADIUM	24 52.0 **Cr** CHROMIUM	25 54.9 **Mn** MANGANESE	26 55.9 **Fe** IRON	27 58.9 **Co** COBALT	28 58.7 **Ni** NICKEL	29 63.6 **Cu** COPPER	30 65.4 **Zn** ZINC
37 85.5 **Rb** RUBIDIUM	38 87.6 **Sr** STRONTIUM	39 88.9 **Y** YTTRIUM	40 91.2 **Zr** ZIRCONIUM	41 92.9 **Nb** NIOBIUM	42 95.9 **Mo** MOLYBDENUM	43 (96) **Tc** TECHNETIUM	44 101.1 **Ru** RUTHENIUM	45 102.9 **Rh** RHODIUM	46 106.4 **Pd** PALLADIUM	47 107.9 **Ag** SILVER	48 112.4 **Cd** CADMIUM
55 132.9 **Cs** CAESIUM	56 137.3 **Ba** BARIUM	57-71 **La-Lu**	72 178.5 **Hf** HAFNIUM	73 181.0 **Ta** TANTALUM	74 183.8 **W** TUNGSTEN	75 186.2 **Re** RHENIUM	76 190.2 **Os** OSMIUM	77 192.2 **Ir** IRIDIUM	78 195.1 **Pt** PLATINUM	79 197.0 **Au** GOLD	80 200.6 **Hg** MERCURY
87 (223) **Fr** FRANCIUM	88 (226) **Ra** RADIUM	89-103 **Ac-Lr**	104 (261) **Rf** RUTHERFORDIUM	105 (262) **Db** DUBNIUM	106 (266) **Sg** SEABORGIUM	107 (264) **Bh** BOHRIUM	108 (277) **Hs** HASSIUM	109 (268) **Mt** MEITNERIUM	110 (281) **Ds** DARMSTADTIUM	111 (272) **Rg** ROENTGENIUM	112 (285) **Cn** COPERNICIUM

The lanthanides and actinides (rare earth metals) are too long to fit on the table so are shown expanded at the bottom.

57 138.9 **La** LANTHANUM	58 140.1 **Ce** CERIUM	59 140.9 **Pr** PRASEODYMIUM	60 144.2 **Nd** NEODYMIUM	61 (145) **Pm** PROMETHIUM	62 (150.4) **Sm** SAMARIUM	63 152.0 **Eu** EUROPIUM	64 157.3 **Gd** GADOLINIUM	65 158.9 **Tb** TERBIUM
89 (227) **Ac** ACTINIUM	90 232.0 **Th** THORIUM	91 231.0 **Pa** PROTACTINIUM	92 238.0 **U** URANIUM	93 (237) **Np** NEPTUNIUM	94 (244) **Pu** PLUTONIUM	95 (243) **Am** AMERICIUM	96 (247) **Cm** CURIUM	97 (247) **Bk** BERKELIUM

ELEMENTAL BLOCKS

The periodic table is divided into blocks containing elements that have similar properties. From left to right the elements change from solid metals to gases. The most well-known metals are in the largest block, the transition metals.

Hydrogen is a gas, but it has one proton so it is placed in group 1.

The first two groups, excluding hydrogen, are reactive metals.

The rare earth metals are below the first group of transition metals.

Transition metals are in the centre.

The last six groups of the table are a block of mainly non-metals.

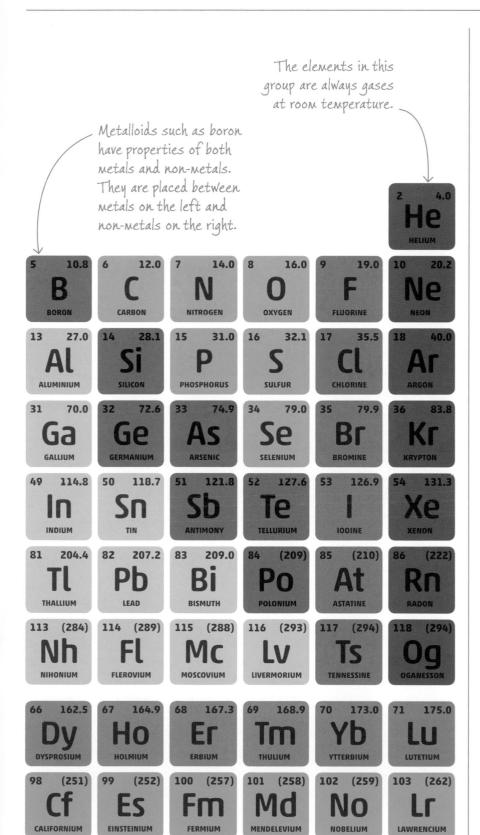

Metalloids such as boron have properties of both metals and non-metals. They are placed between metals on the left and non-metals on the right.

The elements in this group are always gases at room temperature.

					2 4.0 **He** HELIUM
5 10.8 **B** BORON	6 12.0 **C** CARBON	7 14.0 **N** NITROGEN	8 16.0 **O** OXYGEN	9 19.0 **F** FLUORINE	10 20.2 **Ne** NEON
13 27.0 **Al** ALUMINIUM	14 28.1 **Si** SILICON	15 31.0 **P** PHOSPHORUS	16 32.1 **S** SULFUR	17 35.5 **Cl** CHLORINE	18 40.0 **Ar** ARGON
31 70.0 **Ga** GALLIUM	32 72.6 **Ge** GERMANIUM	33 74.9 **As** ARSENIC	34 79.0 **Se** SELENIUM	35 79.9 **Br** BROMINE	36 83.8 **Kr** KRYPTON
49 114.8 **In** INDIUM	50 118.7 **Sn** TIN	51 121.8 **Sb** ANTIMONY	52 127.6 **Te** TELLURIUM	53 126.9 **I** IODINE	54 131.3 **Xe** XENON
81 204.4 **Tl** THALLIUM	82 207.2 **Pb** LEAD	83 209.0 **Bi** BISMUTH	84 (209) **Po** POLONIUM	85 (210) **At** ASTATINE	86 (222) **Rn** RADON
113 (284) **Nh** NIHONIUM	114 (289) **Fl** FLEROVIUM	115 (288) **Mc** MOSCOVIUM	116 (293) **Lv** LIVERMORIUM	117 (294) **Ts** TENNESSINE	118 (294) **Og** OGANESSON

66 162.5 **Dy** DYSPROSIUM	67 164.9 **Ho** HOLMIUM	68 167.3 **Er** ERBIUM	69 168.9 **Tm** THULIUM	70 173.0 **Yb** YTTERBIUM	71 175.0 **Lu** LUTETIUM
98 (251) **Cf** CALIFORNIUM	99 (252) **Es** EINSTEINIUM	100 (257) **Fm** FERMIUM	101 (258) **Md** MENDELEVIUM	102 (259) **No** NOBELIUM	103 (262) **Lr** LAWRENCIUM

ELEMENTAL TILES

Each tile shows an element's chemical symbol in the centre. The atomic number shows how many protons an element has. The atoms of an element always have the same number of protons, but the number of neutrons can vary. Versions of an atom with different numbers of neutrons are known as isotopes. Relative atomic mass is the average amount of all an element's protons and neutrons.

Atomic number: the number of protons

19	39.1
K	
POTASSIUM	

Relative atomic mass is the average mass of all an element's isotopes.

PERIODS

The seven rows of elements running from left to right across the table are called periods. Moving along a period, the atomic number increases by one, so each element have one more electron than the element on its left. The number of electron shells (see page 292) in each period remains the same, so, for example, in period 4 all elements have four electron shells.

Atomic number increases by one.

SOME OF THE ELEMENTS IN PERIOD 4

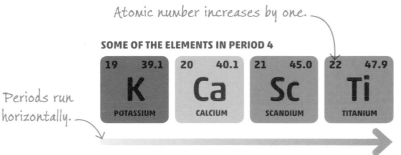

Periods run horizontally.

GROUPS

Columns running from the top to the bottom are known as groups. Elements in a group all have the same number of electrons in their outer shell, even if they have a different number of shells. For example, in group one, all the elements have one electron in their outer shell.

Groups run vertically and elements become larger and heavier the further down the group.

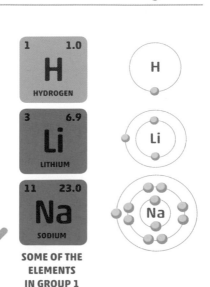

SOME OF THE ELEMENTS IN GROUP 1

ALL ABOUT ATOMS

An atom is the smallest unit of an element and one of the basic units of matter. They are so tiny that 1,000,000 atoms lined up are equal to the width of a human hair. Atoms are made up of even smaller particles called protons, neutrons, and electrons.

ELECTRON SHELLS

An atom is made up of a nucleus of positively charged protons and neutral neutrons, with negatively charged electrons around it. Atoms contain an equal number of positively charged protons and negatively charged electrons, so they have no overall charge. Each element has a different number of protons and electrons. Electrons occupy energy levels or "shells" around the nucleus. Each shell can hold a certain number of electrons before it is full. For example, the first shell can hold two electrons and the second can hold eight. Atoms with partially filled electron shells are less stable. They form bonds with other atoms so that their outermost electron shell is either completely full or empty.

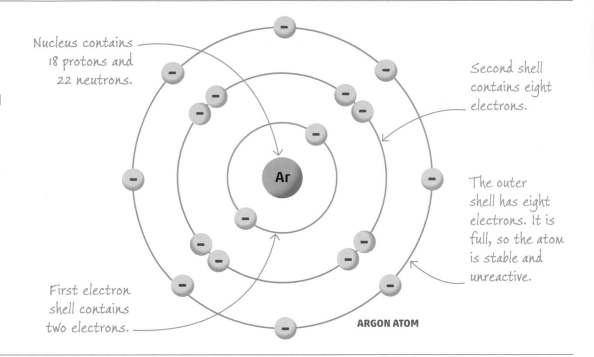

Nucleus contains 18 protons and 22 neutrons.

Second shell contains eight electrons.

The outer shell has eight electrons. It is full, so the atom is stable and unreactive.

First electron shell contains two electrons.

ARGON ATOM

MOLECULES

When two or more atoms join together, they form molecules. Atoms in molecules are held together by covalent bonds – chemical bonds created by the sharing of electrons in the outer shells of atoms, so that each atom has a total of eight electrons in its outer shell. This occurs in most non-metal elements and compounds.

SIMPLE MOLECULES

Simple molecules contain a small number of atoms. The number of bonds an atom can form with other atoms depends on the number of electrons present in the outer shell. Some molecules contain only one type of atom, like this oxygen molecule.

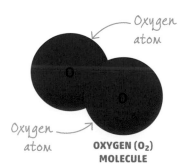

Oxygen atom

Oxygen atom

OXYGEN (O₂) MOLECULE

MACROMOLECULES

Macromolecules are made up of many atoms joined together by covalent bonds. The atoms join in a regular arrangement, but there is no set number of atoms.

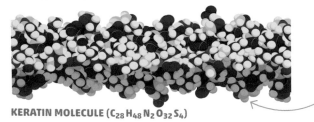

A keratin molecule is made up of lots of atoms from five different elements.

KERATIN MOLECULE ($C_{28}H_{48}N_2O_{32}S_4$)

POLARITY

When two atoms of the same element are joined by covalent bonds, electrons are shared equally between them. When covalent bonds form between atoms of different elements, the shared electrons may be attracted to the nucleus of one atom more than that of the other. As a result, one side of the molecule has a slightly negative charge, while the other has a slightly positive charge. The molecule they form is said to have negative and positive "poles", or "polarity". This is different to ionic bonding, where electrons passed between elements create charged ions that attract each other.

Hydrogen atoms in a water molecule give it positive polarity.

The carbon and hydrogen atoms in butane share electrons fairly equally, so butane is non-polar.

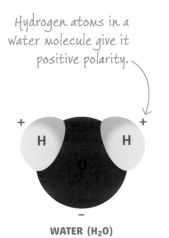

WATER (H_2O)

BUTANE (C_4H_{10})

CHEMICAL FORMULAS AND EQUATIONS

Formulas and equations are used to show what happens to substances in chemical reactions. All elements have a unique symbol. Compounds are represented by formulas made up of these symbols and numbers that denote how much of each element is in a compound. Chemical equations show the changes in the elements and compounds in a reaction. They can be word equations, symbol equations, or represented as diagrams.

WORD	CARBON + OXYGEN	→	CARBON DIOXIDE
SYMBOL	C + O₂	→	CO₂
DIAGRAM	C + O O	→	O C O

IONS

An atom has no overall charge. When an atom loses or gains an electron, it becomes a charged particle called an ion. As electrons have a negative charge of 1^-, if an atom gains an electron, it becomes a negative ion with a charge of 1^-. Gaining two electrons gives it a charge of 2^-. If an atom loses electrons, it becomes a positive ion. Losing one electron results in a charge of 1^+.

HYDROGEN (H)
Neutral atom has one proton and one electron.

HYDROGEN (H⁻)
Negative ion has more electrons than protons.

HYDROGEN (H⁺)
Positive ion has more protons than electrons.

ISOTOPES

While the number of protons in an element's atoms is always the same, the number of neutrons can vary. Atoms that have the same number of protons but different numbers of neutrons are called isotopes. Isotopes of an element all have the same atomic number (the number of protons) but a different atomic mass, as the mass is determined by the number of neutrons and protons in an atom.

HYDROGEN
Also known as hydrogen-1, hydrogen is made up of just one proton and one electron.

DEUTERIUM
Hydrogen-2, or deuterium, is an isotope of hydrogen with one neutron.

TRITIUM
Hydrogen-3, or tritium, is an isotope of hydrogen that has two neutrons.

REDOX REACTIONS

A reduction-oxidation reaction, or redox reaction, is the name given to a chemical reaction where electrons are transferred between two reactants, which can be molecules, atoms, or ions. The reactant that loses electrons is said to be "oxidized", while the reactant that gains electrons is "reduced". The acronym "OILRIG" can be used to remember that "oxidation is loss, reduction is gain". Redox reactions happen all around us, such as when plants use photosynthesis to convert sunlight into food, and cells in the human body convert sugar into energy.

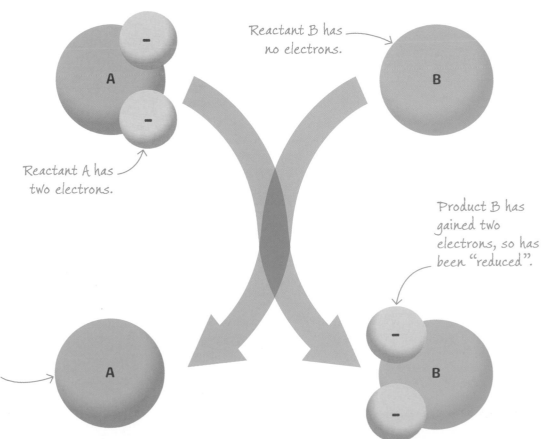

Reactant B has no electrons.

Reactant A has two electrons.

Product B has gained two electrons, so has been "reduced".

Product A has lost its two electrons, so has been "oxidized".

SCIENTIFIC LAWS

A scientific law describes something that is observed to be true every time that it is tested. The well-known laws of science are often named after the scientist who discovered them, and are based on mathematical calculations.

NEWTON'S LAWS OF MOTION

English scientist Isaac Newton published his laws of motion in 1687, in the *Principia Mathematica*. One of the best-known scientific works of all time, it set the direction for physics over the next two centuries. The laws explain the relationship between objects and forces, and how it is complicated by the effects of friction and air resistance.

FIRST LAW OF MOTION

The first law of motion states that any object will continue to remain still, or move in a straight line at a steady speed, unless an external force acts on it. When the forces acting on an object are balanced, there is no change in the way it moves. If the forces are unbalanced, there is a resultant force in one direction, which alters the object's speed or the direction in which it is moving.

The football is motionless.

1 AT REST
A football remains still until it is kicked. The force of gravity acts on the ball, but the ground stops it from moving so it remains at rest. The forces are balanced.

A boot applies force to the football.

2 FORCE APPLIED
When a football is kicked, the forces are unbalanced and the ball starts to move in one direction. The impact of the kick applies a force that accelerates the ball as long as the boot remains in contact with it.

MOTION

A boot stops the football moving.

3 FORCE STOPS MOTION
The ball starts to slow due to the resistance of the air and friction with the ground. It stops when it meets a stationary object (the boot). Once stopped, the forces are balanced again.

SECOND LAW OF MOTION

The second law of motion states that when a force acts on an object, the object will accelerate in the direction of the force. The larger the force, the greater an object's acceleration. The more massive an object is, the greater the force needed to accelerate it.

SMALL FORCE   ACCELERATION

1 SMALL FORCE, SMALL MASS
If you throw an apple, the force causes it to accelerate. Acceleration is the rate the apple's speed is changing over time.

The acceleration doubles

DOUBLE FORCE   ACCELERATION

2 DOUBLE FORCE, SMALL MASS
If you throw the same apple with double the force, the apple will accelerate at twice the rate.

This melon has double the mass of the appple.

DOUBLE FORCE   ACCELERATION

3 DOUBLE FORCE, DOUBLE MASS
If you use the same double force to throw a melon with double the apple's mass, its acceleration will be half that of example 2.

LAW OF CONSERVATION OF MASS
During a chemical reaction, atoms are neither created nor destroyed. Every atom that was part of the reactants is present in the products. This principle is known as the law of conservation of mass, or matter.

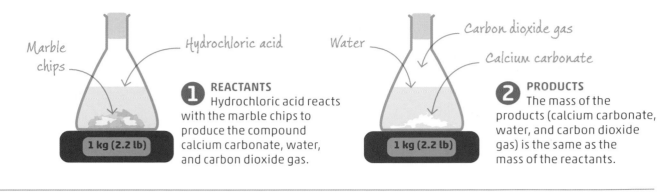

Marble chips — Hydrochloric acid

1 REACTANTS
Hydrochloric acid reacts with the marble chips to produce the compound calcium carbonate, water, and carbon dioxide gas.

Water — Carbon dioxide gas — Calcium carbonate

2 PRODUCTS
The mass of the products (calcium carbonate, water, and carbon dioxide gas) is the same as the mass of the reactants.

1 kg (2.2 lb)

THIRD LAW OF MOTION
The third law of motion says that forces come in pairs. For example, you have weight because Earth's gravity is pulling down on you. You also have gravity, and you are pulling up on Earth, but the effect is too small to notice. Pairs of forces such as this are called action reaction pairs. The forces are always the same kind of force, the same size, and act in opposite directions.

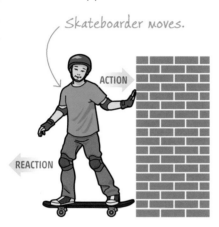

Skateboarder moves.

ACTION

REACTION

ACTION AND REACTION, EXAMPLE 1
If a skateboarder pushes a wall, the wall pushes back with a reaction force that causes the skateboarder to roll away from it.

Skateboarders move in opposite directions.

REACTION   ACTION

ACTION AND REACTION, EXAMPLE 2
If one skateboarder pushes the other, action and reaction cause both skateboarders to roll away from each other.

GAS LAWS
These three main gas laws relate the movements of particles in a gas to its volume, pressure, and temperature, and state how each measure responds when the others change.

BOYLE'S LAW
This law is named after 17th-century Irish chemist Robert Boyle. His law says that if a gas's temperature stays the same, forcing the gas into a smaller volume results in it exerting a higher pressure.

CHARLES'S LAW
This gas law, named after French scientist Jacques Charles, says the temperature of a gas is proportional to its volume. So if the gas is held in a container with an adjustable volume – a gas syringe, for example – increasing the gas's temperature results in an increase in its volume.

GAY-LUSSAC'S LAW
Named after French scientist Joseph Louis Gay-Lussac, this law states that for a fixed volume of gas, pressure is proportional to the temperature. This means that when a gas's temperature rises, the pressure will also increase. An increase in its pressure will cause its temperature to rise too.

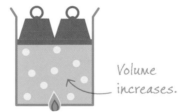
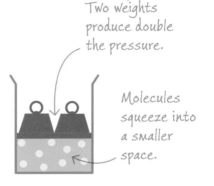
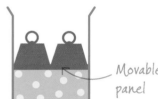
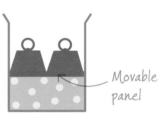
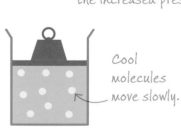
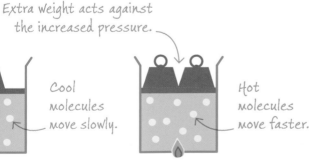

Two weights produce double the pressure.

Weight produces pressure.

Molecules squeeze into a smaller space.

EVENLY SPACED
Gas molecules spread out evenly to fill the container. The force exerted on an area (its pressure) is caused by the molecules hitting the sides.

PRESSURE
Reducing the volume gives the molecules less room to move. They hit the sides more frequently, which increases the pressure.

Movable panel

Volume increases.

TEMPERATURE
Temperature is a measure of the motion of a gas's particles. Increasing the temperature of a gas increases the speed at which the particles move.

MORE MOTION
Heat makes molecules move faster, hitting the sides harder and more often. If one side is able to move, the hits will push it outwards, increasing volume.

Extra weight acts against the increased pressure.

Cool molecules move slowly.

Hot molecules move faster.

FEWER COLLISIONS
In a cool gas, molecules move slowly, hitting the sides of the container infrequently. These few, weak collisions create a low gas pressure.

MORE COLLISIONS
As the gas heats up, the molecules move faster and hit the sides of the container more often and with greater force. Thus the pressure goes up.

HOW LIFE IS CLASSIFIED

Scientists classify organisms based on their similarities. Members are grouped together because they are likely to be related to one another. The field of science that classifies organisms is called taxonomy.

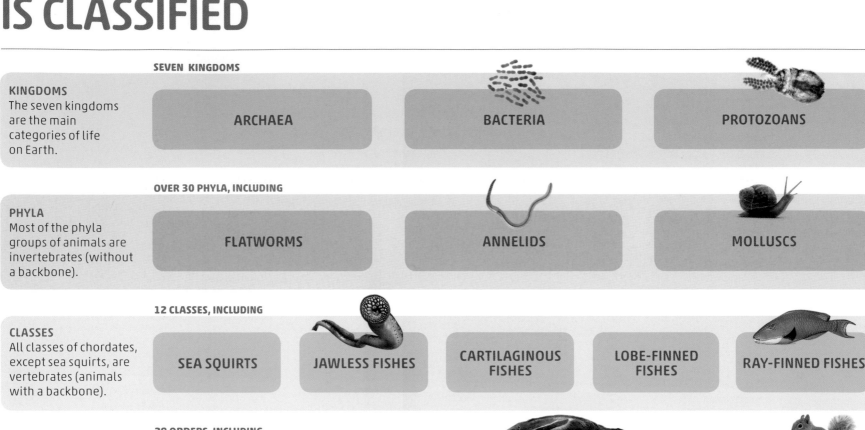

KINGDOMS
The seven kingdoms are the main categories of life on Earth.

SEVEN KINGDOMS

| ARCHAEA | BACTERIA | PROTOZOANS |

PHYLA
Most of the phyla groups of animals are invertebrates (without a backbone).

OVER 30 PHYLA, INCLUDING

| FLATWORMS | ANNELIDS | MOLLUSCS |

CLASSES
All classes of chordates, except sea squirts, are vertebrates (animals with a backbone).

12 CLASSES, INCLUDING

| SEA SQUIRTS | JAWLESS FISHES | CARTILAGINOUS FISHES | LOBE-FINNED FISHES | RAY-FINNED FISHES |

ORDERS
Orders of mammals range from the tiniest mammals, rodents, to the biggest, whales.

29 ORDERS, INCLUDING

| MONOTREMES | MARSUPIALS | ELEPHANTS | SLOTHS AND ANTEATERS | PRIMATES | RODENTS |

FAMILIES
Odd-toed hoofed mammals include horses, asses, zebras, and tapirs.

THREE FAMILIES

| HORSES, ASSES, AND ZEBRAS | RHINOCEROS |

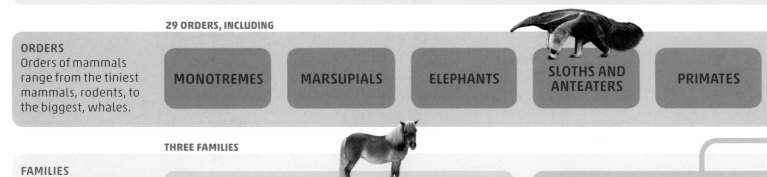

GENERA
The genus forms the first part of an organism's Latin name.

FOUR GENERA

| WHITE RHINOCEROS *CERATOTHERIUM* | BLACK RHINOCEROS *DICEROS* | ONE-HORNED RHINOCEROS *RHINOCEROS* |

SPECIES
The species is indicated by the second part of an organism's Latin name.

TWO SPECIES

The Latin name shows it belongs to the genus Rhinoceros and the species Rhinoceros unicornis.

| GREATER ONE-HORNED RHINOCEROS *RHINOCEROS UNICORNIS* |

CLASSIFYING BIRDS

Although birds are traditionally classified in their own group, studies of their DNA and of fossils show they are actually descended from extinct dinosaurs. This makes them closely related to living crocodiles and alligators. Many scientists now think that birds should be classified as a subgroup of reptiles.

MAMMALS

SEVEN KINGDOMS

TURTLES

LIZARDS AND SNAKES

CROCODILES

BIRDS

ANIMALS

There are around one million known species in the animal kingdom.

FUNGI

ALGAE

PLANTS

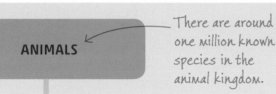

NEMATODES

ARTHROPODS

ECHINODERMS

Chordates phylum includes all animals with a backbone.

CHORDATES

AMPHIBIANS

REPTILES

BIRDS

MAMMALS

Animals in the mammal class grow hair and feed their young with milk.

RABBITS, HARES, AND PIKAS

SHREWS AND MOLES

BATS

CARNIVORES

HORSES, RHINOS AND RELATIVES

DEER, PIGS, AND RELATIVES

WHALES AND DOLPHINS

All members of any classification group are thought to have descended from a single common ancestor.

TAPIRS

The Javan Rhinoceros and the Greater One-horned Rhinoceros both have prominent skin folds, but their difference in size puts them in separate species.

SUMATRAN RHINOCEROS
DICERORHINUS

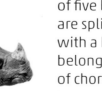

JAVAN RHINOCEROS
RHINOCEROS SONDAICUS

◄ CLASSIFYING A RHINOCEROS

The Javan Rhinoceros (pictured left) is one of five living species of Rhinoceroses, which are split over four genera. As an animal with a backbone, the Javan Rhinoceros belongs to the animal kingdom and phylum of chordates. It is in the class of mammals because it feeds its young with milk. Its three-toed feet put it in the same order as horses and zebras, and its single horn makes it a member of the rhinoceros family in the One-horned Rhinoceros genus.

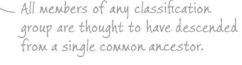

HUMAN BODY SYSTEMS

Organs are parts of the body that perform particular tasks, such as the heart that pumps blood, or the stomach that digests food. But organs do not work alone: they must work with other organs in systems to keep a body alive. Each system is concerned with a different aspect of the body's functions.

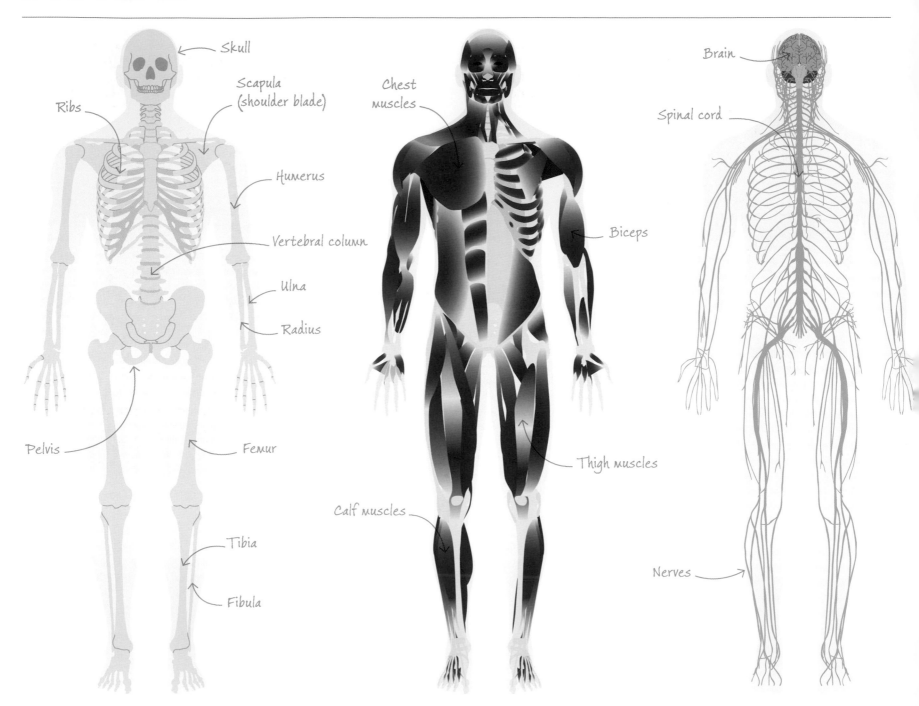

Skull
Scapula (shoulder blade)
Ribs
Humerus
Vertebral column
Ulna
Radius
Pelvis
Femur
Tibia
Fibula

Chest muscles
Biceps
Thigh muscles
Calf muscles

Brain
Spinal cord
Nerves

SKELETAL

Bones are linked together in the skeleton: a framework that keeps the body's shape, helps it to stand upright, and protects the soft organs. At flexible joints, muscles pull on bones to make them move. The soft inner marrow of some bones produces blood cells.

MUSCULAR

Muscles contract (shorten) to cause movement. Many muscles are connected to bones via cords, called tendons, and are under conscious control. Other muscles make up the walls of internal organs, such as the stomach or heart, and work automatically.

NERVOUS

The nervous system includes the brain, spinal cord, nerves, and sense organs. Sense organs fire electrical impulses through sensory nerves to the brain and spinal cord, which send signals through motor nerves to muscles triggering movement. The brain controls how the body behaves.

SKIN SYSTEMS

Some systems of the body defend against invading microbes. The surface of the skin, called the epidermis, forms a protective barrier that prevents many microbes from entering the body. Beneath the epidermis is a second layer of skin called the dermis. The dermis is a thicker layer containing hairs, blood vessels, nerves, and glands.

Hairs grow from roots called follicles deep within the skin.

The epidermis is the tough surface layer of the skin.

Glands, such as this sweat gland, occur in the dermis – the deeper layer of the skin.

A layer of insulating fat lies beneath the skin.

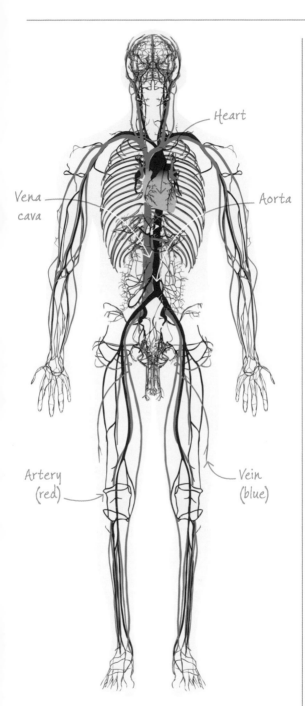

Heart

Vena cava

Aorta

Artery (red)

Vein (blue)

CIRCULATORY

The bloodstream transports materials around the body, such as oxygen from the lungs, and delivers waste to excretory organs. The heart pumps blood through tubes called blood vessels. Arteries carry blood away from the heart, veins carry blood to the heart.

RESPIRATORY

The airways and lungs form the respiratory system. The body uses oxygen and releases waste carbon dioxide in respiration. During breathing, the lungs bring oxygen into the blood and expel carbon dioxide.

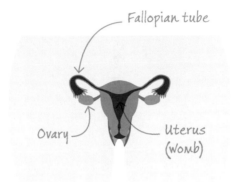

Trachea (windpipe)

Right lung

DIGESTIVE

Food passes through the digestive system, where it is broken down so it is small enough to pass into the blood stream from the intestines. Undigested waste is expelled in a process called egestion.

Oesophagus

Stomach

Intestines

ENDOCRINE

Organs called endocrine glands produce hormones in the endocrine system. Their chemical signals trigger responses around the body, such as adrenalin from the adrenal glands, which speeds up the heart when the body is excited.

Pineal gland

Thyroid gland

Pancreas

Adrenal gland

Testis

Ovary

REPRODUCTIVE SYSTEM

The reproductive system produces gametes (sex cells) inside sex organs. Female gametes are called eggs and male gametes are called sperm. An egg fertilized by a sperm grows into a new person.

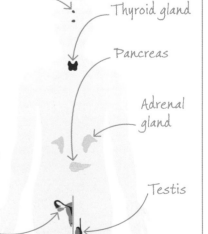

Fallopian tube

Ovary

Uterus (womb)

FEMALE

Organs called ovaries produce eggs. In adult humans, a single egg is released each month, ready for fertilization in the fallopian tube following sexual intercourse. If fertilized, the embryo grows in the uterus.

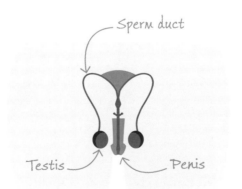

Sperm duct

Testis

Penis

MALE

Sperm are produced in organs called testes and thousands of sperm are released through the penis during sexual intercourse. The sperm swim to the fallopian tube to reach the egg.

EARTH'S GEOLOGICAL TIMELINE

Earth – the third planet from the Sun – is a changeable place. Although the Earth is 4.5 billion years old, life appeared 3.8 billion years ago and has been evolving ever since – just as the landscape and oceans have been changing because of geological forces.

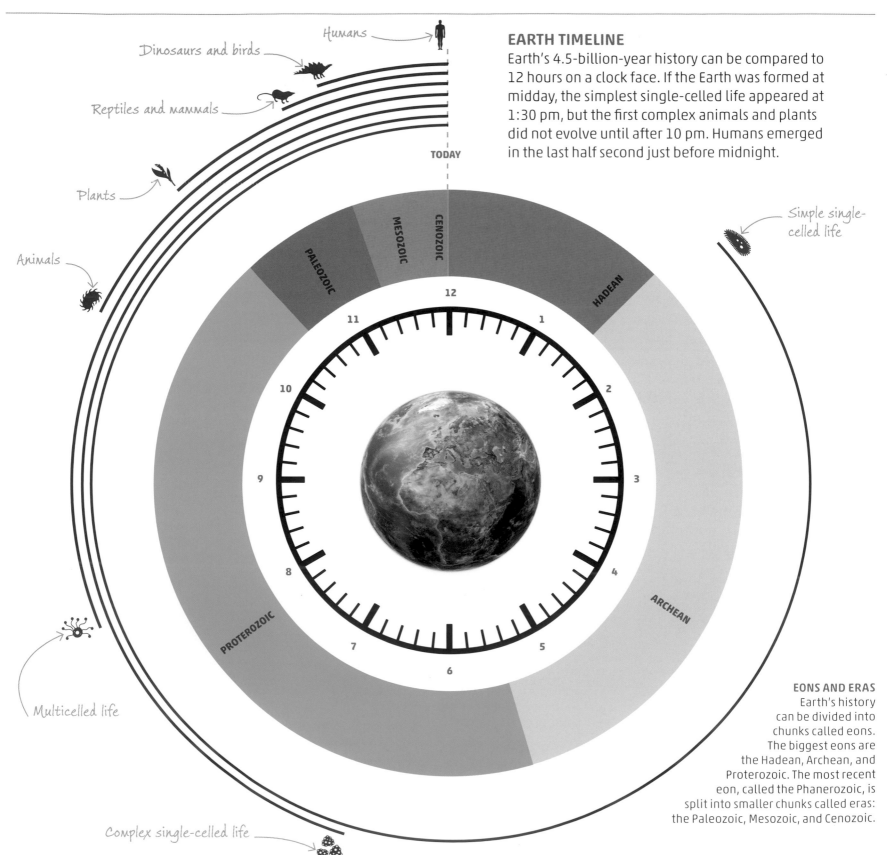

Humans

Dinosaurs and birds

Reptiles and mammals

TODAY

Plants

Animals

PALEOZOIC
MESOZOIC
CENOZOIC
HADEAN

Multicelled life

PROTEROZOIC

ARCHEAN

Complex single-celled life

Simple single-celled life

EARTH TIMELINE
Earth's 4.5-billion-year history can be compared to 12 hours on a clock face. If the Earth was formed at midday, the simplest single-celled life appeared at 1:30 pm, but the first complex animals and plants did not evolve until after 10 pm. Humans emerged in the last half second just before midnight.

EONS AND ERAS
Earth's history can be divided into chunks called eons. The biggest eons are the Hadean, Archean, and Proterozoic. The most recent eon, called the Phanerozoic, is split into smaller chunks called eras: the Paleozoic, Mesozoic, and Cenozoic.

WATER ON EARTH

Liquid water occurs on Earth because, across much of the Earth's surface, it is too cool for the water to evaporate or too warm to freeze. It is the presence of liquid water that helps to make Earth habitable. Most of the Earth's water is found as salt water in the oceans. Less than three per cent is fresh water, and most of that is frozen in ice caps and glaciers.

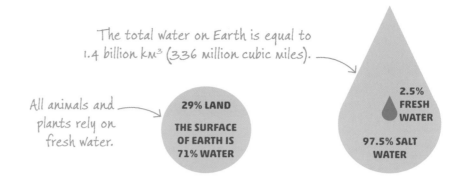

The total water on Earth is equal to 1.4 billion km³ (336 million cubic miles).

All animals and plants rely on fresh water.

29% LAND

THE SURFACE OF EARTH IS 71% WATER

2.5% FRESH WATER

97.5% SALT WATER

OCEAN CURRENTS

As the Earth rotates and the winds blow, the water in the oceans streams in currents whose flow is determined by the positions of the continents. Ocean currents carry warm tropical water and cool polar water around the world, helping to transfer the tropical heat away from the equator. The Gulf stream - one of the strongest ocean currents – carries warm water north from the western Atlantic, for example. Many currents of the ocean form giant circular streams called gyres.

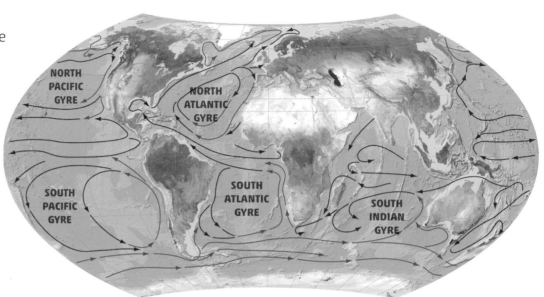

NORTH PACIFIC GYRE

NORTH ATLANTIC GYRE

SOUTH PACIFIC GYRE

SOUTH ATLANTIC GYRE

SOUTH INDIAN GYRE

WARM CURRENT →

COLD CURRENT →

PLATE BOUNDARIES

The strong outer shell of the planet - made up of surface crust and the upper mantle just below it - is divided into sections called tectonic plates. These plates are in constant slow motion. Where their edges meet at places called plate boundaries, the movement and heat from the Earth below can result in volcanic eruptions or sudden earthquakes. Over millions of years this motion produces huge mountain ranges and forms new oceans as continents collide and drift apart.

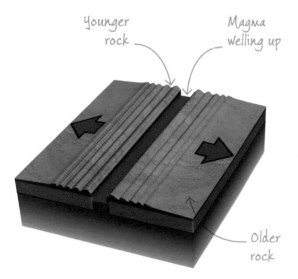

Younger rock

Magma welling up

Older rock

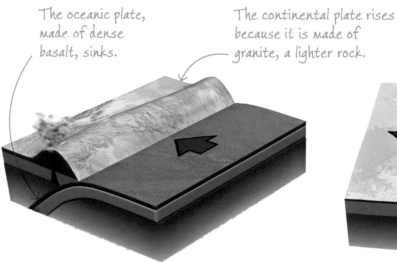

The oceanic plate, made of dense basalt, sinks.

The continental plate rises because it is made of granite, a lighter rock.

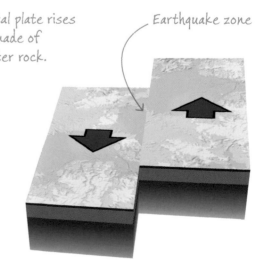

Earthquake zone

DIVERGENT BOUNDARY
When two plates move apart, melted rock called magma rises to the surface between the plates. The magma cools at the surface to form new rock, which builds up to the plate on either side.

CONVERGENT BOUNDARY
Where two plates move towards each other, a denser oceanic plate will move beneath a lighter continental plate, creating an ocean trench. If two continental plates collide, neither sinks so they buckle upwards to form mountain ranges.

CONSERVATION BOUNDARY
Sometimes plates slide past one another, with each one conserved as it is. Friction means that they do not slide smoothly: pressure can build up until the plates suddenly shift, causing an earthquake.

HOW MICROSCOPES WORK

Microscopes are scientific instruments that help to magnify objects so their structure can be examined in more detail. Most microscopes let us see the cells that make up plants and animals, but the most powerful microscopes can reveal individual molecules.

❶ THE EYEPIECE
One eye is used to look through the top of the microscope, called the eyepiece, which usually contains a lens that magnifies ×10. A dial is turned to bring the object into focus.

A set of lenses in the eyepiece usually has ×10 magnification.

The second lens focuses light towards the upper eyepiece lens.

Light beams cross over, which flips the final image.

The dial moves the tube closer to the specimen to bring it into focus.

Objective lenses of different strengths can be rotated into place.

A glass slide containing the specimen is placed on the stage.

Objective lenses usually have a magnification between ×4 and ×100.

An opening called the iris, or diaphragm, controls the intensity of the light shining on the specimen.

A mirror reflects light onto the specimen.

▼ HOW A LIGHT MICROSCOPE WORKS
A light microscope uses glass lenses to focus light coming from an object into our eyes, producing a magnified view of the object when we look through the eyepiece. For most school microscopes the object must be very thin because the light must pass through it from below. A mirror reflects a beam of light up through a specimen placed on a glass slide, then through two sets of lenses before it reaches the eye.

❷ THE SPECIMEN
A thin, transparent object to be observed, called a specimen, is placed on a glass microscope slide. A thin glass square, called a cover slip, is laid on top to keep the specimen flat and stop it touching the objective lens. The specimen is then placed on the stage.

The total magnification of these plant cells is ×400.

❸ THE LIGHT SOURCE
Light rays coming from a lamp are reflected up into the microscope to the eyepiece by an adjustable angled mirror. Some microscopes have a light source built into the bottom, so a mirror is not needed.

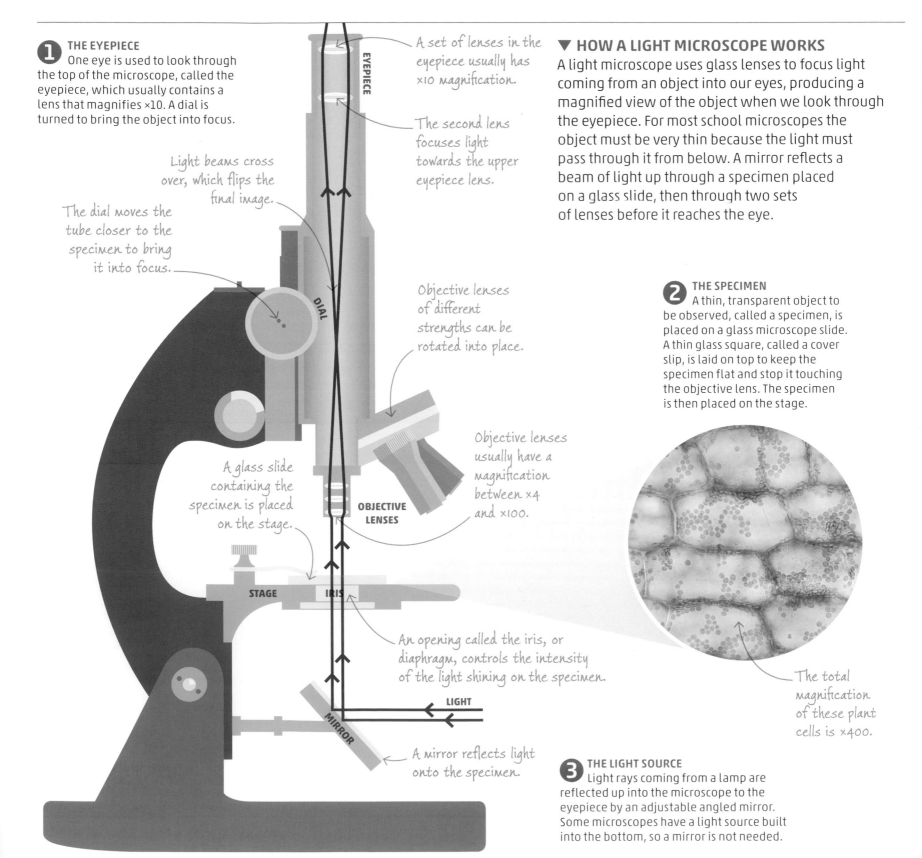

EYEPIECE

DIAL

OBJECTIVE LENSES

STAGE   IRIS

LIGHT

MIRROR

STEREO MICROSCOPE

In stereo microscopes the light shines from above and reflects off the specimen, rather than passing through it. This means that the surface of a thick specimen can be seen in three-dimensions. Stereo microscopes have lower magnifications for looking at larger objects, such as animal dissections or rocks.

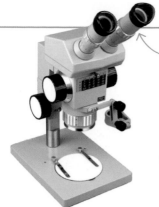

Both eyes are used to look down a stereo microscope.

WEEVIL CLOSE-UP
With a stereo microscope it is possible to see surface detail on the body of an insect – including its eyes, sensory hairs, and the joints of its antennae and legs.

MAGNIFICATION

Light microscopes use different lenses to focus at increasing magnifications. Higher magnifications demand brighter light to see the specimen clearly, so an adjustable hole beneath the microscope stage, called a diaphragm, is opened to let more light through. Special lenses can be used to achieve a maximum magnification of around ×1,000 or ×1,500. Another type of microscope called an electron microscope is used to achieve even higher magnifications.

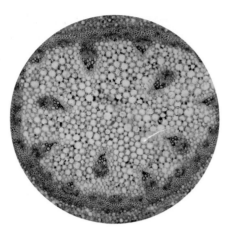

×40 LILY STEM
This section of stem from a lily of the valley is about 1 mm in thickness. The lowest magnification reveals the cell layers of the stem.

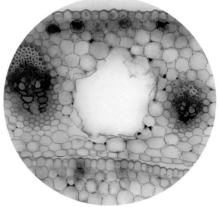

×100 LILY STEM
The ×100 magnification is good enough to see these individual cells, each of which is about a tenth of 1 mm in diameter.

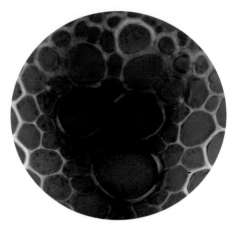

×400 LILY STEM
The ×400 magnification opens up some of the detail found inside individual cells, revealing structures such as this vascular bundle.

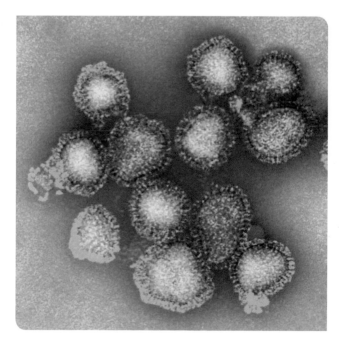

ELECTRON MICROSCOPE

An electron microscope has greater magnification and reveals more detail than is possible with a light microscope. This is because it uses a beam of electrons instead of light. Electrons, which can behave like waves, have a much smaller wavelength than light so they can distinguish much smaller objects. The electron beams are focused with electromagnets, instead of glass lenses, and the specimen must be held in a vacuum to stop air molecules interfering with the beam.

TRANSMISSION ELECTRON MICROSCOPE
Ultra-thin sections of a specimen can be viewed by a transmission electron microscope (TEM). The electron beam passes through the specimen, just as light is transmitted through the specimen in a typical school light microscope. This gives a two-dimensional image, such as this image of the influenza virus.

SCANNING ELECTRON MICROSCOPE
Larger specimens are viewed by a scanning electron microscope (SEM). The electron beam scans the surface of a specimen and is reflected from it. The reflected electrons give a three-dimensional image, showing the surface contours of a specimen, such as this fruit fly.

WEIGHTS AND MEASURES

All scientists use numbers and the same units of weights and measures, no matter where they are in the world. This is so their measurements are taken in the same way and can be compared.

SI UNITS

Scientists use an international system of weights and measures called SI units. "SI" is an abbreviation of the French name for the system, "Système Internationale". There are seven basic units and they are based on the metric system of measurement, with the official standard of each measurement maintained by experts at the International Bureau of Weights and Measures in France.

DERIVED SI UNITS

Combinations of the seven SI units are used to create all other measurements in science and technology. These measurements are called derived SI units, and they have their own names and symbols. As with SI units, the symbols are lower case unless they are named after a person. There are more than 20 derived SI units some of which are shown in the table below.

SI UNITS

UNIT	SYMBOL	QUANTITY MEASURED
metre	m	A metre is the SI unit that measures length and distance. One metre (1 m) equals 100 centimetres (100 cm) and 1,000 millimetres (1,000 mm).
kilogram	kg	A kilogram is the SI unit of mass – the amount of matter that makes up an object or substance. One kilogram (1 kg) equals 1,000 grams (1,000 g).
second	s	A second is the SI unit of time. There are 60 seconds in one minute, 60 minutes in one hour, and 24 hours in a day.
ampere	A	An ampere is the SI unit of electrical current. This is the measure of the amount of charge, carried by flowing electrons, passing any point of a wire per one unit of time.
kelvin	K	A kelvin is the SI unit used by scientists to measure temperature. It begins at absolute zero: 0 kelvin or -273.15°C (459.67°F).
candela	cd	A candela is the SI measure of brightness (how powerful a light source is). One candela (1 cd) is equal to the light given by one candle.
mole	mol	A mole is the SI unit of an amount of a substance (generally very small particles such as atoms and molecules). One mole stands for a quantity equal to 600 sextillion (that is 600,000,000,000,000,000,000,000).

DERIVED SI UNITS

UNIT	SYMBOL	QUANTITY MEASURED
Celsius	°C	Celsius is a unit of temperature, at the same size as a kelvin, but zero (0°C) is at water's freezing point.
cubic metre	m^3	A cubic metre is a measurement of volume. One cubic centimetre (1 cm^3) is the same volume as a millilitre.
hertz	Hz	A hertz is the unit of frequency – the number of cycles or repeating events per second.
joule	J	A joule is a unit of energy. For example, one joule (1 J) is the amount of energy needed to lift an apple one metre (1 m).
newton	N	A newton is a unit of force. One newton (1 N) is about the force of an apple's weight.
pascal	Pa	A pascal is a unit of pressure. This is the force of one newton (1 N) applied across an area of one square metre (1 m^2).
square metre	m^2	A square metre is a measurement of area. The area is equal to a square with each side measuring one metre (1 m).
volt	V	A volt is a unit for electrical potential difference (the energy transferred when electrical charge passes through a component).
watt	W	A watt is the unit used to measure power. One watt (1 W) is one joule (1 J) of energy transferred per second.

HOW FAR IS A LIGHT-YEAR?

Astronomers use light-years to measure huge distances between objects in the Universe. One light-year is the distance light travels in a year, which is about 9.5 trillion km (5.9 trillion miles). The distances are so great that it is not possible to show them to scale.

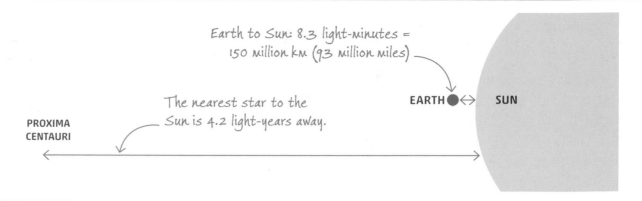

Earth to Sun: 8.3 light-minutes = 150 million km (93 million miles)

The nearest star to the Sun is 4.2 light-years away.

PROXIMA CENTAURI

EARTH ⟷ SUN

TEMPERATURE SCALES

People use three different scales to measure temperature: Kelvin (K), Celsius (°C), and Fahrenheit (°F). Celsius is the temperature scale people use most often, while Fahrenheit is used in the USA and the Caribbean. The SI unit of measurement, kelvin, which has absolute zero as its lowest point, is the scale used by scientists. Unlike Celsius and Fahrenheit, the Kelvin scale is not written or referred to in degrees (°).

RANGE OF TEMPERATURES

TEMPERATURE		EXAMPLE
15 million K (15 million°C; 27 million°F)		Sun's core
30,000 K (29,727°C; 53,540°F)		Lightning bolts
5,800 K (5,527°C; 9,980°F)		Surface of the Sun
5,700 K (5,500°C; 9,932°F)		Earth's core
523 K (250°C; 482°F)		Burning point of wood
373 K (100°C; 212°F)		Boiling point of water
330 K (56.7°C; 134°F)		Highest recorded air temperature on Earth
310 K (37°C; 98.3°F)		Normal human body temperature
273 K (0°C; 32°F)		Freezing point of water
184 K (-89°C; -129°F)		Lowest recorded air temperature on Earth
43 K (-230°C; -382°F)		Surface temperature of Pluto
0 K (-273.15°C; -459.67°F)		Absolute zero

TEMPERATURE CONVERSION

If one temperature on a scale is known, it can be converted to either of the other two scales using set formulas, which are shown below.

CONVERT	FORMULA
Fahrenheit (°F) to Celsius (°C)	$C = (F - 32) \times 5 \div 9$
Celsius (°C) to Fahrenheit (°F)	$F = (C \times 9 \div 5) + 32$
Celsius (°C) to Kelvin (K)	$K = C + 273$
Kelvin (K) to Celsius (°C)	$C = K - 273$

EARTH'S VITAL STATISTICS

Our planet is the largest rocky planet in the Solar System and the third from the Sun. It is the only planet in the Solar System where life exists, being at the right distance for the temperature to be not too hot or too cold. For this reason, it is sometimes known as a "Goldilocks" planet.

STATISTIC	MEASUREMENT
Average diameter	12,742 km (7,918 miles)
Average distance from the Sun	149.6 million km (93 million miles)
Average orbital speed around the Sun	29.8 km/s (18.5 mps)
Sunrise to sunrise (at the equator)	24 hours
Mass	5.98×10^{24} kg
Volume	1.08321×10^{12} km^3
Average density (water = 1)	5.52 g/cm^3
Surface gravity	9.8 N/kg
Average surface temperature	15°C (59°F)
Ratio of water to land	70:30

GLOSSARY

ABSOLUTE ZERO
The lowest possible temperature, defined as zero kelvin or –273.15°C (–459.67°F), at which all atoms stop moving.

ACCELERATION
An increase or decrease in an object's velocity due to a force being applied to it.

ACID
A compound that releases hydrogen ions when it dissolves in water. Vinegar and lemon juice are weak acids.

ADHESION
Attraction between molecules of different substances.

AIR PRESSURE
The force of air molecules pushing against a surface or container.

AIR RESISTANCE
The force that pushes against an object moving through the air, slowing it down; also called drag.

ALKALI
A base that dissolves in water, releasing hydroxide ions. Alkalis neutralize acids.

ALLOTROPES
The different structural forms in which an element can exist.

ALLOY
A mixture of two or more metals, or of a metal and a non-metal.

AMPLITUDE
The distance between the peak or trough of a wave and its undisturbed position.

ANODE
In electrolysis, a positive electrode.

ARTERY
A thick-walled blood vessel that carries blood away from the heart to other parts of the body.

ATMOSPHERE
A layer of gases that surrounds a planet, moon, or star.

ATOM
The smallest unit of an element with the properties of that element.

AXIS
A real or imaginary line through the middle of something.

BACTERIA
Single-celled organisms with no cell nuclei; the most abundant organisms on Earth.

BASE
Any substance that is able to neutralize an acid.

BATTERY
An energy-storing device made of two or more electrical cells that produces an electric current when connected in a circuit.

BLOODSTREAM
The flow of blood through the vessels of a living thing.

BOILING POINT
The temperature at which a liquid turns to gas so quickly that bubbles form. The gas will condense into a liquid at this temperature.

BOND
An attractive force between atoms or ions that holds them together.

CAPILLARY
A small blood vessel that delivers oxygen to body cells.

CARBOHYDRATE
A molecule made up of carbon, hydrogen, and oxygen, which can typically be broken down to produce energy in living things.

CATALYST
A substance that increases the rate of a chemical reaction without being used up in that reaction.

CATHODE
In electrolysis, a negative electrode.

CELL
The basic unit from which all living organisms are made. Also an energy-storing device that produces an electric current when connected in a circuit.

CHEMICAL REACTION
A process in which atoms are rearranged to form at least one new substance.

CHROMOSOME
A structure in the nucleus of cells made up of coils of DNA.

CHLOROPHYLL
A green pigment found in plants that absorbs the energy from sunlight to use in photosynthesis.

CHLOROPLAST
A tiny structure in plant cells that contains chlorophyll.

CLONE
A living thing that is genetically identical to its parent.

COHESION
Attraction between molecules of the same substance.

COLLOID
A mixture made up of tiny particles of one substance dispersed in another substance, in which it does not dissolve.

COMPOUND
A substance made up of two or more different elements joined by chemical bonds.

CONCENTRATION
The amount of one substance mixed or dissolved in a known volume of another. A mixture containing a large amount of the dissolved substance (the solute) compared to the amount of solvent is said to be concentrated.

CONDENSE
To turn from a gas to a liquid.

CONDUCTION
The process by which energy is transferred by heating or electricity, usually through a solid substance. Some materials are better conductors than others.

CONVECTION
The process by which energy is transferred through a liquid or gas by heating. Warm areas rise and cooler ones sink, creating a circulating current known as a convection current.

CONVERGENT BOUNDARY
An area of Earth where two tectonic plates meet as they move towards one another.

COVALENT BOND
A chemical bond in which two atoms share electrons.

CUTICLE
A protective outer skin found on many invertebrates.

CYTOPLASM
The jelly-like fluid inside a cell membrane, which makes up most of the material inside a cell.

DENSITY
The mass (amount of matter) of a substance per unit of volume.

DIFFUSION
The mixing of two or more substances due to the random movement of their molecules.

DILUTE
A mixture containing only small amounts of a solute compared to the amount of solvent is said to be dilute.

DIVERGENT BOUNDARY
An area of Earth where two tectonic plates are moving away from each other.

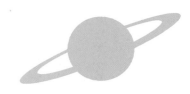

DRAG
The force that slows down an object moving through a fluid, such as air or water.

DNA
A complex molecule found in the cells of all organisms that contains the genetic instructions for how a living thing will look and function.

ELECTRIC CHARGE
A property of ions, electrons, and protons that can cause non-contact forces between objects. Charges can be positive or negative.

ELECTRIC CIRCUIT
A continuous loop of wire around which electric charge can flow. It includes a power source (such as a battery) and other components (such as a light bulb).

ELECTRIC CURRENT
The flow of electric charge.

ELECTRICITY
A form of energy transferred by an electric current.

ELECTRODE
A piece of metal or carbon that collects or releases electrons in an electric circuit.

ELECTROLYTE
A liquid that conducts electricity.

ELECTROMAGNET
A coil of wire that becomes magnetic when electricity flows through it.

ELECTROMAGNETIC SPECTRUM
The range of different types of electromagnetic radiation, from gamma rays to radio waves.

ELECTRON
A negatively charged particle that occupies the outer part of an atom. Moving electrons carry an electrical charge.

ELEMENT
A substance that contains only one type of atom. There are 118 known elements, about 90 of which occur in nature.

EMBRYO
An early stage in the development of an animal or plant.

EMULSIFIER
Something that helps combine substances that do not normally mix, such as oil and water.

ENDOTHERMIC
A chemical reaction that takes in energy from the surroundings.

ENERGY
Energy is what allows things to happen. For example, chemical energy stored in food enables organisms to live and move. Energy can be transferred but not created or destroyed.

ENZYME
A protein that acts as a biological catalyst, speeding up a chemical reaction inside cells.

EVAPORATE
To turn from a liquid to a gas.

EVOLUTION
The process by which populations of living things change their characteristics over the course of many generations.

EXCRETION
The process by which living organisms expel or get rid of the waste produced by cells of the body.

EXOSKELETON
The hard, external skeleton that covers, supports, and protects some invertebrates.

EXOTHERMIC
A chemical reaction that releases energy into the surroundings.

FERTILIZATION
The joining of male and female sex cells.

FISSION
Breaking apart; nuclear fission involves radioactive atoms splitting, releasing a huge amount of energy.

FLUORESCENCE
The emission of light as a result of exposure to radiation of a shorter wavelength.

FLUID
A substance that can flow, such as a gas or liquid.

FORCE
A push or a pull that causes an object to change its speed, direction, or shape.

FREQUENCY
The number of times something happens in a unit of time. Wave frequency is the number of waves per second, measured in hertz (Hz).

FRICTION
A force that occurs between moving objects, where the surfaces rub against each other, opposing their movement.

FULCRUM
The pivot around which a lever turns.

FUSION
Joining together; nuclear fusion involves two small atoms fusing into a single larger one, releasing huge amounts of energy.

GAMMA RAYS
A type of electromagnetic radiation with a very short wavelength.

GENE
A length of DNA that instructs a living cell to make a particular kind of protein, and affects one or more inherited characteristics.

GENERATOR
A device that produces electricity when it spins.

GLUCOSE
A simple sugar used by cells as a source of energy.

GRAVITY
A force of attraction that acts between all masses.

HEMISPHERE
Half of a sphere. Earth is divided into the northern and southern hemispheres by the equator (an imaginary line around the middle of the globe).

HOMEOSTASIS
The process by which conditions within an animal's body, such as temperature, are regulated.

HORMONE
A chemical messenger that travels through the bloodstream to control certain life processes.

HYDROCARBON
A chemical compound made up of hydrogen and carbon atoms.

INFRARED RADIATION
A type of electromagnetic radiation produced by hot objects.

INORGANIC
A substance mostly made up of elements other than carbon.

INSULATOR
A material that reduces or stops the flow of heat, electricity, or sound.

ION
An atom or group of atoms that has lost or gained electrons and therefore carries a positive or negative charge.

IONIC BOND
A chemical bond caused by the attraction between positive and negative ions.

LASER
A beam of intense light consisting of waves that are in step and of equal wavelength. Laser stands for light amplification by stimulated emission of radiation.

LATTICE
An arrangement of particles in a regular, repeating pattern.

LENS
A curved, transparent piece of plastic or glass that can bend, or refract, light rays.

LEVER
A rigid rod that pivots around a fixed point. Levers can multiply forces, making hard jobs easier.

LIFT
The upward force produced by the wing of an object that keeps it airborne.

LIGHT
The visible part of the electromagnetic spectrum.

LUMINESCENCE
The emission of light without using heat.

MAGNETIC FIELD
The area around a magnet in which its effects are felt.

MAGNETISM
An invisible force that can affect materials such as iron. Magnets can attract or repel one another.

MASS
The amount of matter in an object.

MATTER
Anything that has mass and occupies space.

MEIOSIS
The process by which a cell divides to create new cells with only half the usual amount of genetic material. These new cells are called sex cells.

MELTING POINT
The temperature at which a solid turns into a liquid. When the liquid is cooled, it will freeze into a solid at this same temperature.

MEMBRANE
A thin layer that surrounds a cell or other body structure.

METAMORPHOSIS
A major change or changes in an animal's body shape during its life cycle.

MICROBE
A tiny organism that can only be seen with the aid of a microscope. Also known as a microorganism.

MINERAL
A naturally occurring, inorganic, solid chemical. Rocks are made of mineral grains stuck together.

MITOCHONDRIA
Tiny parts in a cell that release the energy needed to power the cell.

MITOSIS
The process by which one cell splits to produce two new cells with the same amount of genetic material.

MIXTURE
A combination of two or more substances that are not chemically bonded.

MOLECULE
Two or more atoms that are joined by a covalent bond.

MOMENTUM
The tendency of a moving object to keep moving until a force stops it.

MONOMER
A small molecule that links with a large number of other molecules to produce a polymer.

MOTOR
A machine that uses electricity and magnetism to produce motion.

MULTICELLULAR
A creature made up of more than one cell.

NERVE
A bundle of nerve cell fibres that carry electrical signals through the body of an animal.

NEURON
A nerve cell. There are three main types of neurons: sensory, motor, and association neurons.

NEUTRON
An uncharged particle located in the nuclei of all atoms except for hydrogen.

NEWTON (N)
The standard unit of force.

NUCLEUS
The central core of something. An atomic nucleus contains protons and neutrons, while a cell's nucleus contains DNA.

NUTRIENT
A substance that is useful for life as a source of energy or as raw material.

OPTICAL FIBRES
Thin glass fibres through which light travels, used to transmit digital signals at high speed.

ORBIT
The path of one body around another, such as a moon orbiting a planet, or an electron moving around an atomic nucleus.

ORE
A naturally occurring rock from which metal can be extracted.

ORGAN
A major structure in an organism that has a specific function.

ORGANIC
A complex substance that is mostly made up of carbon atoms and originates from living things.

ORGANISM
A living thing.

OSMOSIS
The way in which water particles move across a membrane from a low concentration of solute to a high concentration of solute.

PARTICLE
A tiny bit of matter. This can refer to atoms and molecules or to sub-atomic particles such as electron, protons, and neutrons.

PERMEABLE
Something that allows liquids or gases to pass through it.

PHLOEM
A small tube in a plant that carries sugars to all its parts.

PHOSPHORESCENCE
The emission of light as a result of exposure to radiation of a shorter wavelength. Light is emitted once the radiation source is removed.

PHOTOSYNTHESIS
The process by which plants use sunlight, water, and carbon dioxide to make food.

PIGMENT
A chemical that colours an object.

PITCH
How high or low a sound is. Pitch is directly related to the frequency of sound waves.

PLASMA
A state of matter that is a highly energized form of gas. Also the liquid part of blood.

POLYMER
A long, chain-like molecule made up of smaller molecules connected together.

PRESSURE
The amount of force that is applied to a surface per unit of area.

PROTEIN
A chemical containing nitrogen, carbon, and oxygen, which is used by living things for growth and repair.

PROTON
A positively charged particle that is located in the nuclei of all atoms.

RADIATION
Waves of energy that travel through space. Radiation includes gamma rays, ultraviolet, visible light, infrared, X-rays, microwaves, and radio waves. It can also be a stream of particles from a source of radioactivity.

RADIOACTIVITY
The breakdown of atomic nuclei, causing radiation to be released.

RADIO WAVES
A type of electromagnetic radiation that has the longest waves.

REACTIVITY
A description of how likely a substance is to become involved in a chemical reaction.

REFLECTION
When an electromagnetic wave, such as visible light, or a sound wave bounces off a surface.

REFRACTION
When a wave changes direction as it passes from one medium to another. Light waves are refracted as they pass from one transparent medium to another.

REPRODUCTION
The way living things make new individuals of the same kind. Most organisms reproduce by sexual reproduction, which involves combining the genetic material of two parents.

RESPIRATION
The process occurring in all living cells that releases energy from glucose to power life.

ROOM TEMPERATURE
A standard scientific term for comfortable conditions (for humans), usually a temperature of around 20°C (68°F).

SALT
An ionic chemical compound formed from a reaction between an acid and a base. The word is also used to specifically describe sodium chloride.

SATELLITE
An object in space that travels around another in an orbit.

SEDIMENT
Solid material that settles at the bottom of a liquid.

SEED
A tough structure containing a tiny plant embryo, which plants use to reproduce. It will grow into a new plant once in the right conditions.

SEX CELLS
A reproductive cell, such as a sperm or egg.

SOLUTE
A substance that dissolves in a solvent to form a solution.

SOLUTION
A mixture in which the molecules or ions of a solute are evenly spread out among the molecules of a solvent.

SOLVENT
A substance (usually a liquid) in which a solute dissolves to form a solution.

STIMULUS
Something that encourages activity or response in people or things.

STOMATA
Pores in a plant's leaves and other parts that release and take in gases.

SUBLIMATION
The process by which a solid turns directly into a gas.

SUGAR
A usually sweet-tasting, soluble carbohydrate found in living tissues.

SYNTHETIC
A man-made chemical.

TEMPERATE
Regions of Earth with a mild climate, most affected by changes in the seasons.

TISSUE
A group of similar cells, such as muscle tissue or fat.

TRANSPARENT
A term for a material that allows light through, making it possible to see through it.

TROPISM
Movement of part of a plant towards or away from a stimulus.

ULTRAVIOLET
A type of electromagnetic radiation with a wavelength slightly shorter than visible light.

UPTHRUST
The upward force exerted by a liquid or a gas on an object floating in it.

URINE
A substance produced by the human kidneys, mostly containing the waste product urea and any excess water.

UTERUS
The part of a female mammal where a baby grows before it is born.

VACUOLE
A large, fluid-filled sac inside a plant cell that helps to keep the cell firm.

VAPOUR
A substance suspended in the air, especially one which is normally a solid or liquid at room temperature.

VEIN
A tube that carries blood from body tissues to the heart. They contain valves to prevent blood from flowing backwards.

VELOCITY
The speed of something in a particular direction.

VESICLE
A structure within a cell that helps to break down food.

VIBRATION
A quick back-and-forth movement of objects or particles.

VISCOSITY
The measure of how thick or resistant to a change in shape a fluid is.

VOLUME
The amount of space an object or substance takes up.

WAVELENGTH
The distance measured between any point on a wave and the equivalent point on the next wave.

WEIGHT
The force applied to a mass by gravity.

WORK
The amount of energy transferred when a force is applied to a mass over a certain distance.

X-RAY
A type of electromagnetic radiation used to create images of bones and teeth.

XYLEM
A small tube in a plant that carries water and minerals up from its roots to its leaves.

INDEX

F

E

ACKNOWLEDGMENTS

DK would like to thank
Shreya Konnur and Melanie Bottrill at the Wohl Reach Out Lab, Imperial College London, for their assistance during the making of this book.

Special thanks to Michelle Afonso and James Bolanji, who carried out the experiments.

In addition, the publisher would like to extend thanks to the following people for their help with making the book:

Grey Hutton and Flir Systems for thermal photography using T1030sc loaned by Flir Systems; Mark Amey at Ameyzoo Exotic Pets for supply and handling of lizards; Zygmunt Podhorodecki for supply and handling of honey bees; Otto Podhorodecki for modelling; Nigel Wright for assistance with photoshoots; London Terrariums for creating the bottle garden; Carron Brown for editorial assistance; Hazel Beynon for proofreading; and Helen Peters for indexing.

The publisher would like to thank the following for their kind permission to reproduce their photographs:

(Key: a-above; b-below/bottom; c-centre; f-far; l-left; r-right; t-top)

1 Dreamstime.com: Malopes / Mario Lopes (Background). **2-3 Dreamstime.com:** Malopes / Mario Lopes (Background). **4-5 Dreamstime.com:** Malopes / Mario Lopes (r/Background). **6 FLPA:** Paul Bertner / Minden Pictures (tr). **Science Photo Library:** Ted Kinsman (tc). **6-7 Dreamstime.com:** Malopes / Mario Lopes (Background). **7 Caters News Agency:** Chad Weisser (tc). **FLPA:** Paul Bertner / Minden Pictures (tl). **8-9 Dreamstime.com:** Malopes / Mario Lopes (Background). **8 Science Photo Library:** (br). **12-13 Dreamstime.com:** Malopes / Mario Lopes (Background). **14 Dreamstime.com:** Egal / Elena Schweitzer (c). **Science Photo Library:** Biophoto Associates (clb); Science Pictures Limited (bc); Wladimir Bulgar (br). **15 123RF.com:** Thawat Tanhai (cb). **Dreamstime.com:** Blair_witch / Svetlana Larina (tc); Joools (bc). **20 123RF.com:** Milosh Kojadinovich (bc/sandglass). **Science Photo Library:** Dr Jeremy Burgess (bc). **22 iStockphoto.com:** JacobVanHouten (cla). **Science Photo Library:** Eye Of Science (clb); Dirk Wiersma (cl).

23 Dorling Kindersley: Natural History Museum, London / Colin Keates (crb). **25 Alamy Stock Photo:** Gino's Premium Images (br). **26-27 FLPA:** Minden Pictures / Paul Bertner. **27 naturepl.com:** Thomas Marent (tl). **30-31 Getty Images:** Feng Wei Photography / Moment Unreleased. **33 Dreamstime.com:** Alexander Shalamov (br). **iStockphoto.com:** mishooo (bc). **35 123RF.com:** Nataliia Kravchuk (cr); Fabrizio Troiani (cra). **iStockphoto.com:** Lisovskaya (crb). **36 Dreamstime.com:** Otmar Winterleitner (clb). **Science Photo Library:** (cla). **45 Alamy Stock Photo:** Les Wagstaff (cra). **49 NASA:** ESA / and the Hubble Heritage Team (STScl / AURA) (cr). **50-51 iStockphoto.com:** rusm. **52 Science Photo Library:** (bc). **54 Dorling Kindersley:** Museum of London (cla). **Dreamstime.com:** Kaspri (bl); Björn Wylezich (br). **55 Dorling Kindersley:** RGB Research Limited (tl, cr). **Dreamstime.com:** Björn Wylezich (clb, br). **57 Dorling Kindersley:** RGB Research Limited (br). **58 iStockphoto.com:** guenterguni / E+ (clb). **59 iStockphoto.com:** BlackJack3D / E+ (c). **60-61 NASA:** (c). **62 Science Photo Library:** Charles D. Winters (tl, tr, crb). **63 Science Photo Library:** Charles D. Winters (l). **64-65 ©smart-elements. com:** (c). **65 Science Photo Library:** Theodore Clutter (cr). **66-67 Dreamstime.com:**

Malopes / Mario Lopes (Background). **68 Dorling Kindersley:** RGB Research Limited (bc, cb, cra). **69 Dorling Kindersley:** RGB Research Limited (tl, b). **70 Science Photo Library:** (c). **71 Science Photo Library:** Martyn F. Chillmaid (tr). **72 Dreamstime.com:** Jiri Vaclavek (bl). **73 Science Photo Library:** (bl). **74 Dreamstime.com:** Alexander Pladdet (crb). **Science Photo Library:** (cl); Charles D. Winters (cra). **75 Science Photo Library:** (br); Charles D. Winters (l). **78-79 Olivier Grunewald:** (c). **84 Dreamstime.com:** Robert Schneider (ca). **Science Photo Library:** Eye Of Science (cra). **84-85 Alamy Stock Photo:** Arterra Picture Library (b). **85 123RF.com:** Kawisara Kaewprasert (cra); Yotsatorn Laonalonglit (ca); pakete (cra/Rusty bolt). **88 Science Photo Library:** Charles D. Winters (tl, tr). **89 Dorling Kindersley:** RGB Research Limited (cra/Sodium, cra/Magnesium, c/Zinc, crb/Copper, cra/Potassium, cra/Calcium, cra/Aluminium). **Science Photo Library:** Power And Syred (bc); Charles D. Winters (l). **90 Alamy Stock Photo:** Christopher Nash (clb/Kettle). **Science Photo Library:** Power And Syred (clb). **91 Science Photo Library:** Alexandre Dotta (c). **92 Science Photo Library:** Charles D. Winters (tc). **93 Science Photo Library:** Charles D. Winters. **94 Science Photo Library:**

Science Source (c). **100-101 Cris Matthews Photography:** (c). **104-105 Dreamstime. com:** Malopes / Mario Lopes (Background). **107 123RF. com:** akkalak (cra). **Alamy Stock Photo:** Anton Starikov (cb). **Dreamstime.com:** Oleg Dudko (crb); Hannu Viitanen (c); Taaeepang (cr). **108 Dreamstime.com:** Jaromír Chalabala (bc/Rubber tree). **Getty Images:** Xvision / Moment Open (bc). **110 123RF.com:** kungverylucky / Chaovarut Sthoop (bc/Pan). **Dreamstime.com:** Sira Jantararungsan (bc/PVC pipe); Scisettialfio / Alfio Scisetti (bc/ Bottle). **111 Alamy Stock Photo:** Paulo Oliveira (crb). **112 Science Photo Library:** Eye Of Science (c). **112-113 Alamy Stock Photo:** NASA Image Collection. **113 NASA:** NASA / JPL / Cornell University / Maas Digital (br). **114-115 Science Photo Library:** Eye Of Science. **116 Alamy Stock Photo:** kramarek (tl); S.E.A. Photo (clb). iStockphoto.com: DiyanaDimitrova (tr); ilbusca / E+ (crb). **117 iStockphoto. com:** Rocter. **119 Alamy Stock Photo:** Cultura Creative (RF) (crb). **120 iStockphoto.com:** baranozdemir (clb). **121 Dreamstime.com:** Pavel Losevsky (ca). **Getty Images:** Bloomberg Creative Photos (cr). **iStockphoto.com:** enviromantic / E+ (cb); enviromantic (bl). Novelis UK Ltd: Hindalco Industries / Aditya Birla Group (tl). **122-123 Science Photo Library:** National Cancer

Institute. **123 Science Photo Library:** Eye Of Science (br). **124-125 Dreamstime.com:** Malopes / Mario Lopes (Background). **126-127 123RF.com:** Vassiliy Prikhodko (Clouds BG). **Alamy Stock Photo:** David Wall (c). **129 Alamy Stock Photo:** Andrew Paterson (tc). **Science Photo Library:** Aberration Films Ltd (cr, crb, br). **135 Alamy Stock Photo:** Cultura Creative (RF) (br). **136-137 Courtesy of NASA/SDO and the AIA, EVE, and HMI science teams:** (tl). **137 NASA:** SDO (bl). NRAO: (br). **138-139 ESO:** B. Tafreshi (twanight.org) (c). **140 Alamy Stock Photo:** Roy Childs (crb). **142 Dreamstime.com:** Kanthorn Dheerachaikulpanich (tl). **143 Depositphotos Inc:** IzelPhotography (cr). **Dreamstime.com:** Pureradiancephoto (crb). **150 Science Photo Library:** Sebastian Kaulitzki (bc). **154-155 Juan Carlos Casado:** (c). **161 Alamy Stock Photo:** Allover Images (cra). **162-163 Getty Images:** Guillaume Souvant / AFP (c). **165 Science Photo Library:** Ted Kinsman (c). **169 Getty Images:** Achim Thomae / Moment (crb); JaCZhou2015 / Moment (br). **172-173 Science Photo Library:** Ted Kinsman (c). **175 123RF.com:** Roman Samokhin (tr/Aluminium Can); Serezniy (tr). **iStockphoto. com:** Saturated (c). **179 Dreamstime.com:** 44Photography (br). **180-181 Hypoxic:** Mark Kirschenbaum (c). **184 Alamy Stock Photo:**

Martin Harvey (bc). **189 Dreamstime.com:** Ivan Cholakov (tl). **190-191 AirTeamImages.com:** Jorgen Syversen (c). **192-193 Dreamstime.com:** Malopes / Mario Lopes (Background). **193 FLPA:** Paul Bertner / Minden Pictures (c). **194-195 Alamy Stock Photo:** Auscape International Pty Ltd (c). **194 Dorling Kindersley:** Mark Winwood / RHS Wisley (cla/Dryopteris Affinis). **Dreamstime.com:** 72hein71cis (cl); Wei Chuan Liu / Rebelml (cla); Indykb (cl/Algae). **Science Photo Library:** Eye Of Science (bl); Omikron (clb); Steve Gschmeissner (clb/Breast milk bacteria). **196-197 Dreamstime.com:** Peter Hermes Furian (c). **199 Science Photo Library:** Steve Gschmeissner (br). **200 Alamy Stock Photo:** Nobeastsofierce Science (clb). **Science Photo Library:** Dr. Tony Brain & David Parker (bc); Hugh Spencer (cl). **201 Science Photo Library:** Dr. Tony Brain & David Parker (c). **202-203 Tracy Debenport, mycologist & microphotographer:** (c). **207 Science Photo Library:** John Walsh (bl). **208-209 Getty Images:** Vicki Jauron / Babylon and Beyond Photography (c/ Hippopotamus). **212 naturepl.com:** Suzi Eszterhas (crb). **214-215 Science Photo Library:** K H Fung (c). **219 Grey Hutton**/Flir Systems (c). **223 Alamy Stock Photo:** Blickwinkel (cr, crb, br).

224-225 Alamy Stock Photo: Steve Bloom Images (cb). **FLPA:** Paul Bertner / Minden Pictures (b). **Getty Images:** Sirachai Arunrugstichai (ca); Per-Andre Hoffmann (t). **226-227 FLPA:** Minden Pictures / Ralph Pace (c). **228-229 Science Photo Library:** Robert Mcneil / Baylor College Of Medicine (c). **231 123RF.com:** Pavlo Vakhrushev / vapi (cb). **236 Science Photo Library:** Eye Of Science (b). **237 Getty Images:** Brian Mckay Photographyy / Moment (crb). **Science Photo Library:** Dr. Yorgos Nikas (tl, ca, ca/Four-cell embryo, c, clb). **241 Alamy Stock Photo:** Iain Masterton (br). **242-243 Science Photo Library:** Frank Fox (c). **243 Science Photo Library:** Steve Gschmeissner (t). **246 Alamy Stock Photo:** Purple Pilchards (r). **248-249 naturepl.com:** Alex Hyde (ca). **248 Alamy Stock Photo:** blickwinkel (bc). **250-251 Dreamstime.com:** Isselee. **252-253 Science Photo Library:** (c). **255 Caters News Agency:** Chad Weisser (c). **256 Dreamstime.com:** Guenter Purin / Mytrade1 (clb). **256-257 NASA:** Goddard Space Flight Center Image by Reto Stöckli (c). **258-259 Alamy Stock Photo:** Hercules Milas (cb). **Getty Images:** Daniel Viñé Garcia (bc). **iStockphoto.com:** Burachet (t). Mika Wist: (ca). **259 Alamy Stock Photo:** Susan E. Degginger (ca). **Science Photo Library:** Andrew J. Martinez (cb); Trevor Clifford

Photography (tc, bc). **260 Dreamstime.com:** Ruslan Minakryn (bl). **Science Photo Library:** Phil Degginger (c). **260-261 Science Photo Library:** Phil Degginger / Jack Clark Collection (c). **261 Dorling Kindersley:** Oxford University Museum of Natural History (br). **Science Photo Library:** Phil Degginger (tc); Charles D. Winters / Science Source (cra). **262-263 Dorling Kindersley:** Oxford University Museum of Natural History (c). **263 Alamy Stock Photo:** Alberto Paredes (cra). **Dorling Kindersley:** Harry Taylor / Sedgwick Museum of Geology, Cambridge (cr). **Science Photo Library:** Adrian Davies / Nature Picture Library (crb). **264 Alamy Stock Photo:** Tom Pfeiffer (bl). **266 Alamy Stock Photo:** Prisma by Dukas Presseagentur / GmbH (bl). **268 Alamy Stock Photo:** Adam Burton (clb); Stephen Barnes / Plants and Gardens

(cla); Oyvind Martinsen (cl). 270-271 **Getty Images:** R. Duran (rduranmerino@gmail.com) (c). **270 Alamy Stock Photo:** Don Johnston_WC (bc). **272 Alamy Stock Photo:** Fredrik Stenström (bc). **274-275 FLPA:** Minden Pictures / Shane P. White (c). **276-277 Caters News Agency:** Chad Weisser (c). **279 Getty Images:** Blend Images - REB Images (crb). **iStockphoto.com:** Digitalimagination (tr). **282-283 NASA:** GSFC / SDO (c). **284-285 NASA:** ESA / and the Hubble Heritage Team (STScl / AURA) (c). **286-287 Getty Images:** Robert Gendler / Stocktrek Images (c). **288-289 Dreamstime.com:** Malopes / Mario Lopes (Background). **296 Dorling Kindersley:** (cra/Snail, cr). **Dreamstime.com:** 3quarks (cra). **297 Dorling Kindersley:** (clb, cla, ca/Starfish). **Dreamstime.com:** Geckophoto / Rob Stegmann

(cl); Kuenzlen / Torsten Kuenzlen (tc/Turtle); Volodymyrkrasyuk (cb). **302 Science Photo Library:** Michael Abbey (crb). **303 Alamy Stock Photo:** Interfoto (tc); Heiti Paves (tr). **Science Photo Library:** CDC (clb); Marek Mis (ca, ca/Lily, cra); Eye Of Science (cb)

Cover images: Front: **123RF.com:** cobalt (Inner Circle), nick8889 (Outer Circle); **Depositphotos Inc:** cappa (Text); **Dreamstime.com:** Mohammed Anwarul Kabir Choudhury c/ (Flask Clamp), Christos Georghiou (Screws), Malopes / Mario Lopes (Background); **Science Photo Library:** Oliver Burston / Ikon Images c/ (Beaker); Back: **123RF.com:** cobalt (Inner Circle), nick8889 (Outer Circle); **Depositphotos Inc:** cappa (Text); **Dreamstime.com:** Christos Georghiou (Screws), Malopes / Mario

Lopes (Background); Spine: **Depositphotos Inc:** cappa (Text); **Dreamstime.com:** Mohammed Anwarul Kabir Choudhury (Flask Clamp), Malopes / Mario Lopes (Background), Sputanski c/ (Blue Background); **Science Photo Library:** Oliver Burston / Ikon Images (Beaker)

Endpaper images: Front: **123RF.com:** cobalt (Inner Circle), nick8889 (Outer Circle); **Dreamstime.com:** Christos Georghiou (Screws), Malopes / Mario Lopes (Background), Sputanski ; Back: **123RF.com:** cobalt (Inner Circle), nick8889 (Outer Circle); **Dreamstime.com:** Christos Georghiou (Screws), Malopes / Mario Lopes (Background).

All other images © Dorling Kindersley

For further information see: **www.dkimages.com**